100 Speeches

that Changed the World

First published in the United States of America in 2019 by
Universe Publishing
A Division of Rizzoli International Publications, Inc.
300 Park Avenue South
New York, NY 10010
www.rizzoliusa.com

Originally published in the United Kingdom in 2019 by
Pavilion Books
43 Great Ormond Street
London, WC1N 3HZ

Produced by Salamander Books, an imprint of Pavilion Books Group Limited.

2019 2020 2021 2022 / 10 9 8 7 6 5 4 3 2 1

ISBN: 978-0-7893-3558-6

Library of Congress Control Number: 2018957476

Printed in Hong Kong

OVERLEAF: *Pictured in October, 1935, President Franklin D.
Roosevelt prepares to make a national broadcast from the
White House.*

100 *Speeches*
that Changed the World

Colin Salter

UNIVERSE

Contents

Introduction 10

c. 399 BC   Socrates
            "I know that I know nothing" 14

c. 326 BC   Alexander The Great
            Speech by the Hydaspes River 16

63 BC   Cicero
            "O tempora! O mores!" 18

c. 31 AD   Jesus Christ
            Sermon on the Mount 20

1305   William Wallace
            "I have slain the English" 22

1588   Elizabeth I
            "I have the heart and stomach of a king" 24

1649   Charles I
            Execution speech 26

1775   Patrick Henry
            "Give me liberty, or give me death!" 28

1789   William Wilberforce
            Abolition of slavery speech 30

1794   Maximilien Robespierre
            Justification for the "reign of terror" 32

1796   George Washington
            Farewell Address 34

1829   Andrew Jackson
            Speech to Congress on "Indian removal" 36

1851   Sojourner Truth
            "Ain't I a woman?" 38

1852   Frederick Douglass
            "What to the slave is the 4th of July?" 40

1860   Thomas Henry Huxley
            Oxford evolution debate 42

1861   Alexander Stephens
            Cornerstone speech, justifying the
            confederacy 44

1863   Abraham Lincoln
            The Gettysburg Address 46

1865   Abraham Lincoln
            Second Inaugural Address 48

1877   Chief Joseph
            Surrender speech 50

1895   Oscar Wilde
            "The love that dare not speak its name" 52

1901   Mark Twain
            Votes for Women 54

1913   Emmeline Pankhurst
            "Freedom or Death" speech 56

1915   Patrick Pearse
            "Ireland unfree shall never be at peace" 58

1917   Vladimir Lenin
            "Power to the Soviets" speech 60

1918   Woodrow Wilson
            Fourteen Points 62

1931   Mahatma Gandhi
            "My Spiritual Message" 64

1933   Adolf Hitler
            First speech as chancellor of
            Germany 66

1933   Franklin D. Roosevelt
            "The only thing we have to fear is
            fear itself" 68

1936   Edward VIII
            Abdication speech 70

1938   Neville Chamberlain
            "Peace for our time" 72

1939   Lou Gehrig
            "The luckiest man on the face of
            this earth" 74

1939   Adolf Hitler
            Obersalzberg speech 76

1939	George VI Declaration of war against Germany	78
1939	Charles Lindbergh Urging the US to stay neutral in WWII	80
1940	Winston Churchill "Blood, toil, tears and sweat"	82
1940	Winston Churchill "We shall fight on the beaches"	84
1940	Winston Churchill "This was their finest hour"	86
1940	General de Gaulle Appeal of June 18	88
1941	Vyacheslav Molotov Radio speech on Nazi invasion	90
1941	Franklin D. Roosevelt "A date which will live in infamy"	92
1944	Dwight D. Eisenhower Announcing the Allies had landed in France	94
1946	Emperor Hirohito Denouncing divine status	96
1946	Winston Churchill "An iron curtain has descended"	98
1946	Albert Speer Nuremberg Trial Testimony	100
1947	Jawaharlal Nehru "Tryst with Destiny"	102
1948	David Ben-Gurion Israeli Declaration of Independence	104
1948	Aneurin Bevan Speech on the founding of the NHS	106
1949	Chairman Mao Zedong "The Chinese people have stood up!"	108
1951	Eva Perón Speech to the descamisados	110
1953	Queen Elizabeth II Coronation speech	112
1954	Earl Warren Racial segregation US schools ruling	114
1956	Nikita Khruschev "Cult of the individual"	116
1960	Harold Macmillan "The wind of change is blowing through this continent"	118
1960	Elvis Presley "Home from the Army" press conference	120
1960	Fidel Castro United Nations' speech	122
1960	Mervyn Griffith-Jones *Lady Chatterley's Lover* Obscenity Trial	124
1961	John F. Kennedy Inaugural Address	126
1962	John F. Kennedy "We choose to go to the moon"	128
1963	John F. Kennedy "Ich bin ein Berliner"	130
1963	Martin Luther King Jr. "I have a dream"	132
1963	Harold Wilson The White Heat of Technology	134
1964	Muhammad Ali "I am the greatest!"	136
1964	Malcolm X "The Ballot or the Bullet"	138
1964	Nelson Mandela "An ideal for which I am prepared to die"	140
1966	John Lennon "We're more popular than Jesus" apology	142
1967	Timothy Leary "Turn on, tune in, drop out"	144
1967	Earl Warren *Loving vs. Virginia*	146
1967	Eugene McCarthy Denouncing the Vietnam War	148

1968	Martin Luther King Jr. "I've been to the mountaintop"	150
1968	Enoch Powell Rivers of Blood	152
1969	Neil Armstrong "One giant leap for mankind"	154
1969	Max B. Yasgur "This is America and they are going to have their festival"	156
1970	Betty Friedan Strike for Equality	158
1971	John Kerry Vietnam Veterans Against the War	160
1973	Harry Blackmun *Roe vs. Wade*	162
1974	Richard Nixon Announcement of Resignation	164
1978	Harvey Milk "You have to give people hope"	166
1980	Margaret Thatcher "The lady's not for turning"	168
1987	Ronald Reagan "Tear down this wall!"	170
1990	Nelson Mandela "We have waited too long for our freedom"	172
1991	Mikhail S. Gorbachev Farewell Address	174
1993	Maya Angelou "On the Pulse of Morning"	176
1997	Chris Patten "A very Chinese city with British characteristics"	178
1997	Earl Spencer "The most hunted person of the modern age"	180
1998	Bill Clinton "I have sinned"	182
1998	Tony Blair Address to Irish Parliament	184
2001	George W. Bush Address to the Nation	186
2004	Osama bin Laden Address to the United States	188
2004	Barack Obama Keynote Address at the Democratic National Convention	190
2007	Steve Jobs "Today Apple is going to reinvent the phone"	192
2007	Bill Gates Commencement Address at Harvard	194
2008	Barack Obama "Yes, We Can!"	196
2013	Malala Yousafzai "The right of education for every child"	198
2016	"Emily Doe" Stanford Rape Trial statement to court	200
2016	Stephen Hawking Exploring the impact of Artificial Intelligence	202
2017	Ashley Judd "I am a nasty woman"	204
2017	Mark Zuckerberg Commencement Address at Harvard	206
2017	James Comey Senate Testimony	208
2017	Elon Musk Becoming a Multiplanet Species	210
2018	Oprah Winfrey "Their time is up"	212

Introduction

Speeches have always been the greatest form of advocacy. The speaker's careful choice of words, phrases, and sentences to persuade his or her audience is as creative an act as the poet's or the playwright's.

Speeches were at the heart of the earliest Western dramas from ancient Greece. Athenian society already had sophisticated rules for rhetoric and drama more than two and a half thousand years ago, and it's fitting that the oldest speech in this book was given by Athenian philosopher Socrates in 399 BC.

Thanks to the ancient Greeks, speeches have become a formal part of our linguistic life. They can be simple declarations of love, defenses of high principles, or pleas in the pursuit of power—on screen, in court, or at rallies. Speeches may seem artificial but that's precisely why they have their place in our legal and political processes. They are opportunities to think before we speak, to compose ourselves and make what we have to say really count. The 271 words which begin "Four score and seven years ago …" are among the most thoughtful ever spoken. In a few minutes its speaker Abraham Lincoln had a far greater impact at Gettysburg than Edward Everett, whose two-hour, 13,607-word oration preceded him that day.

Speeches invariably have a job to do. They must convince the listener of something; perhaps a speaker's devotion, an apology, a government's decision, or an accused man's innocence. It is no surprise that some of the speeches we've chosen here were landmark legal rulings which advanced the rights of women and African Americans. Speeches really can change the world; but to do so, good speakers must know not only their own mind but all the rich, poetic tools of rhetoric at their disposal. They need to wield the power of language to full effect.

Speeches demand an audience, and above all speakers must be able to tailor their words to that audience—seldom will words simply spoken out loud do the job. Politicians are today schooled in the art of speech-making, but the best speakers in history have had a natural ability. Martin Luther King Jr.'s instinctive feel for rhythm and dynamics, born of the gospel music of his church, made his speeches some of the greatest ever given in the modern age. All the speech writers in the world can't help you speak in public, but a charismatic speaker can turn an average speech or a difficult moment of history into a triumph of rhetoric. In the wrong hands such charisma is not without danger. Adolf Hitler was a mesmeric speaker, however abhorrent his ideas were.

The one hundred speeches presented here span nearly 2,500 years. They mark pivotal moments in the story of humanity, from the birth of nations to

LEFT: *A master of the art, Winston Churchill's wartime speeches helped galvanize an isolated Britain.*

OPPOSITE: *John F. Kennedy received a rapturous welcome when he spoke in Berlin.*

the end of empires. A handful mark significant cultural moments. The speeches were made in defeat or victory, anticipating imprisonment or liberation, sometimes urging cruelty and repression but more often arguing for social equality or scientific advancement. Kennedy's speech declaring that "we choose to go to the moon" may have been motivated in part by the Soviet Union's lead in the space race, but he expressed it in terms of America's pioneering spirit and of a selfless quest for knowledge which could not fail to move his audience (and, importantly, persuade them to pay for it).

Taken together, these one hundred speeches express some of the finest aspirations of the human heart. Of the one hundred, there are perhaps fifty which changed the world, and another fifty that mark the point at which the world changed. Malala Yousafzai's original speech advocating education for girls in her native Pakistan was sufficiently incendiary to have the Taliban attempt her murder. The fact that they failed led to global condemnation and enabled her, once recovered, to deliver another speech at the United Nations.

More recent speeches, delivered after the invention of recording, have an automatic advantage in that we know how they sounded. Fine words are only half the battle, and the strength of many earlier speakers can only be judged by their reputation in the absence of video and audio evidence. We know how Churchill sounded when he defined the defiant British spirit in World War Two; but how did Queen Elizabeth's famous evocation of Englishness come across to ordinary soldiers waiting to fight the Spanish Armada?

There's a popular myth that Zhou Enlai, the Chinese premier, remarked in the 1970s—when asked to comment on the 1789 French Revolution—that it was "too soon to tell." In fact he was commenting on the rather more recent Parisian student uprising of 1968. The final speeches in this book were given in the last ten years, and it is certainly too soon to tell what long-term impact they will have. But who could deny that, for example, Obama's victory speech in 2008 was a profound moment in American and world history?

We close with Oprah Winfrey's speech at the Golden Globes in 2018 which summarized the demands of women for greater respect in the workplace. Some observers believed it hinted at Ms. Winfrey's own ambitions for public office. The "MeToo" movement described by Oprah Winfrey is righting that wrong at last, and perhaps her speech will eventually be seen to mark the greatest of all changes in the world, a move to complete equality between women and men.

Lack of space prevents us from reproducing entire speeches here. Fidel Castro's four-and-a-half-hour lecture to the United Nations was never going to fit, while Neil Armstrong's first words spoken on another planet was not difficult. To convey as much as possible of the longer speeches we have included edited highlights. We hope the original speakers will forgive us and not feel that we have distorted their meaning. The full texts of almost all the one hundred speeches are widely available online.

In the electronic age it sometimes seems as if speeches have had their day. Speeches have given way

LEFT: Eva Perón. 'Evita' was a powerful advocate for her husband, Juan Perón.

to the soundbite, which has been elbowed sideways by the 140 characters of a tweet. So it was reassuring, that at Senator John McCain's memorial service in 2018, Barack Obama was asked to speak, and once again we heard a politician weighing his words carefully and sounding presidential.

Anyone with a vision of a better future still wants to talk about it, whether it's Stephen Hawking talking about Artificial Intelligence or Elon Musk reviving the spirit of Kennedy in his push to Mars. Those seeking change are moved to the finest words, and we should listen.

Colin Salter
2018

ABOVE: Martin Luther King Jr. delivering his "I have a dream" speech in 1967, from in front of the Lincoln Memorial.

BELOW: Oprah Winfrey announces "Their time is up" at the 2018 Golden Globes.

Wherefore, O judges, be of good cheer about death, and know this of a truth, that no evil can happen to a good man, either in life or after death. He and his are not neglected by the gods; nor has my own approaching end happened by mere chance. But I see clearly that to die and be released was better for me; and therefore the oracle gave no sign. For which reason also, I am not angry with my accusers, or my condemners; they have done me no harm, although neither of them meant to do me any good; and for this I may gently blame them.

Still I have a favor to ask of them. When my sons are grown up, I would ask you, O my friends, to punish them; and I would have you trouble them, as I have troubled you, if they seem to care about riches, or anything, more than about virtue; or if they pretend to be something when they are really nothing, then reprove them, as I have reproved you, for not caring about that for which they ought to care, and thinking that they are something when they are really nothing. And if you do this, I and my sons will have received justice at your hands.

The hour of departure has arrived, and we go our ways—I to die, and you to live. Which is better God only knows.

SPEECH GIVEN AT TRIAL, AS RECORDED IN PLATO'S *APOLOGY OF SOCRATES*

LEFT: *A first century sculpture of Socrates held by the Louvre Museum in Paris—believed to be a copy of a lost bronze statue by Lysippos. His last words were, to a wealthy friend, "I owe Asclepius a rooster. Please pay my debt." Thus he sought to fulfill his commercial obligations as, by dying, he was fulfilling his social contract with the state.*

Socrates
"I know that I know nothing"

(c. 399 BC)

Socrates saw himself as an irritant sent by the gods to sting the Athenians into action with his satire and criticism. He was charged with corrupting the youth of the city and with disregarding the city's gods. Plato, a student of Socrates, was present at his mentor's trial and later wrote down Socrates's defense of his actions.

None of Socrates's own writings survive, and we rely on Plato for a sense of the man and his philosophy. Although Plato wrote his record of the trial in the form of dramatized conversations between Socrates and his accusers, his presence at the proceedings must make it a reasonably accurate version of the arguments, if not the words themselves.

Plato's style of writing is known as Socratic, and it is probably how Socrates himself rehearsed his arguments—by encouraging his audience or his characters to ask questions and then answering them philosophically. Although he denied it, Socrates was a follower of sophism, in which wise men were paid to impart their wisdom to rich men's sons using the powers of philosophy and rhetoric. In such relationships, there was a clear opportunity (or danger) of subverting the young with unconventional ideas. Socrates took very public pride in his nonconformity.

At his trial, however, he denied wisdom and protested his ignorance. He had once been told at the Oracle of Delphi that there was no one wiser than him; he claimed that he only believed the assertion because oracles never lie. He searched among the learned, among poets and even among politicians for wise men; but although he found knowledge and even genius in a few, Socrates found no one who used these things wisely.

"Yet," he countered, "each man is thought wise by the people, and each man thinks himself wise; therefore, I am the better man, because I know that I know nothing." This, he argued, was the real reason behind the accusations against him. "For those who I have examined, instead of being angry with themselves [for not being wiser], are angry with me!"

Socrates claimed that he could not have corrupted youth because he was not a sophist; and he was not a sophist because he chose a life of unpaid poverty. He was not paid to teach; young wealthy Athenians simply followed him around and asked him questions, having nothing better to do. None had come forward as witnesses for the prosecution.

In the charge of ignoring Athenian gods in favor of his own, he argued that his gods forbade him from acting unethically, thereby admitting that he followed his own spiritual path and not that of Athens. But he insisted that he was respectful of authority, even though he admitted, "all day long I never cease to settle here, there, and everywhere, rousing, persuading, reproving every one of you."

Socrates demonstrated that respect for his accusers when the verdict was returned by a jury of 500 of his peers: guilty. He was sentenced to death, but by tradition he was allowed to propose an alternative punishment. By convention a condemned man might escape death at this stage by suggesting he be exiled from the city or by the payment of a large fine. Socrates accepted, as his philosophical position dictated, that the city fathers were right to condemn him. Instead of a fine, he suggested that he should be kept in financial security by the city for the rest of his life, since his existence provided such a useful service of questioning its values. When this proved unacceptable to the judges, he offered to pay a desultory sum, a hundred drachmae, as a fine. His supporters quickly tried to avoid offense by raising the amount to three thousand; but the judges had had enough of his wisdom.

The death sentence was upheld. Socrates refused to flee the city as was expected of men in his position. To do so, he said, was to show a fear of death and a disrespect of the rule of law unbecoming of a philosopher. Instead, he drank the offered cup of poison.

Alexander the Great

"The utmost hopes of riches or power ... will be far surpassed"

(c. 326 BC)

In a long and successful campaign, Alexander the Great of Macedonia conquered all of Greece, Egypt, and Persia. Now he stood at the border of a vast prize—India. But his armies, weary from ten years of constant battle, wanted to go home. Alexander had to convince them that it was worth going on.

"I observe, gentlemen, that when I would lead you on a new venture you no longer follow me with your old spirit." We rely largely on a historian called Arrian for the text of this speech, and for our knowledge of Alexander's conquests. Although written down in the second century AD, five hundred years after the events that it describes, Arrian's account of the military life of Alexander the Great is based on earlier histories, now lost. These were written by two men, Ptolemy and Aristobulus, who both served with Alexander. Arrian's version, therefore, has some authority.

Alexander, King of Macedonia, knew that his troops were jaded. So very far from home, they must already have looted wealth beyond their wildest dreams as they swarmed over most of the known world to the east. No wonder the enthusiasm had begun to drain from their battle cries. They were ten years older, and so were their wives and children. Was another notch on the imperial bedpost worth it?

Their leader mustered many arguments to convince them it was. Firstly, it would be easy. "These natives either surrender without a blow or are caught on the run—or leave their country undefended for your taking." Secondly, they had come so far, and there was so little left to conquer, "a small addition to the great sum of your conquests. The area of the country still ahead of us from here to the Ganges is comparatively small." This was not strictly true. Alexander and his troops were on the banks of the Hydaspes River (now the Jhelum River) in northwestern India, some 1,500 miles from the Ganges delta. Furthermore, Alexander's claim that they

would be able to sail home afterward because the Indian Ocean was connected to the Caspian Sea did not hold water.

Alexander reasoned that a soldier's job was to fight, and that a man's work "has no object beyond itself." But he also made a military case for pressing on. To leave the job of conquering the world half done would be to leave the door open to insurgents from territories not yet subdued. It was worth a little extra push, surely? "For well you know that hardship and danger are the price of glory, and that sweet is the savor of a life of courage and of a deathless renown beyond the grave." This was a direct appeal to his men's machismo; after all, if they wanted to avoid danger, they could all just have stayed at home defending Macedonia's borders.

As Alexander reeled off the list of conquered kingdoms, there was no denying the scale of their success so far. He was at pains from the start of the speech to credit his men for it. It had been won "through your courage and endurance." He returned to the theme at the end: "You and I, gentlemen, have shared the labor and shared the danger, and the rewards are for us all."

Finally, Alexander appealed to any fighting soldier's greatest self-interest: loot. "The conquered territory belongs to you; from your ranks the governors of it are chosen; already the greater part of its treasure passes into your hands, and when all Asia is overrun, then indeed I will go further than the mere satisfaction of your ambitions: the utmost hopes of riches or power which each one of you cherishes will be far surpassed."

That individualization—"each one of you"—was a masterstroke. And it worked. The army stayed and won

For a man who is a man, work, in my belief, if it is directed to noble ends, has no object beyond itself; none the less, if any of you wish to know what limit may be set to this particular campaign, let me tell you that the area of country still ahead of us, from here to the Ganges and the Eastern Ocean, is comparatively small. You will undoubtedly find that this ocean is connected with the Hyrcanian Sea, for the great Stream of Ocean encircles the earth.

Moreover I shall prove to you, my friends, that the Indian and Persian Gulfs and the Hyrcanian Sea are all three connected and continuous. Our ships will sail round from the Persian Gulf to Libya as far as the Pillars of Hercules, whence all Libya to the eastward will soon be ours, and all Asia too, and to this empire there will be no boundaries but what God Himself has made for the whole world.

But if you turn back now, there will remain unconquered many warlike peoples between the Hyphasis and the Eastern Ocean, and many more to the northward and the Hyrcanian Sea, with the Scythians, too, not far away; so that if we withdraw now there is a danger that the territory which we do not yet securely hold may be stirred to revolt by some nation or other we have not yet forced into submission.

Should that happen, all that we have done and suffered will have proved fruitless—or we shall be faced with the task of doing it over again from the beginning. Gentlemen of Macedon, and you, my friends and allies, this must not be. Stand firm; for well you know that hardship and danger are the price of glory, and that sweet is the savor of a life of courage and of deathless renown beyond the grave.

SPEECH BY THE HYDASPES RIVER

a tactically brilliant battle to take control of the Punjab. But it sustained relatively heavy losses. When Alexander began to size up Bengal, the next kingdom to conquer, his generals decided that enough was enough. Alexander, unbeaten in battle, conceded defeat and advanced no farther than the banks of the Indus River. King of a vast empire, he died in Babylon three years later, at the age of just thirty-two.

OPPOSITE: A Greek silver tetradrachm coin of Alexander the Great, from around 323 BC.

RIGHT: Charles Le Brun's portrait of Alexander with Hephaestion (in the red cloak) a friend and key general.

Cicero
"O tempora! O mores!"

(63 BC)

Marcus Tullius Cicero was a Roman politician who reached the pinnacle of the political system when he was elected consul for the year 63 BC. When in the course of the year he was handed evidence incriminating a rival in a plot to overthrow the government, he saw an opportunity to make his mark on the political stage.

When, O Catiline, do you mean to cease abusing our patience? How long is that madness of yours still to mock us? When is there to be an end of that unbridled audacity of yours, swaggering about as it does now? Do not the nightly guards placed on the Palatine Hill—do not the watches posted throughout the city—does not the alarm of the people, and the union of all good men—does not the precaution taken of assembling the senate in this most defensible place—do not the looks and countenances of this venerable body here present, have any effect upon you?

Do you not feel that your plans are detected? Do you not see that your conspiracy is already arrested and rendered powerless by the knowledge which every one here possesses of it? What is there that you did last night, what the night before—where is it that you were—who was there that you summoned to meet you—what design was there which was adopted by you, with which you think that any one of us is unacquainted?

Shame on the age and on its principles! The senate is aware of these things; the consul sees them; and yet this man lives. Lives! Aye, he comes even into the senate. He takes a part in the public deliberations; he is watching and marking down and checking off for slaughter every individual among us. And we, gallant men that we are, think that we are doing our duty to the Republic if we simply keep out of the way of his frenzied attacks.

CATILINE ORATIONS; ACCUSING CATILINE OF LEADING A PLOT TO OVERTHROW THE ROMAN GOVERNMENT

OPPOSITE: A bust of Marcus Tullius Cicero held by the Museo Capitolino in Rome.

Cicero is regarded as one of the finest orators of the Roman Age. Reverence for classical Greece and Rome made him a role model for future writers and speakers throughout Europe well into the eighteenth century. The four speeches known as the Catiline Orations, which he made in accusing the leader of the 63 BC conspiracy, are considered among his best.

Lucius Sergius Catilina—Catiline—stood against Cicero in the consular elections for 63 BC, and lost. His campaign platform—debt relief for ordinary Roman citizens—displeased the elite in whose hands the election lay. It was a bitter blow for a man with a long family history of public service to live up to. Catiline wanted revenge and built a secret coalition of soldiers and senators with their own axes to grind, who between them mustered an army of some 10,000 men.

When Cicero learned of the rebellion, he called a special meeting of the senate and ambushed Catiline with a short but hard-hitting speech. His introductory remarks consisted entirely of rhetorical questions—fifteen of them in less than two hundred words. "What is there that you did last night, what the night before, where is it that you were, who was there that you summoned to meet you, what design was there which was adopted by you, with which you think that any one of us is unacquainted?"

These were questions that required no answer, accusations disguised as questions, which rained down on Catiline like hailstones. Cicero continued with a declaration that has become a byword for corruption in society: "O tempora! O mores!" Literally "Oh, the times! Oh, the values!" loosely translated as "What have we come to in this day and age?" Catiline tried to discredit his accuser by comparing Cicero's humble origins with his own noble ones, before yelling threats as he stormed out of the chamber.

In the coming days, Cicero spoke twice in public about the

plot. Aware that Catiline's election platform might have made him popular with the masses, he told them that Catiline had gone not into self-imposed exile as he claimed, but to join his rebel forces. When several of Catiline's co-conspirators were captured and made to confess, Cicero spoke in reassuring terms, declaring the public to be safe because he (with no false modesty) had prevented an uprising that had threatened great loss of life. "You see this day, O Romans, all your lives, your wives and children, this most fortunate and beautiful city, by the great love of the immortal gods for you, by my labors and counsels and dangers, snatched from fire and sword, and almost from the very jaws of fate, and preserved and restored to you."

Finally, in the fourth oration, Cicero addressed the senate again. Consuls were supposed to be impartial in matters of law, but Cicero chose his words with such skill as to enable other speakers to call for the death sentence for all the conspirators. And he was very careful, in the most self-effacing manner, to take as much credit for the successful removal of the threat. "I ask nothing of you but the recollection of this time and of my whole consulship. I recommend to you my little son, to whom it will be protection enough if you recollect that he is the son of him who has saved all these things at his own single risk."

The conspirators were duly executed by strangulation. Catiline was killed in battle while on the run with the rump of his army. Cicero continued to be a political operator in Rome until he misjudged his last opponent, Mark Antony. In revenge for his searing verbal and written attacks, his head and hands were cut off and nailed up in the Roman Forum, where Antony's wife is reported to have pulled out Cicero's persuasive tongue and stabbed it repeatedly with a hairpin.

Jesus Christ
Sermon on the Mount

(c. 31 AD)

Of all the passages of the New Testament of the Bible, chapters five, six, and seven of Matthew's Gospel are among the richest. They contain a detailed account of Jesus's Sermon on the Mount, a speech to his followers that laid out the principles of Christianity.

Blessed are the poor in spirit: for theirs is the kingdom of heaven. Blessed are they that mourn: for they shall be comforted. Blessed are the meek: for they shall inherit the earth. Blessed are they which do hunger and thirst after righteousness: for they shall be filled.

Blessed are the merciful: for they shall obtain mercy. Blessed are the pure in heart: for they shall see God. Blessed are the peacemakers: for they shall be called the children of God. Blessed are they which are persecuted for righteousness' sake: for theirs is the kingdom of heaven. Blessed are ye, when men shall revile you, and persecute you, and shall say all manner of evil against you falsely, for my sake.

Rejoice, and be exceeding glad: for great is your reward in heaven: for so persecuted they the prophets which were before you. Ye are the salt of the earth: but if the salt have lost his savor, wherewith shall it be salted? It is thenceforth good for nothing, but to be cast out, and to be trodden under foot of men.

Ye are the light of the world. A city that is set on a hill cannot be hid. Neither do men light a candle, and put it under a bushel, but on a candlestick; and it giveth light unto all that are in the house. Let your light so shine before men, that they may see your good works, and glorify your Father which is in heaven.

SERMON ON THE MOUNT

OPPOSITE: The most likely site for the Sermon on the Mount is a hill near Tabgha in Israel, overlooking the sea of Galilee. A Roman Cathlic church, the Church of the Beatitudes, was built there in 1938.

Jesus began his ministry at the age of about thirty when he was baptized by John the Baptist. He preached in Galilee and performed miracles, and by the age of thirty-one he had built up a large following. Perhaps in search of a natural amphitheater to amplify his voice, he walked up into the mountains of the region and began to address the multitude.

The Sermon on the Mount is the longest continuous speech by Jesus in the Bible. Phrases and sayings from it have entered the English language and are so widely used that you may not even realize where they come from. "Salt of the earth" and "light of the world" are just two of the metaphors employed, both of them to describe Jesus's followers and their effect on daily life, improving and illuminating its condition.

"Turn the other cheek," "go the extra mile," "no man can serve two masters," "ask, and it shall be given you; seek, and ye shall find." It may seem dismissive or disrespectful to assess the founder of a religion purely in terms of oratory, but the words attributed to Jesus in the Sermon on the Mount show a genius for the simple metaphor, the catchy slogan that encapsulates an entire moral idea.

The Sermon on the Mount reveals a fine orator, capable of holding and persuading an audience. Nowhere are the speaker's rhetorical instincts better revealed than in the opening section on the theme of happiness, known today as the Beatitudes. The title comes from the Latin word "beatus," which is usually translated as "blessed" but also means "happy." "Blessed are the poor in spirit: for theirs is the kingdom of heaven. Blessed are they that mourn: for they shall be comforted. Blessed are the meek: for they shall inherit the earth." In all, the word is used nine times to describe different ways to be morally and spiritually happy, in a rhythmic call and response.

As if all these rhetorical treasures were not enough, the Sermon on the Mount is also used to unveil an example of a good prayer to offer up to God—so good that it has become the central prayer of Christianity, the Lord's Prayer.

The sermon closes with more vivid imagery for its audience, a simple choice that must surely have been illustrated by the mountains at hand: "Whosoever heareth these sayings of mine, and doeth them, I will liken him unto a wise man, which built his house upon a rock: and the rain descended, and the floods came, and the winds blew, and beat upon that house; and it fell not: for it was founded upon a rock. And every one that heareth these sayings of mine, and doeth them not, shall be likened unto a foolish man, which built his house upon the sand: and the rain descended, and the floods came, and the winds blew, and beat upon that house; and it fell: and great was the fall of it."

The Sermon on the Mount remains the single most defining text of Christianity, and many of its moral commandments are common to other religions too. Leo Tolstoy and Mahatma Gandhi corresponded on its message of nonviolence, for example. Although theologians continue to debate its finer points, it is a masterpiece of the spoken word, packed full of big ideas yet presented with poetic simplicity for the masses.

"I can not be a traitor, for I owe him no allegiance. He is not my Sovereign; he never received my homage; and whilst life is in this persecuted body, he never shall receive it. To the other points whereof I am accused, I freely confess them all. As Governor of my country I have been an enemy to its enemies; I have slain the English; I have mortally opposed the English King; I have stormed and taken the towns and castles which he unjustly claimed as his own. If I or my soldiers have plundered or done injury to the houses or ministers of religion, I repent me of my sin; but it is not of Edward of England I shall ask pardon.

TRIAL STATEMENT

LEFT: A painting of William Wallace held by the Stirling Smith Art Gallery, Stirling, Scotland.

William Wallace
"I have slain the English"

(August 23, 1305)

Not all cinematic histories are accurate. Braveheart, the biopic of Scottish ruler William Wallace, is wider of the mark than most. Its very title was not applied to Wallace but to his successor, Robert the Bruce. However, its depiction of Wallace's mock trial and torturous execution are uncomfortably close to the truth.

After the death of King Alexander III of Scotland there was a political vacuum in the country, which Edward I of England was quick to fill. He installed a weak king, John Balliol (now known in Scotland as Toom Tabard, "the empty coat"), then deposed him and invaded Scotland.

Wallace was one of a number of leaders of small, local rebellions throughout the country that eventually joined forces and began to inflict significant defeats on the English both in Scotland and in northern England. He took the title of Guardian of Scotland, since John Balliol was still alive but in exile in France.

But Edward sent another army, which crushed Wallace's forces at Falkirk, and from then on Wallace was a fugitive. He resigned as Guardian but conducted diplomatic missions overseas in search of support for Scotland. In 1305, he was betrayed by a Scottish knight who supported King Edward, and taken to London to be tried.

The trial was a mockery, and William Wallace was not allowed to speak in his own defense. But when one of the charges was read out—of treason against the English king—he could bite his tongue no longer:

"I can not be a traitor, for I owe him no allegiance. He is not my Sovereign; he never received my homage; and whilst life is in this persecuted body, he never shall receive it. To the other points whereof I am accused, I freely confess them all. As Governor of my country I have been an enemy to its enemies; I have slain the English; I have mortally opposed the English King; I have stormed and taken the towns and castles which he unjustly claimed as his own. If I or my soldiers have plundered or done injury to the houses or ministers of religion, I repent me of my sin; but it is not of Edward of England I shall ask pardon."

The decision of the judge was a foregone conclusion, and he was sentenced to the traitor's death; to be hung, drawn, and quartered. In a gratuitous process of barbaric cruelty the prisoner was strangled with a rope but not killed. Then, still alive, he was made to watch as he was mutilated and his severed organs burned in fire. Finally, he was beheaded and his body cut into four pieces, in Wallace's case, to be displayed at four northern towns.

One man's terrorist is another man's freedom fighter. Edward of England may have disposed of a troublesome revolutionary; but the Scots, taunted by the show of Wallace's arms and legs in Newcastle, Berwick, Stirling, and Perth, became more determined than ever to regain their independence. Led by Robert the Bruce, now King Robert, they did so decisively in 1314 at the Battle of Bannockburn.

Scotland's fortunes waxed and waned in the following centuries, and in 1707, after the disastrous Darien Scheme almost bankrupted the country, decided their future prosperity was better served by joining England in the United Kingdom. The memory of Wallace, Bruce, and Bannockburn has been romanticized since then, not only by Hollywood but authors of historic fiction, such as Sir Walter Scott and Nigel Tranter. Robert Burns wrote the ballad "Scots Wha Hae" in 1796; and the National Wallace Monument, a Gothic tower near Stirling, was erected in 1869. William Wallace was no saint, but his memory is still invoked by Scottish nationalists today.

Elizabeth I
"I have the heart and stomach of a king"

(August 9, 1588)

England was under threat, and ill-prepared to defend itself. There was not enough money in the coffers to maintain a large standing army; the one that Elizabeth I addressed at Tilbury had been hastily assembled to face an attack by the approaching Spanish Armada. The queen's speech is one of the earliest on record to appeal to the Englishman's sense of his country, his sovereign, and his God.

Let tyrants fear. I have always so behaved myself that, under God, I have placed my chiefest strength and safeguard in the loyal hearts and goodwill of my subjects; and therefore I am come amongst you, as you see, at this time, not for my recreation and disport, but being resolved, in the midst and heat of the battle, to live and die amongst you all; to lay down for my God, and for my kingdom, and my people, my honor and my blood, even in the dust.

I know I have the body but of a weak and feeble woman; but I have the heart and stomach of a king, and of a king of England too, and think foul scorn that Parma or Spain, or any prince of Europe, should dare to invade the borders of my realm: to which rather than any dishonor shall grow by me, I myself will take up arms, I myself will be your general, judge, and rewarder of every one of your virtues in the field.

I know already, for your forwardness you have deserved rewards and crowns; and We do assure you in the word of a prince, they shall be duly paid you. In the mean time, my lieutenant general shall be in my stead, than whom never prince commanded a more noble or worthy subject; not doubting but by your obedience to my general, by your concord in the camp, and your valor in the field, we shall shortly have a famous victory over those enemies of my God, of my kingdom, and of my people.

<small>SPEECH TO THE TROOPS AT TILBURY IN PREPARATION FOR THE ANTICIPATED INVASION BY THE SPANISH ARMADA</small>

OPPOSITE: The portrait of Elizabeth I, circa 1588, held by the National Portrait Gallery in London.

Elizabeth's predecessor on the English throne was her Catholic half-sister Mary I, who was married to the Spanish king Phillip II. With Mary's death Phillip lost his influence over the English throne and sought to regain it by deposing the Protestant Queen Elizabeth. The Spanish Armada was a fleet of 130 ships whose mission was to carry troops from Flanders (modern-day northern Belgium) to invade England in support of the claim to the English throne of another Mary, Queen of Scots, a devout Catholic.

Elizabeth responded by supporting Protestant rebellion in the Spanish-held territories in northern Europe centered on Brussels, and in 1587, she ordered the execution of the Scottish queen after the discovery in 1856 of an assassination plot. The Armada set sail from northern Spain in May 1588, and on July 19 was sighted off Cornwall. A series of skirmishes with the English navy forced the Armada into a weak defensive position off Calais. The Spanish fleet was dispersed in a final English assault on July 29 and fled to the North Sea.

Deprived of their transport for the time being, the Spanish troops in Flanders nevertheless remained a threat. Elizabeth's job in speaking to the ragged assembly of English recruits was to fire them up with a sense of nationality and superiority. In her speech, she placed herself firmly both at the head of her troops and by their side in battle; in a speech of just over 300 words, she used the word "my" fifteen times, five of them in variations of the protective notion of "my people."

When she said that, "We shall shortly have a famous victory," it was not the royal "We" but an implied alliance between the people and the Crown. At the beginning and at the end of the speech she drew together her religion, her country, and its citizens in the

phrase, "my God, my kingdom, and my people."

She had by then been on the English throne for twenty-nine years, and displayed in her Tilbury speech a surprisingly good understanding of the common people of her kingdom. Having appealed to their patriotism, she gets down to the nitty-gritty: "I know already, you have deserved rewards and crowns; and we do assure you, they shall be duly paid you." Plunder and the queen's shilling were great motivators for the soldiers in a volunteer army.

It's a remarkably personal speech from a monarch who, in the Tudor period, would have had very little direct contact with the ordinary population. Its most intimate moment is the point, at the very heart of the speech, when she confronted the question of her sex. She was a woman, not a warrior, after all; a queen (and a virgin queen at that), not a battle-hardened general. She met her critics head on: "I know I have the body of but a weak and feeble woman; but I have the heart and stomach of a king, and of a king of England too." She emphasized the point by wearing a helmet and a breast plate of armor. Combined with a white velvet cloak and mounted on a white horse, her appearance must have been dazzling to the unwashed masses who heard the speech.

The survival of many contemporary accounts of the queen's performance at Tilbury confirms its effect. Its patriotic rallying cry made an immediate impact, one which only grew in the weeks and years that followed. Although the threatened invasion of England never came, Elizabeth's impassioned appeal has become a defining moment of Englishness to rival any drafted by Shakespeare or Churchill.

For the King, indeed I will not argue. The Laws of the Land will clearly instruct you for that; therefore, because it concerns My Own particular, I only give you a touch of it.

For the people, and truly, I desire their Liberty and Freedom as much as any Body whomsoever. But I must tell you that their Liberty and Freedom consists in having of Government; those Laws, by which their Life and their goods may be most their own. It is not for having share in government, Sir; that is nothing pertaining to them. A subject and a sovereign are clean different things, and therefore until they do that, I mean, that you do put the people in that liberty as I say, certainly they will never enjoy themselves.

Sirs, It was for this that now I am come here. If I would have given way to an Arbitrary way, for to have all Laws changed according to the power of the Sword, I needed not to have come here; and therefore, I tell you, and I pray God it be not laid to your charge, that I am the Martyr of the People.

In troth, Sirs, I shall not hold you much longer, for I will only say thus to you. That in truth I could have desired some little time longer, because I would have put then that I have said in a little more order, and a little better digested than I have done. And, therefore, I hope that you will excuse Me.

I have delivered my Conscience. I pray God, that you do take those courses that are best for the good of the Kingdom and your own Salvations.

EXECUTION SPEECH

LEFT: The triple portrait of Charles I, painted by Sir Anthony van Dyck around 1635, part of the Royal Collection.

Charles I
"I go from a corruptible to an incorruptible crown"

(January 30, 1649)

Charles I was the latest in a virtually unbroken line of monarchs who ruled Britain by divine right. He occupied the throne, he believed, by the authority of God, not of man. His high-handed approach to the government of his country led to civil war and, ultimately, his own execution. As he awaited the executioner's ax he addressed the expectant crowd with remarkable royal dignity.

Believing in his absolute authority to rule the country as he saw fit, Charles I had found many ways to anger his subjects. He imposed taxes directly, without consulting Parliament. As king he was also Head of the Church of England, a Protestant denomination. But he tried to impose a very high Anglican version of Christianity on England, and he married a Catholic French princess. Many of his more puritanical Presbyterian subjects were offended.

In Scotland, where he tried to install bishops in a country generally opposed to such a church hierarchy, war broke out. Armed opposition to his style of rule then spread to the whole of Britain, which became bitterly divided by civil war from 1642 onward. When he was at last captured, Charles was tried for treason, an offense that carried the death penalty. He was found guilty, and the death warrant was signed by Oliver Cromwell, leader of the Parliamentarian forces.

Charles accepted the ruling as an act of God, although he protested his innocence. He wore two shirts on the cold January morning of the execution, lest his shivering be mistaken for fear. He had refused to defend himself at his trial on the grounds that he did not recognize the court. Now, however, as the moment of his death approached, he spoke thoughtfully about his religion and his hopes for his country and its people. "My charity commands me to endeavour to the last gasp the peace of the kingdom."

He was critical of the use of force to govern and insisted that it was the Parliamentarians who started the armed conflict. He suggested a national synod to debate the form that national religion should take. As for the people, he called for "laws by which their life and their goods may be most their own." But he drew the line at democracy. "It is not for having share in government, Sir; that is nothing pertaining to them."

Charles broke off twice during his speech to warn other people on the scaffold about the ax. He wasn't concerned so much for their safety as for the sharpness of the blade—any chip or blow to it would dull the edge and make for a messier execution. In a final exchange with his executioner, he told him, "I go from a corruptible to an incorruptible crown where no disturbance can be."

The decision to kill a king was a shocking one and his enemies had to go back to the Roman Empire to find a law that might justify it. Many, even in Cromwell's camp, were opposed to carrying it out; and when the deed was done, the crowd of 10,000 did not roar in a bloodthirsty manner but gasped as one, "a moan as I never heard before and desire I may never hear again" according to one onlooker.

Following Charles's death, the monarchy was formally abolished and Britain became for a few years a republic, and then a protectorate under the supreme leadership of Oliver Cromwell. Cromwell closed down first the House of Lords and then the House of Commons. The irony was plain for people to see—one absolute ruler had been replaced by another—and within a year of Cromwell's death the monarchy was restored in the person of Charles's son, Charles II.

They tell us, sir, that we are weak. Sir, we are not weak if we make a proper use of those means which the God of nature hath placed in our power. Three millions of people, armed in the holy cause of liberty, and in such a country as that which we possess, are invincible by any force which our enemy can send against us.

Besides, sir, we shall not fight our battles alone. There is a just God who presides over the destinies of nations; and who will raise up friends to fight our battles for us. The battle, sir, is not to the strong alone; it is to the vigilant, the active, the brave.

Besides, sir, we have no election. If we were base enough to desire it, it is now too late to retire from the contest. There is no retreat but in submission and slavery! Our chains are forged! Their clanking may be heard on the plains of Boston! The war is inevitable and let it come! I repeat it, sir, let it come.

It is in vain, sir, to extenuate the matter. Gentlemen may cry, 'Peace, Peace,' but there is no peace. The war is actually begun! The next gale that sweeps from the north will bring to our ears the clash of resounding arms! Our brethren are already in the field! Why stand we here idle? What is it that gentlemen wish? What would they have? Is life so dear, or peace so sweet, as to be purchased at the price of chains and slavery? Forbid it, Almighty God! I know not what course others may take; but as for me, give me liberty or give me death!

"GIVE ME LIBERTY, OR GIVE ME DEATH!" SPEECH

"GIVE ME LIBERTY, OR GIVE ME DEATH!"

LEFT: A Currier & Ives hand-colored lithograph of the speech, published in 1876 to commemorate the centenary of the Revolution.

Patrick Henry
"Give me liberty, or give me death!"
(March 23, 1775)

At the second of a series of conventions in Virginia that campaigned for American independence from Britain, Patrick Henry called for the state's militia to be used against occupying British troops. His powerful words carried the day and set in motion the events that culminated in the American Revolution.

Patrick Henry already had a reputation as a fiery speaker. In 1760, as a young attorney he successfully upheld a new law enacted in Virginia, which had been overruled by the British king. His sense of the injustice of London rule may have stemmed from that moment. In 1765, he was a vocal opponent of the Stamp Act, by which the paper used in the American colonies for everything from newspapers to playing cards had to come from Britain and bear a British stamp to prove it.

In 1775, he was a delegate at the Second Virginia Convention, a gathering of those actively seeking an end to the state's colonial status. Tensions were high in the thirteen colonies ruled from London; there were British soldiers everywhere, so the Convention met in Richmond, not Williamsburg, which was the state capital at the time. A petition calling for reconciliation had earlier been handed to the British governor, and some delegates believed it would be sensible to wait for his response before deciding on any further action.

For Patrick Henry, however, enough was enough. "It is natural to man," he began, "to indulge in illusions of hope." But what, he asked his more cautious colleagues, were they hoping for? His argument against hope took the simple rhetorical form of a series of questions and answers, mostly addressing the presence of British troops in such historically high numbers. "Are fleets and armies necessary to a work of love and reconciliation? Have we shown ourselves so unwilling to be reconciled, that force must be called in to win back our love? Let us not deceive ourselves. These are the implements of war and subjugation—the last arguments to which kings resort."

It was clear, he reasoned, that all peaceful attempts at reconciliation over the past ten years had failed. "There is no longer any room for hope." He paused, before confronting his audience with a crescendo of their shared dreams. "If we wish to be free—if we mean to preserve inviolate those inestimable privileges for which we have been so long contending—if we mean not basely to abandon the noble struggle in which we have been so long engaged, and which we have pledged ourselves never to abandon until the glorious object of our contest shall be obtained—" and if they really wanted all this, he declared, "We must fight! I repeat it, sir, we must fight!"

There were more questions. "They tell us, sir, that we are weak, unable to cope with so formidable an adversary. But when shall we be stronger? Will it be the next week, or the next year? Will it be when we are totally disarmed, and when a British guard shall be stationed in every house . . . ? Shall we acquire the means of effectual resistance, by lying supinely on our backs, and hugging the delusive phantom of hope, until our enemies shall have bound us hand and foot?" The alternative to battle was slavery, he suggested. It was a persuasive image, given that most of his audience were Virginia plantation owners who possessed many slaves. "Is life so dear, or peace so sweet, as to be purchased at the price of chains and slavery? Forbid it, Almighty God! I know not what course others may take; but as for me, give me liberty, or give me death!"

Patrick Henry won the day, and the Virginia militia was committed to a revolutionary war, which led the following year to a declaration of independence. Henry would serve two terms as governor of post-colonial Virginia. Also in the room that night in Richmond were two future presidents of the United States: George Washington and Thomas Jefferson, both Virginian tobacco growers whom Patrick Henry's vision must have guided through the years.

William Wilberforce

"A trade founded in iniquity, and carried on as this was, must be abolished"

(May 12, 1789)

A great many people got rich on the back of the slave trade, whether in the buying and selling of human beings, the use of them as cheap labor, or the sale of goods produced from their crops. Wealthy British politicians turned a blind eye to the barbarity of slavery, until William Wilberforce forced them to look.

William Wilberforce was a reluctant parliamentary poster boy for the anti-slavery movement. He accepted the role because speaking out against the trade was a moral imperative. Slavery had been illegal on English soil following a 1772 court case, but slavery in the colonies and the business of slave trading was not. Others in Wilberforce's circle were far better informed, and he relied on their research as he threw himself into the task, "provided that no person more proper could be found." Eventually, it was his friend Prime Minister William Pitt the Younger who persuaded him to address Parliament on the matter. "Do not lose time," Pitt argued, "or you will lose the ground to another."

He was nervous when he rose for the first time to address the issue in the House of Commons. He had been an MP for seven years by then, but was daunted not only by his new mission, but by the weight of opposition that he knew he faced from the House. He was at pains to be dispassionate, simply to present the facts, not to blame. "I mean not to accuse any one, but to take the shame upon myself, in common, indeed, with the whole parliament of Great Britain, for having suffered this horrid trade to be carried on under their authority. We are all guilty."

He excused the merchants of Liverpool, who greatly profited from the trade, by allowing that the business of slavery was such a large one that they may have lost sight of slaves as individuals. He described conditions aboard the slave ships: "If the wretchedness of any one of the many hundred negroes stowed in each ship could be brought before their view, and remain within the sight of the African merchant, that there is no one among them

whose heart would bear it." But he was not so generous with a certain Mr. Norris of Liverpool, an apologist for the slave trade for whom "interest [has drawn] a film across the eyes so thick that total blindness could do no more."

Norris, in a deposition to the Privy Council, had made the voyage from Africa to the West Indies sound like a picnic of African and European cookery, with singing and dancing, hobbies and perfume. The truth, as Wilberforce noted line by line, was very different. The European food was horse beans; the songs were heart-breaking laments, the dances were forced on the slaves by men with whips; and the perfume was to cover the stench of ill-treated humanity in a confined space.

Finally, he said, "I will call the attention of the House to one species of evidence which is absolutely infallible. Death." Wilberforce reeled off the statistics: 12½ percent of slaves died during the voyage from Africa; 4½ percent died ashore before they were sold; a third died in their first year of slavery. In all, more than half of all Africans captured for the slave trade died as a result of their capture and sale. Hearing this statistic, he concluded, had made his mind up for him. "I from this time determined that I would never rest till I had effected [the trade's] abolition."

It was, as he had promised, a dispassionate speech, a calm laying-out of the facts. It won few hearts at the time, and his first few attempts to introduce an abolition bill to the House were defeated. The great success of Wilberforce's first salvo in the anti-slavery crusade was to expose the slave trade for what it really was. Parliament could no longer pretend it did not know what was going on. It took a long time before it began to

Not less than 12½ percent perish in the passage. Besides these, the Jamaica report tells you, that not less than 4½ percent die on shore before the day of sale, which is only a week or two from the time of landing. One third more die in the seasoning, and this in a country exactly like their own, where they are healthy and happy as some of the evidences would pretend.

The diseases, however, which they contract on shipboard, the astringent washes which are to hide their wounds, and the mischievous tricks used to make them up for sale, are, as the Jamaica report says, (a most precious and valuable report, which I shall often have to advert to) one principle cause of this mortality. Upon the whole, however, here is a mortality of about 50 percent and this among negroes who are not bought unless (as the phrase is with cattle) they are sound in wind and limb.

How then can the House refuse its belief to the multiplied testimonies before the privy council, of the savage treatment of the negroes in the middle passage? Nay, indeed, what need is there of any evidence? The number of deaths speaks for itself, and makes all such enquiry superfluous. As soon as ever I had arrived thus far in my investigation of the slave trade, I confess to you sir, so enormous so dreadful, so irremediable did its wickedness appear that my own mind was completely made up for the abolition.

A trade founded in iniquity, and carried on as this was, must be abolished, let the policy be what it might, let the consequences be what they would, I from this time determined that I would never rest till I had effected its abolition.

ABOLITION OF SLAVERY SPEECH

reflect the growing public opinion in favor of abolition. But in 1807, the trade in slaves was abolished; and in 1833, a month after Wilberforce's death, the ownership of slaves in the colonies also became illegal.

RIGHT: *An antislavery medallion, first produced in 1787 by Staffordshire pottery manufacturer Josiah Wedgwood. Above the kneeling figure are the words, "AM I NOT A MAN AND A BROTHER?" It was a popular image in the British movement for the abolition of the slave trade in the late eighteenth and early nineteenth century and was used on pendants, bracelets, and snuff box lids.*

Maximilien Robespierre
"Lead the people by reason and the people's enemies by terror"

(February 5, 1794)

In the aftermath of the 1789 French Revolution the optimism of the new Republic gave way to in-fighting and argument. From 1792, paranoia and revenge brought about a reign of terror as personal and political rivals were guillotined for alleged treason. Robespierre's justification for the purge was a dark masterpiece.

Maximilien Robespierre rose to power during the French Revolution, and was appointed the first deputy of the National Convention, the new republican government established in 1792. In that position he exerted ever greater influence on the political color of the revolution. He worked hard to secure the vote of Convention delegates, which resulted in the execution of Louis XVI on January 21, 1793. This, it seemed to Robespierre, was not the end of the revolution, but merely the beginning of a virtuous purification of France.

The mildly named Committee of Public Safety—on which Robespierre, his friend Georges Danton,

M.M.J. ROBERSPIERRE
Députée de l'Artois.

and others served—effectively hijacked the legislative powers of the Convention in the course of 1793. It was very successful in stabilizing the country's chaotic economy and efficiently restructuring the French army. But not everyone supported the revolution and the committee also turned its attention to internal divisions in France.

Robespierre believed that in turbulent times a strong, single-minded government was required. Anyone who did not wholeheartedly subscribe to the revolutionary agenda—his revolutionary agenda—was an enemy. As he cast his net ever wider in search of opponents, his counterrevolutionaries came to include followers of the left wing and the right, moderates within and without the Convention, "false revolutionaries," foreigners, priests, nobles, the weak, the corrupt—and almost anyone could be accused of one of these "vices." In February 1794, Robespierre sought to justify to the Convention the ruthlessness with which he disposed of such enemies of the state; 270 citizens had already been executed and 5,500 were in prison awaiting trial.

His report to the Convention was a remarkable statement—politically brilliant but radically unhinged. It had a taut internal logic, but turned everything upside down. Speaking in vague idealistic terms about liberty and equality—but not fraternity—he defined revolution as "at the same time [both] virtue and terror: virtue, without which terror is fatal; terror, without which virtue is impotent. Terror is nothing but prompt, severe inflexible justice." This, he claimed with no sense of irony, would bring about "the peaceful enjoyment of liberty and equality, the reign of that eternal justice whose laws have been inscribed, not in marble and stone,

We must smother the internal and external enemies of the Republic or perish with them. Now, in this situation, the first maxim of your policy ought to be to lead the people by reason and the people's enemies by terror.

If the mainspring of popular government in peacetime is virtue, amid revolution it is at the same time [both] virtue and terror: virtue, without which terror is fatal; terror, without which virtue is impotent. Terror is nothing but prompt, severe, inflexible justice; it is therefore an emanation of virtue. It is less a special principle than a consequence of the general principle of democracy applied to our country's most pressing needs.

It has been said that terror was the mainspring of despotic government. Does your government, then, resemble a despotism? Yes, as the sword which glitters in the hands of liberty's heroes resembles the one with which tyranny's lackeys are armed. Let the despot govern his brutalized subjects by terror; he is right to do this, as a despot. Subdue liberty's enemies by terror, and you will be right, as founders of the Republic. The government of the revolution is the despotism of liberty against tyranny. Is force made only to protect crime? And is it not to strike the heads of the proud that lightning is destined?

To punish the oppressors of humanity is clemency; to pardon them is barbarity. The rigor of tyrants has only rigor for a principle; the rigor of the republican government comes from charity.

SUBDUE LIBERTY'S ENEMIES BY TERROR, GIVING JUSTIFICATION FOR THE "REIGN OF TERROR"

but in the hearts of all men."

But almost in the same breath he distanced ordinary men and women from that justice: "The citizen is subject to the magistrate, the magistrate to the people, and the people to justice." The speech was the work of a zealot who thought only of revolution and had lost sight of the people for whom the revolution was fought. It is no wonder that in 1920s Russia, Stalin held Robespierre up as the ideal revolutionary figure.

Robespierre was proud to be a despot. "The government of the revolution is the despotism of liberty against tyranny. Democracy perishes by popular scorn for the authorities whom the people themselves have established, scorn which makes each individual take unto himself the public power and bring the people to

annihilation or to the power of one man."

He could have been talking about himself. Two months after this tirade he turned on his friend and colleague Georges Danton, who had called for a moderation of the terror, and beheaded him. He signed a new law permitting execution without trial of those merely suspected of counterrevolution. No one was safe, not even other members of the Convention, for whom their comrade had finally overplayed his hand. Robespierre was arrested and convicted (without trial) of tyranny, and on July 28, 1794, guillotined.

OPPOSITE: An etching of Robespierre, made in 1794, by Franz Gabriel Freisinger. Before he was arrested, he received a pistol shot in the jaw, many believe was a botched attempt at suicide.

George Washington
"These counsels of an old and affectionate friend"

(September 19, 1796)

George Washington's valedictory address, in the form of an open letter to the nation, used to be considered as important an American historical document as the Declaration of Independence. The first president of the United States reflected at length on the state of the nation that he had helped to build and counselled against political infighting after he had gone.

Harmony, liberal intercourse with all nations, are recommended by policy, humanity, and interest. But even our commercial policy should hold an equal and impartial hand; neither seeking nor granting exclusive favors or preferences; consulting the natural course of things; diffusing and diversifying by gentle means the streams of commerce, but forcing nothing; … constantly keeping in view that it is folly in one nation to look for disinterested favors from another; that it must pay with a portion of its independence for whatever it may accept under that character; that, by such acceptance, it may place itself in the condition of having given equivalents for nominal favors, and yet of being reproached with ingratitude for not giving more. There can be no greater error than to expect or calculate upon real favors from nation to nation. It is an illusion, which experience must cure, which a just pride ought to discard.

In offering to you, my countrymen, these counsels of an old and affectionate friend, I dare not hope they will make the strong and lasting impression I could wish; that they will control the usual current of the passions, or prevent our nation from running the course which has hitherto marked the destiny of nations. But, if I may even flatter myself that they may be productive of some partial benefit, some occasional good; that they may now and then recur to moderate the fury of party spirit, to warn against the mischiefs of foreign intrigue, to guard against the impostures of pretended patriotism; this hope will be a full recompense for the solicitude for your welfare, by which they have been dictated.

FAREWELL ADDRESS

OPPOSITE: A detail from the Lansdowne portrait by Gilbert Stuart, painted in 1796, Washington's final year in office.

George Washington originally intended to step down from the presidency of the newly formed United States in 1792, after just one term in office. He was persuaded to stand for a second term by conflicts within government between Secretary of State Thomas Jefferson and Treasury Secretary Alexander Hamilton. The text of the statement announcing his decision not to stand for a third was largely prepared by Hamilton, his aide-de-camp in the Revolutionary War, and published in the columns of a Pennsylvania daily newspaper. From there it was quickly taken up by other newspapers across the states.

The intention of the letter was to reassure Americans about the future of their country while alerting them to the potential threats to it that Washington perceived. He was passing on "the disinterested warnings," as he put it, "of a parting friend, who can possibly have no personal motive to bias his counsel."

Nevertheless, he had strong views based on experience. He presciently urged Americans to be united by their shared interests in commerce and defense, but to avoid "those overgrown military establishments which, under any form of government, are inauspicious to liberty." They should endeavor not to be divided along geographical lines, "northern and southern, Atlantic and western, whence designing men may endeavor to excite a belief that there is a real difference of local interests and views." His message was clear: Divisive party politics, by which each scored points off the other in the guise of serving the people, should be avoided.

Religion and education were essential, Washington affirmed, to the morality of a free country. Without enlightened morality, how could public opinion, in the form of an elected government, be enlightened? He had advice for government too—the importance

of not running up national debt by, for example, fighting wars; and of paying off such debts as soon as possible. To avoid debt, credit must be maintained by taxes, which, although always unpopular, should be rendered for the good of the country.

Having helped lead the United States to independence from Britain, Washington understandably urged caution in relations with foreign powers. He advised against giving any trading partner the status of favored nation, or entering into any permanent treaty with them, in order to avoid their undue influence on America. "It is our true policy," he wrote, "to steer clear of permanent alliances with any portion of the foreign world." Indeed, it wasn't until the formation of NATO (North Atlantic Treaty Organization) in 1949 that America did such a thing.

The whole letter is infused with the dignity of a Founding Father, full of wisdom and insight into potential threats to America that, inevitably, have appeared in the centuries since. Although Washington did not intend to set a precedent, subsequent presidents have generally adhered to the convention of serving only two terms. Although some have stood for a third, Franklin Delano Roosevelt is the only president to have succeeded. After he died during his fourth term in office, the Twenty-Second Amendment was passed, formally restricting service to two.

Washington's lengthy address is a blueprint for young republics. One historian has said that if Abraham Lincoln's Gettysburg Address is America's New Testament, George Washington's farewell is its Old. Although it is no longer memorized, as it once was, by the schoolchildren of America, it is read out every year in the Senate on the anniversary of his birthday as a reminder of the principles on which the American republic was founded.

Humanity has often wept over the fate of the aborigines of this country, and philanthropy has been long busily employed in devising means to avert it, but its progress has never for a moment been arrested, and one by one have many powerful tribes disappeared from the earth. To follow to the tomb the last of his race and to tread on the graves of extinct nations excite melancholy reflections.

But true philanthropy reconciles the mind to these vicissitudes as it does to the extinction of one generation to make room for another. In the monuments and fortresses of an unknown people spread over the extensive regions of the West, we behold the memorials of a once powerful race, which was exterminated or has disappeared to make room for the existing savage tribes.

Nor is there anything in this which, upon a comprehensive view of the general interests of the human race, is to be regretted. Philanthropy could not wish to see this continent restored to the condition in which it was found by our forefathers. What good man would prefer a country covered with forests and ranged by a few thousand savages to our extensive republic, studded with cities, towns, and prosperous farms, embellished with all the improvements which art can devise or industry execute, occupied by more than twelve million happy people, and filled with all the blessings of liberty, civilization, and religion?

The tribes which occupied the countries now constituting the eastern states were annihilated or have melted away to make room for the whites. The waves of population and civilization are rolling to the westward, and we now propose to acquire the countries occupied by the red men of the South and West, and to send them to a land where their existence may be prolonged and perhaps made perpetual.

SPEECH TO CONGRESS ON "INDIAN REMOVAL"

LEFT: Andrew Jackson painted by D. H. Carter and subsequently engraved in 1860 by A. H. Ritchie.

Andrew Jackson
"The waves of population and civilization are rolling to the westward"

(December 8, 1829)

In a move designed to clear Native Americans from the southeast of the United States, in 1830, President Andrew Jackson signed the Indian Removal Act into law. In so doing he reversed the policy established by Washington who had encouraged them to remain and adopt the white man's culture, language, and religion.

The so-called Five Civilized Tribes east of the Mississippi—the Cherokee, Chickasaw, Choctaw, Muscogee-Creek, and Seminole Nations—were allowed to stay in their ancestral homelands after America's independence. They were, however, encouraged to adopt European ways, to speak English, to practice agriculture, to pursue individual ownership of property, and to convert to Christianity.

In the south, calls had been growing to move the natives out since the turn of the century. There was pressure on land use; there were clashes of culture; and legal conflicts between the tribes and the settlers, notably in Georgia. The northern states were, however, generally opposed to the action. In his State of the Union address on December 8, 1829, Jackson chose his words carefully to promote the idea.

His key strategy was a fundamentally racist one, to draw a clear distinction between the white man and the "red men." Humanity's progress, he argued, "has never for a moment been arrested, and one by one have many powerful tribes disappeared from the earth." The extinction of the "savage tribes" was inevitable, he believed, and to be regretted no more than "the extinction of one generation to make room for another."

He heaped blame for the situation on the Indian himself, "unwilling to submit to the laws of the States," "discontented in his ancient home," and for preferring "a country covered with forests to our extensive republic, studded with cities, towns, and prosperous farms." The tribes were ungrateful for being sent "to a land where their existence may be prolonged and perhaps made perpetual," where they might "pursue happiness in their own way and under their own rude institutions." And

they were weak: Hadn't America's white settlers done just the same thing, leaving behind in Europe the graves of their ancestors?

At heart, the new policy was a naked land grab, which would "relieve the whole State of Mississippi and the western part of Alabama of Indian occupancy, and enable those States to advance rapidly in population, wealth, and power," Jackson boasted. "The waves of population and civilization are rolling to the westward."

It was to modern ears a speech of monumental arrogance that showed the settler as in every way the man of progressive humanity, the native as inferior. "Toward the aborigines of the country no one can indulge a more friendly feeling than myself, or would go further in attempting to reclaim them from their wandering habits and make them a happy, prosperous people." Jackson judged them entirely on the white man's terms and ignored the fact that the settlers had chosen to travel far from their homelands in search of space and wealth; the tribes had not. It was blind racism.

Nevertheless, Jackson swayed Congress, and the Indians were driven west of the Mississippi—some reluctantly, some forcibly. The Seminoles resisted and won the right to remain in Florida. For the rest, the heartbreaking exodus west under armed escort became known as the Trail of Tears. Many died on the way, unaccustomed to strange diet and climate. The Cherokees, last to leave in 1838, are believed to have lost about a quarter of their number. One Georgian soldier who took part in their forcible relocation declared in his memoirs: "I fought through the War Between the States and have seen many men shot, but the Cherokee Removal was the cruelest work I ever knew."

Sojourner Truth
"Ain't I a woman?"

(May 29, 1851)

Freed slave Sojourner Truth's impromptu speech at a women's convention in Akron, Ohio, challenged not only sexism but racism. Not the carefully crafted product of a team of writers, her words came instinctively and from the heart. So why is the speech we remember now the version written by a white woman twelve years later?

I want to say a few words about this matter. I am a woman's rights. I have as much muscle as any man, and can do as much work as any man. I have plowed and reaped and husked and chopped and mowed, and can any man do more than that? I have heard much about the sexes being equal. I can carry as much as any man, and can eat as much too, if I can get it. I am as strong as any man that is now.

As for intellect, all I can say is, if a woman have a pint, and a man a quart—why can't she have her little pint full? You need not be afraid to give us our rights for fear we will take too much—for we can't take more than our pint'll hold. The poor men seems to be all in confusion, and don't know what to do. Why children, if you have woman's rights, give it to her and you will feel better. You will have your own rights, and they won't be so much trouble.

I can't read, but I can hear. I have heard the bible and have learned that Eve caused man to sin. Well, if woman upset the world, do give her a chance to set it right side up again. Jesus, he never spurned woman from him. When Lazarus died, Mary and Martha came to him with faith and love and besought him to raise their brother. And Jesus wept and Lazarus came forth. And how came Jesus into the world? Through God who created him and the woman who bore him. Man, where was your part?

"Ain't I a Woman," delivered at the Ohio Women's Rights Convention [Marcus Robinson]

OPPOSITE: When Sojourner Truth left the farm she was working on with her daughter, she had to leave behind her son Peter, who was sold illegally by the owner. In 1828, with help from the Van Wagenen family, she became one of the first black women to go to court and win the case against a white man.

A family of abolitionists bought Sojourner Truth's freedom in 1827, a year before slavery was ended in her native New York State. Truth became a preacher and an active antislavery campaigner, achieving a degree of national celebrity. After publishing her autobiography in 1850, she undertook a speaking tour, which brought her to Akron, Ohio, at the time of a conference on women's rights in the town.

Responding to a defense from a male speaker of acts of chivalry by men toward the weaker sex, she spoke with admirable directness and indisputable logic. The speech was transcribed three weeks later in the *Anti-Slavery Bugle* by Marius Robinson, an abolitionist friend of Truth's who had discussed the speech with her and was the secretary of the Akron event. Although Robinson may have cleaned up the language a little for his audience, it is probably a fairly accurate account. According to him she said, "I have plowed and reaped and husked and chopped and mowed, and can any man do more than that? . . . I can carry as much as any man, and can eat as much too, if I can get it. I am as strong as any man that is now."

Compare that with the version recorded twelve years later by Frances Dana Barker Gage, a campaigner for both abolition and women's suffrage. "Nobody eber helps me into carriages, or ober mud puddles, or gibs me any best place! And ar'n't I a woman? Look at me! Look at my arm! I have ploughed, and planted, and gathered into barns, and no man could head me! And ar'n't I a woman? I could work as much and eat as much as a man—when I could get it—and bear de lash as well! And ar'n't, I a woman?"

Gage, whether deliberately or with fading memory, transformed Truth from a New York State resident into a stereotype of a simple illiterate Southern slave. According to Gage, Truth prefaced her remarks by saying, "Wall, chilern, whar dar is so much racket dar must be somethin' out o' kilter. I tink dat 'twixt de nigger of de Souf and de womin at de Norf, all talkin' 'bout rights, de white men will be in a fix pretty soon. But what's all dis here talkin' 'bout?"

In Robinson's version, Truth makes a witty biblical reference: "I have . . . learned that Eve caused man to sin.

Well, if woman upset the world, do give her a chance to set it right side up again. . . . And how came Jesus into the world? Through God who created him and the woman who bore him. Man, where was your part?"

In Gage's revision: "If de fust woman God ever made was strong enough to turn de world upside down all alone, dese women togedder ought to be able to turn it back, and get it right side up again! Whar did your Christ come from? From God and a woman! Man had nothin' to do wid Him."

As there is no definitive account of Truth's speech, historians have relied on Gage's printed versions. Gage rewrote Truth's speech several times subsequently, and the extracts here are from an 1881 printing. Whether Truth's words were recorded verbatim or not, Gage's use of the recurring refrain "Ain't I a woman?" gave the speech its title and much of its rhetorical power.

Frederick Douglass
"What to the American slave is the Fourth of July?"

(July 5, 1852)

Frederick Douglass was a sensation in his day, a runaway slave who became a gifted orator. He spoke with intellectual fire, proving a slave could be the equal of a white man in mental as well as physical strength. In a speech following Independence Day 1852, he gave the slave's perspective on a white celebration of freedom.

After running away from his owner, Frederick Douglass published his autobiography in 1845. It was a best seller, but fearing that the publicity might encourage his former owner to reclaim him, Douglass fled to Great Britain for two years. There he refined his oratory on speaking tours of the nation's churches and marveled at the equality with which he was treated. "I employ a cab—I am seated beside white people—I reach the hotel—I enter the same door—I am shown into the same parlor—I dine at the same table—and no one is offended."

On his return to the United States he settled in liberal Rochester NY and launched the *North Star*, an abolitionist newspaper, giving it the slogan, "Right is of no Sex—Truth is of no Color—God is the Father of us all, and we are all brethren." As that implied, Douglass used the paper to argue for women's suffrage as well as slaves' liberation. Thus it was that he was invited in 1852 to give an Independence Day address to the Rochester Anti-Slavery Sewing Society.

He began by appearing to hail America's independence and applauding the annual celebration of it. But, he said, giving voice to the millions of African Americans still enslaved, "I am not included within the pale of this glorious anniversary. This fourth of July is yours, not mine. Above your national, tumultuous joy I hear the mournful wail of millions whose chains are today rendered more intolerable by the jubilant shouts which reach them."

There was a split in the abolitionist movement at the time between those who believed the US Constitution supported slavery and should be torn up; and those, like Douglass, who thought that it should be used as a weapon in the fight. Douglass used much of his address to argue that slaves were men, not lower forms of life. Therefore, because the Declaration of Independence insists that all men are equal, slaves should have equal rights and treatment.

He gave uncomfortable examples. On rights: "There are seventy-two crimes in the State of Virginia which, if committed by a black man, subject him to the punishment of death; while only two of these same crimes will subject a white man to like punishment." And on treatment: "Am I to argue that it is wrong to make men brutes, to rob them of their liberty, to work them without wages, to keep them ignorant of their relations to their fellow men, to beat them with sticks, to flay their flesh with the lash, to load their limbs with irons, to hunt them with dogs, to sell them at auction, to sunder their families, to knock out their teeth, to burn their flesh, to starve them into obedience and submission to their masters?" These truths were self-evident; Frederick Douglass spoke from experience.

He concluded, "What, to the American slave, is your Fourth of July? I answer: A day that reveals … the gross injustice and cruelty to which he is the constant victim. … A thin veil to cover up crimes which would disgrace a nation of savages."

It would take another fifteen years and a civil war to end slavery. After the war, in which Douglass encouraged black men to fight for the unionist side, three amendments to the Constitution were passed, outlawing slavery and guaranteeing equal rights of voting and citizenship for all races. Douglass continued to campaign for the upholding of these rights, and for women's suffrage, right up to his death in 1895.

What, then, remains to be argued? Is it that slavery is not divine; that God did not establish it; that our doctors of divinity are mistaken? There is blasphemy in the thought. That which is inhuman cannot be divine. Who can reason on such a proposition? They that can, may—I cannot. The time for such argument is past.

What, to the American slave, is your Fourth of July?

I answer: a day that reveals to him, more than all other days in the year, the gross injustice and cruelty to which he is the constant victim. To him, your celebration is a sham; your boasted liberty, an unholy license; your national greatness, swelling vanity; your sounds of rejoicing are empty and heartless; your denunciation of tyrants, brass-fronted impudence; your shouts of liberty and equality, hollow mockery; your prayers and hymns, your sermons and thanksgivings, with all your religious parade and solemnity, are, to Him, mere bombast, fraud, deception, impiety, and hypocrisy—a thin veil to cover up crimes which would disgrace a nation of savages.

There is not a nation of savages. There is not a nation on the earth guilty of practices more shocking and bloody than are the people of the United States at this very hour. Go where you may, search where you will, roam through all the monarchies and despotisms of the Old World, travel through South America, search out every abuse, and when you have found the last, lay your facts by the side of the everyday practices of this nation, and you will say with me that, for revolting barbarity and shameless hypocrisy, America reigns without a rival.

"WHAT TO THE SLAVE IS THE 4TH OF JULY?"

LEFT: *A daguerreotype of Frederick Douglass, taken around 1850, by Samuel J. Miller.*

Thomas Henry Huxley
Oxford evolution debate

(June 30, 1860)

Charles Darwin's book *On the Origin of Species* was a direct challenge both to the orthodox science of its day and to the religious teachings of the church. Seven months after its publication, an informal debate in Oxford produced spirited arguments both for and against his revolutionary theory.

"**Do you consider yourself descended from an ape through your grandmother or grandfather?**"

HUXLEY: Man has no reason to be ashamed of having an ape for his grandfather. If there were an ancestor whom I should feel shame in recalling, it would be a man, a man of restless and versatile intellect, who, not content with an equivocal success in his own sphere of activity, plunges into scientific questions with which he has no real acquaintance, only to obscure them by an aimless rhetoric, and distract the attention of his hearers from the real point at issue by eloquent digressions, and skilled appeals to religious prejudice.

OXFORD UNIVERSITY EVOLUTION DEBATE

LEFT: Thomas Huxley, around 1870, with a drawing of a gorilla skull. Apart from acting as "Darwin's bulldog" he developed the theory of agnosticism: That the existence of god is unknown or unknowable.

OPPOSITE: Today there is a monument outside the Oxford University Museum of Natural History celebrating the Great Debate.

Since 1831, the British Association for the Advancement of Science has held an annual public conference to promote discussion of scientific matters. The 1860 event was the first since Darwin's groundbreaking publication, and its wide-ranging implications were discussed in a number of papers presented during the week. Among them were reviews of "the sexuality of plants" and "the intellectual development of Europe," both in the light of Darwin's theory of evolution.

Thomas Huxley was a biologist with his feet firmly in the pro-Darwin camp. He and Darwin worked together, and Huxley was one of the few people to read *On the Origin of Species* before it was published. He had already been forced to defend his colleague's work earlier in the week, and was persuaded to do so again on the morning of Saturday June 30, when Samuel Wilberforce, the Bishop of Oxford, was due to speak against Darwinism.

Wilberforce was also a scientist—a mathematician—and he insisted that his objections were scientific, not religious. As a clergyman he was an experienced public speaker with a national reputation. Both men had written reviews of Darwin's book, and Wilberforce now got up to repeat his arguments against it. Accustomed to large congregations, he used the full range of oratorical tricks to carry the thousand-strong crowd with him. At the end of his speech he had entertained his audience, and he sat down to a deafening cheer.

Sadly, no verbatim account of what was said by either man that day exists. But from accounts reported in correspondence, in the days and weeks following the debate, it is possible to piece together the tone, particularly of the handover from

Wilberforce to Huxley. The bishop's final insulting taunt to the biologist before sitting down was something like this: "Do you consider yourself descended from an ape through your grandmother or grandfather?"

Huxley rose from his seat as Wilberforce's applause died down. He cleared his throat. He had prepared a few remarks, but first he replied to the bishop's closing salvo. "If then the question is put to me whether I would rather have a miserable ape for a grandfather or a man as highly endowed by nature and possessed of great means of influence and yet employs these faculties and that influence for the mere purpose of introducing ridicule into a grave scientific discussion, I unhesitatingly affirm my preference for the ape." The audience, who were already worked up into a vocal frenzy by the bishop's oratory, erupted with delight at Huxley's riposte.

The rest of Huxley's remarks were unremarkable. He was no public speaker and struggled to fill the large hall of the Oxford University Museum of Natural History in which the event was being held. Both men felt afterward that they had won the debate. It seems that the Bishop of Oxford may have drawn the largest cheers on the day, but that Huxley's support for Darwin was the more convincing scientific argument.

The organization is now called the British Science Association, and its annual conference is now the British Science Festival. Despite overwhelming evidence to the contrary since the exchanges that took place in Oxford, some religious fundamentalists still wish to continue the debate. But since Wilberforce insisted his objections were scientific and not doctrinal, perhaps his ghost has by now accepted Huxley's defense of Darwin's work.

Alexander Stephens
Cornerstone Speech

(March 21, 1861)

Ten days after the seceding Southern states declared their desire for "permanent federal government," their vice president of four weeks, Alexander Stephens, addressed a huge crowd at the Athenaeum in Savannah, Georgia. He was not the last VP to make remarks that his president might wish he hadn't.

"The constitution . . . rested upon the assumption of the equality of races. This was an error. It was a sandy foundation, and the government built upon it fell when the storm came and the wind blew.

Our new government is founded upon exactly the opposite idea; its foundations are laid, its cornerstone rests upon the great truth, that the negro is not equal to the white man; that slavery—subordination to the superior race—is his natural and normal condition. This, our new government, is the first, in the history of the world, based upon this great physical, philosophical, and moral truth. . . .

This truth has been slow in the process of its development, like all other truths in the various departments of science. It has been so even amongst us. Many who hear me, perhaps, can recollect well, that this truth was not generally admitted, even within their day. The errors of the past generation still clung to many as late as twenty years ago.

Those at the North, who still cling to these errors, with a zeal above knowledge, we justly denominate fanatics. All fanaticism springs from an aberration of the mind—from a defect in reasoning. It is a species of insanity. One of the most striking characteristics of insanity, in many instances, is forming correct conclusions from fancied or erroneous premises; so with the anti-slavery fanatics; their conclusions are right if their premises were. They assume that the negro is equal, and hence conclude that he is entitled to equal privileges and rights with the white man. If their premises were correct, their conclusions would be logical and just—but their premise being wrong, their whole argument fails."

ALEXANDER STEPHENS'S "CORNERSTONE SPEECH" JUSTIFYING THE CONFEDERACY

OPPOSITE: Alexander Stephens photographed between 1865 and 1880.

Alexander Stephens was a Georgia man who had represented his state in Congress. He was a moderate who opposed not only war but also secession, which he likened to Adam and Eve leaving the Garden of Eden. Raised in poverty but blessed with a fine mind, Stephens was a self-made man, a lawyer who invested his wealth in land—and slaves, of whom he owned over thirty. He was, it seems, a relatively kindly owner; but he had no reservations about the institution of slavery, the issue that dominated the 1860 presidential campaign eventually won by Abraham Lincoln.

The seceding states each made a Declaration of Causes, which cited economic favoritism toward the North, or a failure of central government to honor its frontier obligations, or in Alabama's case hostility "to the domestic institutions and to the peace and security of the people of Alabama." But when Stephens got up to speak in Savannah, he was all too clear about the central issue that had brought about the secession—slavery.

He attacked the fundamental premise of the Declaration of Independence—that "All men are created equal"—with a counterargument that gave the speech its name: "Our new government is founded upon exactly the opposite idea . . . its cornerstone rests on the great

truth that the negro is not equal to the white man. . . . This, our new government, is the first, in the history of the world, based upon this great physical, philosophical, and moral truth."

He continued, "They assume that the negro is equal, and hence conclude that he is entitled to equal privileges and rights with the white man. Their premise being wrong, their whole argument fails. They were attempting to make things equal which the Creator had made unequal." The South, in contrast, was simply following the laws of nature in enslaving the inferior black man.

Stephens spoke at length and also addressed the constitutional differences between the two sides, before concluding, "If we are true to ourselves, true to our cause, true to our high mission in presenting to the world the highest type of civilization ever exhibited by man, there will be found no word in our lexicon for 'fail.'"

It's important to remember that Stephens was saying nothing remarkable for his time and place. He was merely describing his audience's normality. There was what one reporter described as "a burst of enthusiasm and applause such as the Athenaeum had never displayed within its walls" when Alexander Stephens sat down. But to twenty-first-century ears it is a shocking position to take.

Jefferson Davis, the Confederate president, was not pleased at such an explicit description of the South's position. It suited the landed leaders of the Confederacy to have reasons that went beyond mere self-interest, and Davis and Stephens never got on. Stephens remained opposed to the war, and to the conscription, which later perpetuated it; and he had a secret meeting with his former congressional colleague Abraham Lincoln in efforts to find peace.

After the war, he continued to serve his fellow Georgians when they returned him to Congress from 1866 onward until they elected him State Governor in 1882. He died in office after only four months, having represented his state for over forty years. Remarkably, Alexander Stephens's slaves remained with him after abolition, and some were by his side when he died.

Abraham Lincoln
The Gettysburg Address

(November 19, 1863)

President Lincoln's address at the dedication of the Soldiers' National Cemetery consisted of little more than a few remarks. He was not the main speaker of the day—that honor belonged to Edward Everett, a Massachusetts pastor and orator who preceded Lincoln with a two-hour, 13,500-word speech. It is, however, Lincoln's 272 words that we remember today.

The Battle of Gettysburg, fought in July 1863 during the American Civil War, resulted in a victory for the Union and halted the advance northward of the Confederate forces. It was a milestone in the conflict, and its bloodiest engagement. From both sides a total of over 50,000 lay dead or injured in its aftermath. Burials of the estimated 9,000 dead were hasty and scattered across the battlefield and beyond.

A hill on which part of the battle had been fought was designated soon afterward as a cemetery in which to re-bury fallen Union soldiers. It was a complicated task to locate so many graves and was by no means complete when, four and half months after the battle, the cemetery was to be consecrated.

Edward Everett delivered a well-crafted address about the glory of battle and the dust of heroes. When Lincoln stood up to speak, the assembled dignitaries, troops, and gravediggers crowded round to hear what he had to say. He wore, eyewitnesses reported, an expression of infinite sadness. When he had finished there was no applause, just thoughtful, respectful silence. The following day, Everett wrote to Lincoln: "I should be glad if I could flatter myself that I came as near to the central idea of the occasion, in two hours, as you did in two minutes."

Lincoln began by evoking the spirit that had founded America with a simple statement. "Four score and seven years ago our fathers brought forth on this continent, a new nation, conceived in Liberty, and dedicated to the proposition that all men are created equal." In that one sentence he transformed the Civil War from a political struggle over the Union to a moral campaign for equality.

He continued by suggesting that the place where they stood was already consecrated, by the blood of the fallen. And then he returned to the bigger picture—America, an idea worth dying for: "That we here highly resolve that these dead shall not have died in vain—that this nation, under God, shall have a new birth of freedom—and that government of the people, by the people, for the people, shall not perish from the earth."

Lincoln's poetic language—"not have died in vain," "a new birth of freedom," "shall not perish"—in a place of graves was profoundly moving. His encapsulation of egalitarian republicanism in nine words—"of the people, by the people, for the people"—was the perfect definition of the ideal. Translated, it would later inspire the constitutions of France, China, and Japan.

Within eighteen months of the speech, the war was over. The Union had been preserved, slavery was abolished—and President Lincoln had been assassinated in Ford's Theatre. The words he spoke in Gettysburg were once learned by heart by American schoolchildren, and they are carved in stone on the Lincoln Memorial at the heart of the nation's capital. Although president and populace may from time to time lose sight of their country's founding principles of liberty and equality, those principles endure.

Four score and seven years ago our fathers brought forth on this continent, a new nation, conceived in Liberty, and dedicated to the proposition that all men are created equal.

Now we are engaged in a great civil war, testing whether that nation, or any nation so conceived and dedicated, can long endure. We are met on a great battlefield of that war. We have come to dedicate a portion of that field, as a final resting place for those who here gave their lives that that nation might live. It is altogether fitting and proper that we should do this.

But, in a larger sense, we can not dedicate—we can not consecrate—we can not hallow this ground. The brave men, living and dead, who struggled here, have consecrated it, far above our poor power to add or detract. The world will little note, nor long remember what we say here, but it can never forget what they did here. It is for us the living, rather, to be dedicated here to the unfinished work which they who fought here have thus far so nobly advanced. It is rather for us to be here dedicated to the great task remaining before us—that from these honored dead we take increased devotion to that cause for which they gave the last full measure of devotion—that we here highly resolve that these dead shall not have died in vain—that this nation, under God, shall have a new birth of freedom—and that government of the people, by the people, for the people, shall not perish from the earth.

GETTYSBURG ADDRESS

LEFT: Recreations of the famous speech have Lincoln standing on a formal stage to address the crowd, but in reality it was a more chaotic affair. This detail taken from a photograph of the event, shows a bare-headed Lincoln in the center, toward the top of the photo, to the left and below a man in a prominent top hat and sash.

Abraham Lincoln
Second Inaugural Address

(March 4, 1865)

During his first term as president, Abraham Lincoln faced many questions about his handling of the war with the South. Victory for the Union at the Battle of Atlanta swung an uncertain 1864 election campaign in his favor. Many expected that, triumphant in war, he would use his second inaugural address to answer his critics.

Although victory was assured, the last actions of the American Civil War were still being fought on Inauguration Day. Those who had attended the previous occasion in 1861 could see that the war had aged Lincoln. Much of his first inaugural speech had been devoted to appeals to the South not to start a war. "We are not enemies, but friends. We must not be enemies." As many as a million Americans had been killed since then.

Relief that the war was ending was therefore tempered by loss, and also by the atrocious weather that had persisted for weeks before Inauguration Day, turning the streets of Washington into rivers of mud. Magically, as Lincoln rose to speak, the sun which had been obscured all day (as one journalist reported it) "burst forth in its unclouded meridian splendor, and flooded the spectacle with glory and with light." No one could miss the symbolism. Lincoln himself remarked the next day: "Did you notice that sunburst? It made my heart jump."

If the waiting crowd and press expected a note of triumphalism from their reelected president, they were to be disappointed. What they got instead was a speech of dignified magnanimity anchored in a profound Christian faith. Lincoln, anxious to heal the nation's divisions, was determinedly evenhanded and in reporting on his first term he said little more than this: "Both parties deprecated war; but one of them would make war rather than let the nation survive; and the other would accept war rather than let it perish. And the war came."

The root of the war, he said, was slavery and the powerful interests invested in it. Rather than blame slave owners, he allowed that both sides believed they had God on their side, and "neither party expected for the war the magnitude or the duration which it has already attained." Lincoln accepted that an all-powerful God may have allowed the "offense" of slavery to be committed in America and that: "He gives to both North and South this terrible war as the woe due to those by whom the offense came. If God wills that it continue until every drop of blood drawn with the lash shall be paid by another drawn with the sword," then so be it.

He closed with moving reconciliation: "With malice toward none; with charity for all; let us strive on to finish the work we are in; to bind up the nation's wounds; to care for him who shall have borne the battle, and for his widow, and his orphan—to do all which may achieve and cherish a just and lasting peace, among ourselves, and with all nations."

The address received only scattered applause, and Lincoln did not feel it had gone down well. "Men are not flattered," he thought, "by being shown that there has been a difference of purpose between the Almighty and them." But it is now regarded as one of Lincoln's finest speeches, and like his Gettysburg address, it is carved in stone on the Lincoln Memorial. It ushered in an era of reconstruction in America: Emancipation of those enslaved, realignment of southern economies that had been dependent on them, and reconciliation of former enemies, all encouraged by Lincoln's moderate, evenhanded tone.

Abraham Lincoln's own role in the Reconstruction was tragically short. Less than six weeks after his second inauguration, he was shot dead in Ford's Theatre by the actor John Wilkes Booth, who had acted as a Confederate spy before and during the war. Lincoln was only fifty-six.

The Almighty has his own purposes. Woe unto the world because of offenses! For it must needs be that offenses come; but woe to that man by whom the offense cometh! If we shall suppose that American Slavery is one of those offenses which, in the providence of God, must needs come, but which, having continued through His appointed time, He now wills to remove, and that He gives to both North and South, this terrible war, as the woe due to those by whom the offense came, shall we discern therein any departure from those divine attributes which the believers in a Living God always ascribe to Him?

Fondly do we hope—fervently do we pray—that this mighty scourge of war may speedily pass away. Yet, if God wills that it continue, until all the wealth piled by the bond-man's two hundred and fifty years of unrequited toil shall be sunk, and until every drop of blood drawn with the lash, shall be paid by another drawn with the sword, as was said three thousand years ago, so still it must be said, the judgments of the Lord, are true and righteous altogether.

With malice toward none; with charity for all; with firmness in the right, as God gives us to see the right, let us strive on to finish the work we are in; to bind up the nation's wounds; to care for him who shall have borne the battle, and for his widow, and his orphan—to do all which may achieve and cherish a just and lasting peace, among ourselves, and with all nations.

ABRAHAM LINCOLN'S SECOND INAUGURAL ADDRESS

RIGHT: In an 1862 letter to Horace Greeley, Lincoln admitted: "My paramount object in this struggle is to save the Union, and is not either to save or to destroy slavery. If I could save the Union without freeing any slave I would do it." However, by the time of his 1865 inaugural speech in Washington, he was just weeks away from achieving both.

Chief Joseph
"From where the sun now stands, I will fight no more forever"
(October 5, 1877)

Joseph, born Hin-mah-too-yah-lat-kekt ("Thunder Rolling down the Mountain"), was not a warrior chief. He and his band of Nez Perce Indians lived peacefully in a fertile valley in Oregon until a series of events forced him to fight a war not of his making. Under his leadership, his people conducted a tactically brilliant campaign along 1,300 miles of territory, until they were, inevitably, overwhelmed.

> **T**ell General Howard I know his heart. What he told me before, I have it in my heart. I am tired of fighting. Our chiefs are killed; Looking Glass is dead, Too-hul-hul-sote is dead. The old men are all dead. It is the young men who say yes or no. He who led on the young men is dead. It is cold, and we have no blankets; the little children are freezing to death. My people, some of them, have run away to the hills, and have no blankets, no food. No one knows where they are, perhaps freezing to death. I want to have time to look for my children, and see how many of them I can find. Maybe I shall find them among the dead. Hear me, my chiefs! I am tired; my heart is sick and sad. From where the sun now stands, I will fight no more forever.

SURRENDER SPEECH

LEFT: *Chief Joseph, photographed by Edward Curtis.*

OPPOSITE: *Chief Joseph (center left with white headdress) and the Nez Perce tribe, including Looking Glass, photographed in 1872.*

Chief Joseph was named after his father, who took the name when he was converted to Christianity in Idaho by some missionaries from the east. Joseph Senior helped establish a Nez Perce reservation, which ran from Idaho to Oregon. But he renounced his faith and burned his bible when the US government took back six million square miles of it because gold had been found on Nez Perce land.

When they tried to clear Joseph Senior from his lush Oregon valley, he refused, and a tense standoff developed between the Nez Perce and impatient settlers. This was the situation that Joseph Junior inherited in 1871, after his father's death. He successfully negotiated an orderly withdrawal, but it was not respected by the settlers; and when the anger of some young Nez Perce warriors boiled over and they attacked and killed some white men, the government had no choice but to send in the cavalry.

Joseph set out for Montana, where he hoped to forge an alliance with the Sioux and Cheyenne nations led by Sitting Bull. To get there he had to lead his people—800 men, women, and children—across nearly 1,400 miles of harsh country, pursued by General Oliver Howard's cavalrymen and volunteers who were unencumbered by family or possessions. It was an unequal war, but Joseph's warriors fought a cunning strategic retreat, laying false trails and decoys and delaying the cavalry advance with surprise attacks.

Joseph arrived in Montana and set up camp to rest and recover from the fifty-day trek. But Howard had planned ahead, and a second cavalry force under General Nelson Miles now descended on the Nez Perce, scattering the women and children into the hills as the surviving men regrouped in a strong defensive position.

But Joseph, for the sake of the people under his care, had had enough. He surrendered. "Our chiefs are killed," he instructed his messenger to tell Howard. "Looking Glass is dead. Too-hul-hul-sote is dead. The old men are all dead. . . . He who led on the young men is dead."

He was concerned for those of his group who were not fit warriors. It was October, and "the little children are freezing to death. My people . . . have run away to the hills and have no blankets, no food. No one knows where they are, perhaps freezing to death. I want to have time to look for my children and see how many of them I can find. Maybe I shall find them among the dead." His fifteen-year-old daughter was among the missing.

He had lost his homeland, his best men and many women and children, the future of the tribe. The fight had gone out of him. His message ended with this: "I am tired; my heart is sick and sad. From where the sun now stands, I will fight no more forever." It was the voice of a weary old man; but Joseph was only thirty-seven.

Howard had the greatest respect for the way in which the Nez Perce had fought, and assured Joseph that he and his people would be returned to their reservation to live in peace. But the government, afraid that Joseph would lead his men in further attacks on white men, had other ideas. The Nez Perce were moved first to an insanitary, swampy field in east Kansas; then to Oklahoma where epidemics ran rife; and finally, to poor land on a different tribe's reservation in Washington State. Once again the Nez Perce were betrayed by the false word of the Christian white man.

Joseph never did get home to his lush valley, but from Washington State, he was a vocal and articulate critic of the government's treatment of Native Americans up to his death in 1904.

Oscar Wilde
"The love that dare not speak its name"

(May 1, 1895)

Much lampooned for his sharp, foppish wit, Oscar Wilde was one of the finest playwrights of the nineteenth century. His masterpiece *The Importance of Being Earnest* premiered in London on St. Valentine's Day 1895. Just weeks later he was facing personal and financial ruin, on trial for gross indecency, when the prosecutor, Mr. C. F. Gill, asked him directly, "What is 'the love that dare not speak its name'?"

> What is 'the Love that dare not speak its name'?
>
> WILDE: 'The Love that dare not speak its name' in this century is such a great affection of an elder for a younger man as there was between David and Jonathan, such as Plato made the very basis of his philosophy, and such as you find in the sonnets of Michelangelo and Shakespeare. It is that deep, spiritual affection that is as pure as it is perfect. It dictates and pervades great works of art like those of Shakespeare and Michelangelo, and those two letters of mine, such as they are.
>
> It is in this century misunderstood, so much misunderstood that it may be described as 'the Love that dare not speak its name,' and on account of it I am placed where I am now. It is beautiful, it is fine, it is the noblest form of affection. There is nothing unnatural about it. It is intellectual, and it repeatedly exists between an elder and a younger man, when the elder man has intellect, and the younger man has all the joy, hope, and glamour of life before him. That it should be so the world does not understand. The world mocks at it and sometimes puts one in the pillory for it.

'THE LOVE THAT DARE NOT SPEAK ITS NAME'

RIGHT: Oscar Wilde photographed in New York by Napoleon Sarony during his 1882 lecture tour. His subject was aestheticism, incorporating art into everyday life. It didn't go down well with the American press.

"The love that dare not speak its name" is a phrase from a poem called *Two Loves* by Lord Alfred Douglas, with whom Wilde had been having an intense affair since 1891. It was an illegal relationship under British law at the time, and therefore could not be publicly acknowledged, or in other words "speak its name."

Wilde and Douglas were flamboyantly indiscreet about their friendship, much to the anger of Douglas's father, the Marquis of Queensberry, who repeatedly demanded of both men that they end the affair. Four days after the opening of *The Importance of Being Earnest*, Queensberry left a calling card at the playwright's club addressed to "Oscar Wilde, posing somdomite." Although the spelling of sodomite was incorrect, the note was a public accusation of homosexuality, which Wilde unwisely sought to refute by taking Queensberry

to court. The Scottish nobleman who had formulated the rules of boxing was more than eager for a fight with the Irish playwright.

The evidence for Wilde's homosexuality was overwhelming. Queensberry was acquitted of libel on the grounds that what he had written was true, and Wilde faced bankruptcy in paying his opponent's legal costs. Worse still, the evidence for his homosexuality resulted in him being arrested and tried for the offense. It was during this second trial that the prosecuting counsel, after calling innumerable male prostitutes as witnesses to Wilde's behavior, asked the defendant, "What is 'the Love that dare not speak its name'?"

Wilde had been discomfited by the trial so far, but now he summoned up his full powers of eloquence: "It is that deep, spiritual affection," he replied, "that is as pure as it is perfect. … It is in this century misunderstood, so much misunderstood that it may be described as 'the Love that dare not speak its name,' and on account of it I am placed where I am now."

Thus far he might have maintained his innocence. But, warming to his theme, he continued: "There is nothing unnatural about it. It is intellectual, and it repeatedly exists between an elder and a younger man, when the elder man has intellect, and the younger man has all the joy, hope and glamour of life before him."

It was his truth, but under the prevailing law it left little doubt of his guilt. Although at the end of the trial he was acquitted by a hung jury, his fame and the details of his activities had aroused a great deal of scandalized public interest. The government was determined to make a public example of him, and at a third trial he was found guilty. Imprisoned for two years, his health suffered, and he spent his final years in exile. He died in Paris, only three years after his release from a traumatic experience in Reading Gaol.

The frenzy of prurient interest whipped up by the English press during Wilde's trials intensified public opinion against homosexuality. His staunch defense of 'the love that dare not speak its name' may actually have delayed society's acceptance of it; homosexuality in Britain was not decriminalized until 1967.

Referring to woman's sphere in life, I'll say that woman is always right. For twenty-five years I've been a woman's rights man. I have always believed, long before my mother died, that, with her gray hairs and admirable intellect, perhaps she knew as much as I did. Perhaps she knew as much about voting as I.

I should like to see the time come when women shall help to make the laws. I should like to see that whiplash, the ballot, in the hands of women. As for this city's government, I don't want to say much, except that it is a shame—a shame; but if I should live twenty-five years longer—and there is no reason why I shouldn't—I think I'll see women handle the ballot. If women had the ballot to-day, the state of things in this town would not exist.

If all the women in this town had a vote to-day they would elect a mayor at the next election, and they would rise in their might and change the awful state of things now existing here.

VOTES FOR WOMEN

LEFT: Mark Twain was an ardent convert to women's suffrage and also a long-time critic of the New York political system and its corrupt Tammany Hall government.

Mark Twain
Votes for Women
(January 20, 1901)

Mark Twain was not always the ardent feminist he became in later life. "I never want to see the women voting, and gabbling about politics, and electioneering," he wrote in a letter to the *Missouri Democrat* newspaper of St. Louis in 1867. But with marriage, maturity, and the passage of time, Twain brought his twin weapons of humor and satire to bear in support of the cause.

A year after his letter to the *Missouri Democrat,* Mark Twain met Olivia Langdon, a genteel daughter of affluent, sophisticated East Coast society. Her father disapproved of Twain, a rough straight-talking western journalist; and so naturally, the couple were soon married. In his wife's company, Twain was exposed to the enlightened arguments of liberal thinkers, and in 1875, he told an audience at the Monday Evening Club of Hartford: "We brag of our universal, unrestricted suffrage; but we are shams after all, for we restrict when we come to the women."

Twain wrote his best-loved novels and short stories in the two decades after he met Livy (as Olivia was always called). He also became the father of three daughters, who may have further influenced his attitude to women's suffrage. Success brought fortune, which Twain invariably plowed into schemes that caught his fancy if not his good judgment—his own publishing house for example, or an "Improvement in Adjustable and Detachable Straps for Garments," his response to his frustration with traditional suspenders. Despite his continuing popularity he was declared bankrupt in 1894.

Just as he seemed to be getting back on his feet, Twain was struck a cruel personal blow. His eldest daughter Susy contracted meningitis and in 1896, she died. The loss drove Twain into a bout of depression from which he never fully emerged for the rest of his life. At about the same time, his youngest daughter Jean was diagnosed with epilepsy. His writing took on a noticeably more bitter tone. His celebrated comic speeches sometimes slipped into sarcasm, as when he famously introduced a young Winston Churchill as guest speaker at the Waldorf-Astoria in 1900 with an anti-imperialist tirade. He strongly objected to the British treatment of Boers in South Africa, a campaign hitting the headlines at the time.

By contrast, his short talk on Votes for Women, given in early 1901 at the Hebrew Technical School for Girls in Manhattan, was a light and witty affair very much in the classic Twain mold. Speaking after an appeal for donations to the work of the school, Twain opened with a humorous story about the delay in passing a collection plate, which caused Twain once to cut back on his offering. Therefore, he quipped, "I adjure you all to give while the fever is on you."

On the matter of women's rights—"I'll say that woman is always right"—he spoke relatively briefly, informally, but in full support. "I should like to see the time come when women shall help to make the laws. I should like to see that whiplash, the ballot, in the hands of women. . . . If women had the ballot to-day, the state of things in this town would not exist."

American women had been agitating for equal rights since the 1840s. He prophesied at the Hebrew Technical School for Girls that "if I should live twenty-five years longer—and there is no reason why I shouldn't—I think I'll see women handle the ballot."

They did, but he didn't. Nineteen years later, in 1920, the Nineteenth Amendment was passed, stating that: "The right of citizens of the United States to vote shall not be denied or abridged by the United States or by any State on account of sex." Livy died in 1904, and in 1909, Twain's daughter Jean died in the bath during a fit on Christmas Eve. Mark Twain, brokenhearted, passed away only four months later.

Emmeline Pankhurst
Freedom or Death
(November 13, 1913)

In the United States, suffrage campaigners were still agitating through political channels for it; but in Britain, some had abandoned peaceful means and chosen direct action, as Emmeline Pankhurst explained to an audience in Hartford, Connecticut.

In Britain, as in America, opinion was divided on the best way to achieve women's suffrage. The questions that split the many factions of the movement included whether or not to align with particular political parties, whether to seek a gradual transition to universal suffrage, whether to ally with other causes such as trade unionism, whether to be militant or not, and whether to be violent or not.

Emmeline Pankhurst, the autocratic leader of the Women's Social and Political Union (WSPU), was on the extreme wing of the movement. Having lost patience with the political process, the WSPU was, by 1913, notorious for throwing stones through windows (including the prime minister's official residence, 10 Downing Street), arson attacks, and even explosions. WSPU members were the object of violent attacks by the police and members of the public. Frequently imprisoned, they undertook hunger strikes and were brutally force-fed.

In 1913, Pankhurst traveled through America on her second speaking tour. She may well have taken her audience by surprise when she told them at the start that she wasn't going to argue for suffrage, which "American suffragists can do very well for themselves." Fully aware of America's battle-torn history, she told them that the issue in Britain had become "the subject of revolution and civil war," and that she was there "as a soldier who has temporarily left the field of battle."

Revolution had worked for America, she argued, and for Russia and China, but always in the hands of men. What, she asked, if the men of Hartford could not vote, "that they were governed without their consent being obtained, that the legislature turned an absolutely deaf ear to their demands?" American men had become revolutionaries in the past. She cited the example of the Boston Tea Party, the first militant incident in the campaign for American independence.

Noncombatants suffered in civil war, Pankhurst acknowledged. Wryly, she noted that women had gone without tea after the Boston Tea Party, but that the men "did not follow it up by throwing the whiskey overboard." The acts of criminal damage perpetrated by the WSPU were necessary to force men in power to pay attention. Golf courses had been vandalized, works of art slashed, and telegraph wires sabotaged. "You cannot make omelettes without breaking eggs; you cannot have civil war without damage to something. You do just as much as will arouse feeling to bring about peace.

"You won the civil war by the sacrifice of human life when you decided to emancipate the negro. You have left it to women in your land—the men of all civilized countries have left it to women—to work out their own salvation. . . . We will put the enemy in the position where they will have to choose between giving us freedom or giving us death."

This was a defiant, well-argued speech. Emmeline Pankhurst's grasp of American history was designed to win friends, and its conclusion, echoing the words of American revolutionary Patrick Henry, must have touched American hearts in Hartford. It might not have played so well back in Britain, where little English blood had been shed since the seventeenth century.

All that was about to change. When war erupted in Europe the following year, the WSPU suspended its campaign so that the nation could focus on the greater threat, Germany. Their reward was the Representation of People Act of 1918, which extended the vote to British women over the age of thirty who were occupiers of property or married to occupiers—a first step on the road to universal suffrage.

They little know what women are. Women are very slow to rouse, but once they are aroused, once they are determined, nothing on earth and nothing in heaven will make women give way; it is impossible.—There are women who are being carried from their sick beds on stretchers into meetings. They are too weak to speak, but they go amongst their fellow workers just to show that their spirits are unquenched, and that their spirit is alive, and they mean to go on as long as life lasts.

Now, I want to say to you who think women cannot succeed, we have brought the government of England to this position, that it has to face this alternative: either women are to be killed or women are to have the vote. I ask American men in this meeting, what would you say if in your state you were faced with that alternative, that you must either kill them or give them their citizenship? Well, there is only one answer to that alternative, there is only one way out—you must give those women the vote.

You won your freedom in America when you had the revolution, by bloodshed, by sacrificing human life. You won the civil war by the sacrifice of human life when you decided to emancipate the negro. You have left it to women in your land—the men of all civilized countries have left it to women—to work out their own salvation. That is the way in which we women of England are doing. Human life for us is sacred, but we say if any life is to be sacrificed it shall be ours; we won't do it ourselves, but we will put the enemy in the position where they will have to choose between giving us freedom or giving us death.

"FREEDOM OR DEATH" SPEECH

ABOVE: *In 1913, suffragettes burned down the teahouse at Kew Gardens.*

LEFT: *Emmeline Pankhurst.*

Patrick Pearse
"Ireland unfree shall never be at peace"

(August 1, 1915)

Patrick Pearse, a lawyer with a degree in modern languages, was good with words. When an oration was called for at the graveside of a stalwart of early Irish republicanism, he was chosen for the job. His words perfectly captured the mood of those fighting for independence from British rule.

In 1915, Jeremiah O'Donovan Rossa died in exile in New York, having promised in 1870 never to return to Ireland if he was released from a life sentence. He had been plotting to overthrow the British government in Ireland, and at liberty in New York he continued his work through fund-raising and the publication of a republican newspaper *The United Irishman*. He was a role model for later generations of Irish freedom fighters, who saw his death as an opportunity to rally support for the cause.

His body was flown back to Dublin, given a hero's welcome, and guarded day and night by soldiers of the republican Irish Volunteers (IV). Patrick Pearse, a member of the IV, was asked to speak at the interment. His lifelong commitment to Irish independence had seen

him rise rapidly through the ranks of the secret Irish Republican Brotherhood (IRB). Having joined in 1913, he was already on its Supreme Council. He was also on its Military Council, which with the utmost secrecy was already planning the rebellion that became known as the Easter Rising.

Pearse's brief for his graveside speech, from his fellow IRB councillor Thomas Clarke, was "make it hot as hell, throw discretion to the winds." And he did. Republicanism was experiencing a resurgence of interest, and from the outset Pearse sought to bind all present together in common cause, which they shared with the dead man. He was speaking, he said, "on behalf of a new generation that has been re-baptised in the Fenian faith, and that has accepted the responsibility of carrying out the Fenian program."

Baptism was one of several religious metaphors with which he punctuated his words. They were all in communion with O'Donovan, working for a holy cause. Adopting the Gaelic grammatical construction "of him," he had the orator's instinct for rhythm and repetition. "Splendid and holy causes are served by men who are themselves splendid and holy. O'Donovan Rossa was splendid in the proud manhood of him, splendid in the heroic grace of him, splendid in the Gaelic strength and clarity and truth of him."

Pearse's final remarks that day became a rallying cry for the rebellion to come. "They think that they have pacified Ireland. They think that they have purchased half of us and intimidated the other half. They think that they have foreseen everything, think that they have provided against everything; but the fools, the fools, the fools! They have left us our Fenian dead, and while Ireland holds these graves, Ireland unfree shall never be at peace."

In communion of spirit too with our own dear comrades who suffer in English prisons to-day, and speaking on their behalf as well as our own, we pledge to Ireland our love, and we pledge to English rule in Ireland our hate.

This is a place of peace, sacred to the dead, where men should speak with all charity and with all restraint; but I hold it a Christian thing, as O'Donovan Rossa held it, to hate evil, to hate untruth, to hate oppression, and, hating them, to strive to overthrow them.

Our foes are strong and wise and wary; but, strong and wise and wary as they are, they cannot undo the miracles of God who ripens in the hearts of young men the seeds sown by the young men of a former generation. And the seeds sown by the young men of '65 and '67 are coming to their miraculous ripening to-day.

Rulers and Defenders of Realms had need to be wary if they would guard against such processes. Life springs from death; and from the graves of patriot men and women spring living nations. The Defenders of this Realm have worked well in secret and in the open. They think that they have pacified Ireland. They think that they have purchased half of us and intimidated the other half. They think that they have foreseen everything, think that they have provided against everything; but the fools, the fools, the fools!—They have left us our Fenian dead, and while Ireland holds these graves, Ireland unfree shall never be at peace.

"IRELAND UNFREE SHALL NEVER BE AT PEACE" SPEECH

On April 24, 1916, Pearse read the Proclamation of the Republic from the steps of the Post Office on Sackville Street in Dublin, launching the Easter Rising. He had been chosen to be the new republic's first president. But after six days of heavy fighting in the city, it was Pearse who gave the order to surrender. The rebellion had failed; Pearse, Clarke, and thirteen other of its leaders were summarily executed in Kilmainham Gaol. Their bodies were withheld from their families for fear that their graves might be as inspirational as O'Donovan Rossa's.

Nevertheless, the fuse had been lit, and the Irish War of Independence, begun in 1919, ended in 1921, with the birth of the Irish republic of which Pearse, O'Donovan Rossa, and other Fenians had dreamed.

ABOVE: Patrick Pearse speaking at Dolphin's Barn on August 30th.
OPPOSITE: The 1915 funeral of Jeremiah O'Donovan Rossa.

Vladimir Lenin
"Power to the Soviets"

(September 1917)

In February 1917, factory workers in St. Petersburg and other cities, overworked and underfed in support of Russian involvement in World War I, rose up in revolt and forced Tsar Nicholas II to abdicate. Vladimir Ilyich Lenin and other exiles were jubilant, but on his return to Russia, Lenin was dismayed to find that the revolution did not support his socialist goals.

A courageous and resolute government steering a firm course is nothing but the dictatorship of the proletariat and the poor peasants. What would such a dictatorship mean in practice? Two days after its creation ninety-nine percent of the army would be enthusiastic supporters of this dictatorship. This dictatorship would give land to the peasants and full power to the local peasant committees.

How can anyone in his right senses doubt that the peasants would support this dictatorship? What Peshekhonov only promised, this dictatorship would put into effect, would translate into reality. At the same time the democratic organizations of food supply, control, etc., that have already begun to form, would in no way be eliminated. They would, on the contrary, be supported and developed, and all obstacles in the way of their work would be removed.

Only the dictatorship of the proletariat and the poor peasants is capable of smashing the resistance of the capitalists, of displaying truly supreme courage and determination in the exercise of power, and of securing the enthusiastic, selfless and truly heroic support of the masses both in the army and among the peasants.

Power to the Soviets—this is the only way to make further progress gradual, peaceful and smooth, keeping perfect pace with the political awareness and resolve of the majority of the people and with their own experience. Power to the Soviets means the complete transfer of the country's administration and economic control into the hands of the workers and peasants, to whom nobody would dare offer resistance and who, through practice, through their own experience, would soon learn how to distribute the land, products, and grain properly.

"POWER TO THE SOVIETS" SPEECH

OPPOSITE: Lenin speaking at a rally in 1917. Leon Trotsky stands to the right of the stage.

After the fall of the tsar, the provisional government formed by the country's middle class, the bourgeoisie, struggled to solve the problems that had brought them to power. In particular its continuing support of Russia's involvement in the war was unpopular. The working classes, the proletariat, formed workers' councils called soviets, which took control of some areas of transport and industry. However, they were poorly organized, and when they tried to rise up against the government, they were defeated.

The passing of power from the imperial court to the provisional government was enough for some revolutionaries. Lenin, however, saw it as merely the first stage of a complete revolution, the second being the handing of power to the proletariat. During his journey back to St. Petersburg from exile, he wrote four doctrinal essays, known now as the April Theses, in which he set out the requirements and results of such a revolution. His proposal was encapsulated in four words: "Power to the Soviets."

The slogan was taken up by the Bolsheviks and their supporters. In the second half of 1917, a war of words raged between the two revolutionary factions, the moderate Mensheviks and the hardline Bolsheviks, for the hearts and minds of ordinary people. Lenin was tireless in campaigning, delivering speech after speech. In one address, given in Moscow in September, he explained that his idea meant far more than merely electing members of Soviets to parliament.

"'Power to the Soviets' means radically reshaping the entire old state apparatus," he said, "removing this apparatus and substituting for it a new, popular one, a truly democratic apparatus of Soviets, the organized and armed majority of the people—the workers, soldiers, and peasants."

Although Lenin had previously argued that the proletariat should only be given power when they were

ready for it, he was now agitating for immediate change. "Let those who say, 'We have no apparatus to replace the old one, which inevitably gravitates towards the defense of the bourgeoisie' be ashamed of themselves. For this apparatus exists: it is the Soviets. Put your faith in their revolutionary organizations and you will see in all realms of state affairs the strength, majesty, and invincibility of the workers and peasants."

Lenin believed that all over Europe, soldiers and workers wearied by the deadly war, were on the verge of joining Russia in revolution. The time, he felt, was now, and his sense of urgency was infectious. "There is no middle course. Either all power goes to the Soviets both centrally and locally, and all land is given to the peasants immediately; or the landowners and capitalists obstruct every step. Power to the Soviets means the complete transfer of the country's administration and economic control into the hands of the workers and peasants. . . ."

The Bolsheviks gained momentum under Lenin's leadership and ousted the provisional government in an almost bloodless coup in October, a month after this speech. The reality of life under a communist government was very different from the egalitarian picture he painted. Power never reached the peasants, and a new ruling class emerged of senior Communist leaders who were as out of touch with the working classes as the tsar had been. After Lenin's death, his successor, Stalin, ruled the country through terror.

Lenin's admirable notion of all men as equals proved to be unsustainable; the maxim "from each according to his ability, to each according to his need" omitted an important part of the human psyche—ambition. With no incentive to work hard except fear of the Party, the Soviet Union became notoriously inefficient and corrupt. The Communist state was finally dismantled on December 26, 1991, less than seventy-five years after its establishment.

Woodrow Wilson
Fourteen Points

(January 8, 1918)

As the tide of World War I turned in favor of the Allied powers, their leaders began to consider the shape of Europe's future. Prime Minister Lloyd George made a public statement on the matter on January 5, 1918. US president Woodrow Wilson addressed Congress on the subject three days later.

Woodrow Wilson built his reputation on a series of progressive economic and fiscal reforms, including the introduction of antitrust laws and income tax. He maintained a policy of neutrality toward the conflict in Europe, until in 1917, Germany declared that American shipping was a legitimate target for its submarine warfare. America's entry into the theater of war "to make the world safe for democracy" undoubtedly affected its outcome.

Wilson set up a study group to identify America's formal war aims. It undertook an exhaustive review of the foreign policies of America and its allies, including the many secret treaties between European nations that had dragged some countries into the war because of their obligations to others. The group of 150 men included philosophers, historians, lawyers, and cartographers, as well as intelligence chiefs and economists. In consultation with Wilson, this Council of the Wise produced a fourteen-point plan as progressive as the president's domestic policy had been.

It is somewhat surprising that leaders of the Allied Powers did not consult with each other about the goals that they wished to achieve, postwar. But Lloyd George's speech outlining the British position was broadly in tune with Woodrow Wilson's; and Wilson was almost persuaded not to bother with his own. The chairman of the study group, Edward House, convinced him to go ahead.

"The day is gone by," Wilson began, "of secret covenants entered into in the interests of particular governments and likely at some unlooked-for moment to upset the peace of the world. What we demand is that the world be made safe and fit to live in."

First among his list of fourteen goals was a peace that would not be undermined by private agreements between governments. He also sought a reduction in arms and freedom on the seas outside territorial waters, something that Britain, ruler of the waves, opposed. He proposed free trade between nations as a way of preserving the peace, a model later adopted by Europe after World War II.

He called for the withdrawal of all invading troops, the creation of Turkey and Poland out of the former Ottoman and Prussian Empires, the redrawing of certain borders of France and Italy, and guarantees of independence for Balkan states, which had, before the war, been imperial territories in someone else's empire. In this wide-ranging and complex redrawing of the geo-political map, a forum would be required for discussion and compromise. The fourteenth and last item on Wilson's shopping list was this: "A general association of nations must be formed under specific covenants for the purpose of affording mutual guarantees of political independence and territorial integrity to great and small states alike."

The idealistic and highly moral speech was not universally well received, either at home or abroad, but by the end of the summer, France and Italy had signed up for it, and Britain too, except for its maritime concerns. Lloyd George insisted on the need for Germany to make war reparations. Thus modified, Woodrow Wilson's Fourteen Points formed the basis for the Treaty of Versailles, which formally concluded the war after the German surrender. The "association of nations" that he called for was established as the League of Nations.

It was a triumph for the president, who in 1919 was awarded the Nobel Prize for Peace. But despite his pleas that the United States ratify the treaty and join the League, opposition from the Senate meant that

T**he program of the world's peace, therefore, is our program; and that** program, the only possible program, as we see it, is this:

I. Open covenants of peace, openly arrived at.

II. Absolute freedom of navigation upon the seas, outside territorial waters.

III. The removal, so far as possible, of all economic barriers.

IV. Adequate guarantees given and taken that national armaments will be reduced to the lowest point consistent with domestic safety.

V. A free, open-minded, and absolutely impartial adjustment of all colonial claims.

VI. The evacuation of all Russian territory [by foreign troops].

VII. Belgium, the whole world will agree, must be evacuated and restored.

VIII. All French territory should be freed and the invaded portions restored.

IX. A readjustment of the frontiers of Italy should be effected along clearly recognizable lines of nationality.

X. The peoples of Austria-Hungary, whose place among the nations we wish to see safeguarded and assured, should be accorded the freest opportunity to autonomous development.

XI. Rumania, Serbia, and Montenegro should be evacuated.

XII. The Turkish portion of the present Ottoman Empire should be assured a secure sovereignty.

XIII. An independent Polish state should be erected which should include the territories inhabited by indisputably Polish populations.

XIV. A general association of nations must be formed under specific covenants for the purpose of affording mutual guarantees of political independence and territorial integrity to great and small states alike.

THE FOURTEEN-POINT PLAN

America, the very country that had secured the peace, did neither. The reparations demanded by the Allies and the restrictions placed on rebuilding Germany's armed forces stirred up resentment, which fueled the rise of National Socialism in Germany. The League collapsed with the outbreak of World War II, but it paved the way for the United Nations, which was created at the end of that second global conflict.

RIGHT: Woodrow Wilson addresses Congress in December 1918.

That law then which governs all life is God. Law and the Lawgiver are one. I may not deny the Law or the Lawgiver because I know so little about it or Him, just as my denial or ignorance of the existence of an earthly power will avail me nothing. Even so, my denial of God and His law will not liberate me from its operation. Whereas, humble and mute acceptance of divine authority makes life's journey easier even as the acceptance of earthly rule makes life under it easier.

I do dimly perceive that whilst everything around me is ever dying, ever guiding, there is—underlying all that change—a living power that is changeless, that holds all together; that creates, dissolves, and recreates. That informing power of spirit is God. And since nothing else that I see merely through the senses can or will persist, He alone is.

And if this power is benevolent or malevolent, I see it as purely benevolent. For, I can see that in the midst of death, life persists. In the midst of untruth, truth persists. In the midst of darkness, light persists. Hence I gather that God is life, truth, light. He is love. He is the supreme good.

But, He is no God who merely satisfies the intellect, if He ever does. God to be God must rule the heart and transform it. He must express himself in ever smallest act of His votary. This can only be done through a definite realization more real than the five senses can ever prove use. Sense perceptions can be and often are false and deceptive, however real they may appear to us. Where there is realization outside the senses it is infallible.

"MY SPIRITUAL MESSAGE"—KINGSLEY HALL, LONDON

LEFT: Gandhi addressing the crowds that had flocked to see him at Kingsley Hall, in London's impoverished East End.

Mahatma Gandhi
"My Spiritual Message"
(October 17, 1931)

Mohandas K. Gandhi, the Mahatma Gandhi, was a thorn in the side of India's British rulers. He coordinated many campaigns against social injustice. His strategy of nonviolent civil disobedience won him a seat at the Round Table Conferences held in London to consider constitutional reform in India.

While he was in London attending the second of the three conferences in late 1931, Gandhi stayed for three months in Kingsley Hall as the guest of Muriel Lester. Kingsley Hall was not a stately home but a thriving community center in the East End of London, run by Muriel and her sister Doris. It had developed out of a nursery school the sisters opened in 1912, and expanded to serve all ages in the development of mind, body and spirit. The center was conceived "as a place of fellowship in which people can meet for social, educational and recreational intercourse without barriers of class, color or creed."

Muriel, a committed socialist, fed the hungry at Kingsley Hall during the General Strike of 1926. As a fervent pacifist she admired Gandhi's nonviolent approach and made several visits to him in India in the late 1920s. They became friends, and Gandhi once teased her: "I think of all my English friends, known and unknown; you are by no means the least."

Gandhi was very content to stay at Kingsley Hall, where he walked and slept, as he did in India, among the poor. Although everyone from Charlie Chaplin to Prime Minister Lloyd George beat a path to his door, the largest crowds to meet him there attended a talk he gave during his visit entitled "My Spiritual Message."

In it he described the natural law and orderliness in the world, which, he argued, was evidence for a spiritual power and he conceded ". . . just as my denial or ignorance of the existence of an earthly power will avail me nothing. Even so, my denial of God and His law will not liberate me from its operation."

One's five senses were not infallible," he admitted. "But I do dimly perceive that whilst everything around me is ever dying, ever guiding, there is—underlying all that change—a living power that is changeless, that holds all together; that creates, dissolves, and recreates. That informing power of spirit is God. . . . Hence I gather that God is life, truth, light. He is love. He is the supreme good."

It was a deeply moving speech for those who heard it. This slight, gentle, round-faced man in simple robes, who spoke in soft, measured tones, seemed to be the embodiment of passive acceptance of his God's benevolent power.

He seemed, however, by implication, to be recommending an acceptance of the earthly order of things—an attitude that quite contradicted his own example of civil disobedience. Only in the final paragraph of his talk was there the slightest hint that the authority of a spiritual power might overrule that of a lesser. "Exercise of faith will be the safest where there is a clear determination summarily to reject all that is contrary to truth and love."

On his return to India, Gandhi was, not for the first or last time, arrested and imprisoned. In Britain, Winston Churchill mocked him in racist terms for daring to "stride half-naked up the steps of the Vice-regal palace to parley on equal terms with the representative of the King-Emperor." It was a remark that perpetuated Britain's imperial attitude well into the 1940s.

During World War II, Gandhi urged nonviolent non-cooperation with Britain's military effort to stave off Japanese advance into the subcontinent through his Quit India campaign. He was imprisoned again. But by the end of the war, he had won a moral victory, and on August 15, 1947, India became an independent nation state. Gandhi lived to see his faith in a moral order justified. As he said in his closing remarks at Kingsley Hall sixteen years earlier, "Faith transcends reason. All that I can advise is not to attempt the impossible."

Adolf Hitler
First speech as chancellor of Germany

(February 10, 1933)

Reeling from runaway inflation, a punitive reparations bill from World War I, and the global Depression of the 1920s, Germany was a country in ruins where resentment and poverty provided the perfect breeding ground for extremism. Adolf Hitler's Nationalsozialistische Deutsche Arbeiterpartei (NSDAP), the National Socialist German Workers' Party, rode this wave of anger to power in 1933.

In addition to decency in all areas of our life: decency in our administration, decency in public life, and decency in our culture as well, we want to restore German honor, to restore its due respect and the commitment to it, and we want to engrave upon our hearts the commitment to freedom.

In doing so, we desire to bestow once more upon the Volk a genuinely German culture with German art, German architecture, and German music, which shall restore to us our soul, and we shall thus evoke reverence for the great traditions of our Volk; evoke deep reverence for the accomplishments of the past, a humble admiration for the great men of German history.

We want to lead our youth back to this glorious Reich of our past. Humbled shall they bow before those who lived before us and labored and worked and toiled so that they could live today. And we want most of all to educate this youth to revere those who once made the most difficult sacrifice for the life of our Volk and the future of our Volk. For all the damage these fourteen years wrought, their worst crime was that they defrauded two million dead of their sacrifice, and these two million shall rise anew before the eyes of our youth as an eternal warning, as a demand that they be revenged.

We want to educate our youth to revere our time-honored army, which they should remember, which they should admire, and in which they should once more recognize the powerful expression of the strength of the German nation, the epitome of the greatest achievement our Volk has ever accomplished in its history.

FIRST ADDRESS AS CHANCELLOR OF GERMANY

OPPOSITE: Adolf Hitler addressing supporters on February 10, 1933, at the Berlin Sports Palace.

The NSDAP was a minority party, in decline in the 1920s until the financial crisis at the end of the decade brought disaffected voters flocking to it. In four years its support rose from under 3 percent of the population to over 37 percent. Two general elections in 1932 failed to produce a stable government. Although the NSDAP was not in the majority, Germany's president Paul von Hindenburg reluctantly appointed Hitler as chancellor, in the hope that Hitler's personal magnetism might bring about a government of unity.

His appointment as chancellor gave Hitler the opportunity he had been waiting for. He installed members of the NSDAP in key roles, and his first speech in office spoke of what was to come. His theme was "Volk und Erde"—the People and the Land. Before a huge crowd of Berliners in the city's Sports Palace, he promised "to bestow once more upon the Volk a genuinely German culture, with German art, German architecture and German music, which shall restore to us our soul," evoking reverence "for the great traditions of our Volk, for the accomplishments of the past . . . for the great men of German history."

There is no evidence that German culture or history was under threat, but the country certainly felt emasculated. Hitler sought to turn that sense of powerlessness on its head by portraying Germany as the victim in a hostile Europe. It was Us against Them—"we shall never believe in foreign help, never in help which lies outside our own nation, outside our own race."

He described the worker and the peasant as the two pillars of national tradition, who had been brought low by "Marxist economic theories" and "a rotten democracy," the peasantry impoverished and "the most industrious class driven to ruin." This was a drive toward isolationist totalitarianism in which all individuals must serve the greater good of the German nation.

Twice he used the word "alien"—"we

rebuild our people not according to theories hatched by some alien brain"; "the German worker must no longer be an alien in the German Reich." Although he didn't mention the Jews, his hideous song of racial purity was already composed. "The future of the German race lies in itself alone."

There is no doubt that Hitler was a mesmerizing speaker. He spoke forcefully and fluently, conveying a sense of a man in command of his world. His strong physical presence and his undeniably violent rhetorical style projected an image of ruthless ability—he looked and sounded like a man who would get things done. He empowered a directionless German people; but he led them to death, destruction, and crimes against humanity, rather than harnessing that energy to recovery and peaceful trade with nations. Ironically, the ruinous war he fought allowed a shattered Germany to rebuild itself into the economic powerhouse it is today.

Hitler's first speech as chancellor bears fascinating comparison with Franklin D. Roosevelt's first inaugural speech given only three weeks later. Both men were the new leaders of countries in the grip of recession. Both sought to energize their farmers and workers with new goals and optimism. Hitler extoled German "Volk und Erde;" and Roosevelt, in an altogether more benign and effective way, put America first.

I am certain that my fellow Americans expect that on my induction into the Presidency I will address them with a candor and a decision which the present situation of our Nation impels. This is pre-eminently the time to speak the truth, the whole truth, frankly and boldly. Nor need we shrink from honestly facing conditions in our country today. This great Nation will endure as it has endured, will revive and will prosper.

So, first of all, let me assert my firm belief that the only thing we have to fear is fear itself—nameless, unreasoning, unjustified terror which paralyzes needed efforts to convert retreat into advance. In every dark hour of our national life a leadership of frankness and vigor has met with that understanding and support of the people themselves which is essential to victory. I am convinced that you will again give that support to leadership in these critical days.

We face the arduous days that lie before us in the warm courage of national unity; with the clear consciousness of seeking old and precious moral values; with the clean satisfaction that comes from the stern performance of duty by old and young alike. We aim at the assurance of a rounded and permanent national life.

We do not distrust the future of essential democracy. The people of the United States have not failed. In their need they have registered a mandate that they want direct, vigorous action. They have asked for discipline and direction under leadership. They have made me the present instrument of their wishes. In the spirit of the gift I take it.

"THE ONLY THING WE HAVE TO FEAR IS FEAR ITSELF"—OPENING AND CLOSING SECTIONS OF INAUGURAL ADDRESS,

LEFT: President Franklin D. Roosevelt making his 1933 inaugural address to an audience before the East Portico of the Capitol.

Franklin D. Roosevelt
"The only thing we have to fear is fear itself"

(March 4, 1933)

The 1932 US election saw Franklin D. Roosevelt elected to the highest office in the land by a population on its knees. One in four Americans was unemployed, and the economy had ground to a halt. Crushed in the grip of the Great Depression, what they needed from him, more than anything, was hope and jobs.

Roosevelt had defeated his opponent Herbert Hoover in a landslide vote, and the American people expected him to deliver them from their despair. "For the trust reposed in me," he promised, "I will return the courage and the devotion that befit the time. I can do no less."

FDR knew about courage. Paralyzed from the waist down by an unidentified disease in 1921, he avoided the use of his wheelchair in public; but his condition was public knowledge. One of the bravest aspects of his inaugural speech was contained not in his fine words but in the sight of him overcoming his disability to walk down the steps from the Capitol to the inaugural stage.

This was a speech about bravery in the face of poverty and hunger. FDR's speech was peppered with metaphors of war—the need to "convert retreat into advance," "the lines of attack" that FDR laid out; his call for "a unity of duty hitherto evoked only in time of armed strife;" his promise to use Executive powers if need be, "as great as would be given to me if we were invaded by a foreign foe."

It was fighting talk from the opening salvo, which included the speech's most famous line: "the only thing we have to fear is fear itself." By his entrance to the stage and his words from it, FDR showed that he would, with the people's support, lead them from the front. "If we are to go forward we must move as a trained and loyal army willing to sacrifice for the good of a common discipline."

To mobilize this civilian army FDR had to identify the enemy. He could not afford to shy away from "the dark realities of the moment." He spoke directly therefore about the collapse of the economy and its impact on farmers, savers, and workers of all kinds.

The blame, in a situation that would be repeated in the early twenty-first century, lay squarely with the banks: "Faced by failure of credit they have proposed only the lending of more money. They know only the rules of a generation of self-seekers. They have no vision, and when there is no vision the people perish."

The president's tone changed in the second half of his address, as he said, "Restoration calls however not for changes in ethics alone. This nation asks for action, and action now." He suggested a number of ways in which action might be taken to stimulate the domestic economy, a priority over the need to boost international trade, which had fallen by 50 percent.

The actions that FDR proposed to take coalesced during his first term into America's New Deal, a program of legislation and regulation that reformed the financial sector, boosted agriculture, and undertook federally funded public works to relieve unemployment. "With this pledge taken," Roosevelt promised at his 1933 inauguration, "I assume unhesitatingly the leadership of this great army of our people dedicated to a disciplined attack upon our common problems."

His parting thought was this: "The people of the United States have not failed." At a time when so many Americans had been made to feel weak and useless by poverty and unemployment, this was exactly the bold, positive speech that his audience wanted to hear, from a father figure determined to restore their country's optimism, unity, and prosperity. Undoubtedly, it contributed to his popularity, and to the electorate's choice in sending him back to the White House another three times.

Edward VIII
Announcement of abdication

(December 11, 1936)

The relationship of a British king with a married American woman scandalized the British Empire and created a constitutional dilemma for the British government. Edward VIII's steadfast love for Wallis Simpson in the face of popular and political opposition left him only one course of action.

> **At long last I am able to say a few words of my own. I have never wanted to** withhold anything, but until now it has not been constitutionally possible for me to speak.
>
> A few hours ago I discharged my last duty as King and Emperor, and now that I have been succeeded by my brother, the Duke of York, my first words must be to declare my allegiance to him. This I do with all my heart.
>
> You all know the reasons which have impelled me to renounce the throne. But I want you to understand that in making up my mind I did not forget the country or the empire, which, as Prince of Wales and lately as King, I have for twenty-five years tried to serve.
>
> But you must believe me when I tell you that I have found it impossible to carry the heavy burden of responsibility and to discharge my duties as King as I would wish to do without the help and support of the woman I love.
>
> And I want you to know that the decision I have made has been mine and mine alone. This was a thing I had to judge entirely for myself. The other person most nearly concerned has tried up to the last to persuade me to take a different course.
>
> I have made this, the most serious decision of my life, only upon the single thought of what would, in the end, be best for all.

ABDICATION SPEECH AS BROADCAST ON RADIO

OPPOSITE: Edward VIII broadcasting to the Empire in 1936.

Edward, Prince of Wales, had been conducting an affair with Wallis Simpson for two years when the early death of his father, George V, elevated him to the British throne. Edward announced his intention to marry Wallis, who had divorced her first husband and was about to divorce her second, the shipping executive Ernest Simpson.

This brought his personal and public lives into direct conflict. As head of state he was now also head of the Church of England, the established church of the country. The Church of England did not allow divorcees to remarry as long as their former spouses were still alive, as both of Wallis's were. Furthermore, the grounds for Wallis's first divorce were not recognized by the Church of England; so in English eyes she was already a bigamist. As head of the Church, Edward was bound to uphold its views. As a man in love, he could not.

British public opinion was split broadly along class lines. Edward, who was a modernizer with little respect for the archaic traditions of royalty and government, won the support of the working people of the country. Unsurprisingly, the conservative middle classes were horrified at his nonconformity. The governments of Britain and all its dominions were universally opposed to the marriage. In the end, to avoid causing damage to the nation and to the institution of the monarchy, Edward abdicated, stepping down from the throne in favor of his brother who then became George VI.

Although the constitutional crisis was thereby averted, it was a sensational step to take. Earlier British monarchs had been forced to abdicate by opposing forces, but this was the first time a king had done so voluntarily in a thousand years of history. And he did it for love. When he addressed the nation by radio, he memorably declared, in a speech carefully edited by Winston Churchill, "I have found it impossible to carry the heavy burden of responsibility and to discharge my duties as King as I would wish to do without the help and support of the woman I love."

It was a dignified speech, in which he was at pains to state his allegiance to the new king, and to deny any rift with the government of the day. The truth was very different. Although George VI quickly made Edward the Duke of Windsor and allowed him to be spoken to as "His Royal Highness," he specifically denied Wallis the address "Her Royal Highness." Nor could it be claimed that Edward and the government were united in their views—the prime minister, Stanley Baldwin, had ordered a secret investigation of Mrs. Simpson's past and present in an effort to discredit her.

Quite apart from his affair with Wallis, it was generally agreed that unconventional Edward would not have made a good king. George VI stepped up to the role and with his wife, Elizabeth, provided genuine comfort and leadership to their subjects during World War II.

It is George's descendants who now carry the royal line. His daughter is Elizabeth II, the longest reigning monarch in British history. And his great grandson Harry, although not first in line to the throne after Charles, has caused no stir at all by marrying a woman who is not only American, not only divorced, but of mixed race. It's too late for Edward VIII, but times have changed.

Neville Chamberlain
"Peace for our time"

(September 30, 1938)

Neville Chamberlain was not the greatest orator of his generation, overshadowed by Winston Churchill among others. His reputation in history rests on two speeches made in the late 1930s. One declared peace for our time; the other declared war.

Neville Chamberlain entered parliamentary politics late in life, driven by a desire to help the poor. He was fifty when he was first elected a member of Parliament, and sixty-eight when he became prime minister. It was his misfortune to be in that post as the threat of war grew in Europe.

Chamberlain was a good man in a bad world. No one suffers in war so much as the common man and woman, and so his desire to avoid war at all costs was entirely in line with his principles. But it may have blinded him to the danger that Adolf Hitler, his counterpart in Germany, presented to continental stability.

At a Munich conference in September 1938, Hitler, Chamberlain, and the leaders of Italy and France resolved what Chamberlain called "the Czechoslovakian problem." The problem was that Hitler wanted to annex the Sudetenland, the large German-speaking area of Czechoslovakia. The solution in Munich was to let him, in the hope that it would satisfy Germany's lust for Lebensraum ("living space").

At the end of the conference, Chamberlain and Hitler signed an agreement that peace in Europe was in everyone's interest. The British prime minister was so pleased that he showed it off to the waiting crowd of reporters when he returned to England. "Here is the paper," he demonstrated, "which bears his name upon it as well as mine." Then he read its contents, a resolution outlining "the desire of our two peoples never to go to war with one another again … thus to contribute to assure the peace of Europe." Later he recited it again outside 10 Downing Street, adding, "for the second time in our history that there has come back from Germany to Downing Street peace with honor. I believe it is peace for our time."

He was echoing the remarks of his predecessor, Prime Minister Benjamin Disraeli, who returned from Berlin in 1878 with a similar declaration and also remarked, "I have returned from Germany with peace for our time." Disraeli was hailing an agreed solution to the disputed borders of the Balkan Peninsula, a compromise that satisfied no one and led ultimately to World War I. Chamberlain's agreement with Germany was similarly unsatisfactory and unconvincing. Large crowds protested in Trafalgar Square, and politicians, including Churchill, disagreed with Chamberlain's appeasement of Hitler's imperial ambitions.

A little less than a year later Hitler destroyed any hope of European peace by invading Poland. A sorrowful Chamberlain made a radio broadcast to the British nation on September 3, 1939, announcing that although Britain had asked Germany to withdraw its troops, "I have to tell you now that no such undertaking has been received, and that consequently this country is at war with Germany."

His appeasement had failed. He limped on in office until May 1940 when he lost the confidence of Parliament and resigned in favor of Churchill, who provided the country with strong leadership and rousing speeches for the rest of the war. Chamberlain's spirit was broken by his rapid fall from power and the subsequent attacks on his reputation. His health declined, and he died only six months later, forever remembered as the man whose peace was not worth the paper it was written on.

We, the German Führer and Chancellor, and the British Prime Minister, have had a further meeting today and are agreed in recognizing that the question of Anglo-German relations is of the first importance for our two countries and for Europe.

We regard the agreement signed last night and the Anglo-German Naval Agreement as symbolic of the desire of our two peoples never to go to war with one another again. We are resolved that the method of consultation shall be the method adopted to deal with any other questions that may concern our two countries, and we are determined to continue our efforts to remove possible sources of difference, and thus to contribute to assure the peace of Europe.

My good friends, for the second time in our history, a British Prime Minister has returned from Germany bringing peace with honor. I believe it is peace for our time. Go home and get a nice quiet sleep.

"PEACE FOR OUR TIME" SPEECH CONCERNING THE MUNICH AGREEMENT

RIGHT: Neville Chamberlain at Heston Aerodrome in 1938, waves his agreement with Adolf Hitler to waiting reporters.

Lou Gehrig
"The luckiest man on the face of this earth"

(July 4, 1939)

Lou Gehrig was a baseball legend in the early twentieth century. His early retirement from the game, forced by illness, was met with public tributes, and the speech he gave when he announced it has been described as "baseball's Gettysburg Address."

Fans, for the past two weeks you have been reading about the bad break I got. Yet today I consider myself the luckiest man on the face of this earth. I have been in ballparks for seventeen years and have never received anything but kindness and encouragement from you fans.

Look at these grand men. Which of you wouldn't consider it the highlight of his career just to associate with them for even one day? Sure, I'm lucky. Who wouldn't consider it an honor to have known Jacob Ruppert? Also, the builder of baseball's greatest empire, Ed Barrow? To have spent six years with that wonderful little fellow, Miller Huggins? Then to have spent the next nine years with that outstanding leader, that smart student of psychology, the best manager in baseball today, Joe McCarthy? Sure, I'm lucky.

When the New York Giants, a team you would give your right arm to beat, and vice versa, sends you a gift—that's something. When everybody down to the groundskeepers and those boys in white coats remember you with trophies—that's something. When you have a wonderful mother-in-law who takes sides with you in squabbles with her own daughter—that's something. When you have a father and a mother who work all their lives so you can have an education and build your body—it's a blessing. When you have a wife who has been a tower of strength and shown more courage than you dreamed existed—that's the finest I know.

So I close in saying that I may have had a tough break, but I have an awful lot to live for.

NEW YORK YANKEES FAREWELL ADDRESS

OPPOSITE: Lou Gehrig delivering his July 4 speech at Yankee Stadium.

After showing early promise, Lou Gehrig signed with the New York Yankees in 1923. His career there overlapped with that of an earlier Yankee superstar, Babe Ruth. The side in which both Gehrig and Ruth played in 1927 is known to this day as Murderers' Row, considered by historians to be the greatest team the sport has ever seen. Gehrig was "Mr. Consistency," holding the record of 2,130 consecutive games played, a record only beaten in the mid-1990s.

Quite suddenly, in the second half of 1938, his fitness declined. He was diagnosed with incurable amyotrophic lateral sclerosis (ALS). It slowly paralyzes the muscles, making even breathing difficult. It is a cruel disease for a top sportsman, and although Gehrig struggled on into 1939, he could not continue. His record-breaking uninterrupted run of appearances with the Yankees came to an end on May 2 that year.

When his illness became known, there was an outpouring of grief, with calls for his great career to be acknowledged in some way. Taking the lead from his shirt number, 4, the club declared July 4, 1939, to be Lou Gehrig Appreciation Day. A crowd of over 61,000 packed Yankee Stadium, and a succession of dignitaries, including New York Mayor Fiorello La Guardia,

gave speeches from the Yankee diamond in Gehrig's honor. Most moving was that from Yankee manager Joe McCarthy, who had guided the last nine years of Gehrig's career.

Gehrig was presented with many memorial gifts during the speeches, before finally stepping up to the microphone himself. The stadium fell silent. "Fans," he began, "for the past two weeks you have been reading about the bad break I got. Yet today I consider myself the luckiest man on the face of this earth." He listed the reasons: first of all, the fans themselves; then his illustrious teammates, including many members of Murderers' Row present for the occasion; his managers at the Yankees, Joe McCarthy and Miller Huggins.

"When you have a wonderful mother-in-law who takes sides with you in squabbles with her own daughter—that's something. When you have a father and a mother who work all their lives so you can have an education and build your body—it's a blessing. When you have a wife who has been a tower of strength and shown more courage than you dreamed existed—that's the finest I know."

From a seriously ill man, these were powerful words. Perhaps only in saying them did Gehrig realize the enormity of the moment. As he stepped back from the microphone, the crowd roared, and their standing ovation lasted for over two minutes. Babe Ruth was among the first to go to Gehrig and embrace him.

Out of respect for the great man, the Yankees retired his shirt number, the first time such a gesture was made in the sport, and now a tradition among MLB teams. Gehrig died less than two years later, but for Yankee fans, July 4 remains Lou Gehrig Appreciation Day. A monument erected in his memory in Yankee Stadium in 1941 was joined all too soon in 1949 by another, to Babe Ruth. Thanks to the campaigning work of Gehrig's widow, Eleanor, ALS is commonly known today as Lou Gehrig's disease.

Adolf Hitler
"Our strength lies in our quickness and our brutality"

(August 22, 1939)

Ten days before Hitler's invasion of Poland, he summoned his commanders to his Bavarian home, the Berghof near Berchtesgaden. There he discussed his plans, making clear his willingness to deceive enemies and allies alike. The survival of a transcript proves the complicity of his generals in his proposed atrocities.

Behind the rhetoric and charisma of Adolf Hitler stood a ruthless egomaniac with an almost cartoonlike craving for world domination. While his public utterances appealed to the German people's resentment after defeat in 1918, the candid meeting that he had with high-ranking officers on the eve of war was brutally frank. "Our strength lies in our quickness and our brutality. Genghis Khan sent millions of women and children to death knowingly and with a light heart: history sees him only as the great founder of states. Poland will be depopulated and settled with Germans."

That matter-of-fact admission of a planned genocide of the Polish people was a consequence of Hitler's adoption of the fifty-year-old concept of Lebensraum, literally "living space." It was developed in the 1890s by a German geographer named Friedrich Ratzel, who argued that successful civilizations spread their culture and influence because of their ability to adapt to different environments. Expansion into new environments gave them the room to live, to thrive.

He was scathing about the possibility of opposition. "Those poor worms Daladier [of France] and Chamberlain [of Britain]" were too cowardly to attack; Turkey was governed by "cretins and half-idiots"; the Japanese emperor was "weak, cowardly, undecided"; Belgians and Scandinavians were overfed and tired.

He had made an earlier pact with Poland only to gain time, he admitted. And now the time was right. He was sending in German troops disguised as Polish ones, and so "the attack upon and destruction of Poland begins." Alliances meant nothing to him. Although he admired the Russian leader Joseph Stalin—"Stalin and I are the only ones who visualise the future"—nevertheless after Stalin's death "the fate of Russia will be exactly the same as the one I am now going through with in the case of Poland."

One chilling train of thought is so shocking to modern ears that it has been inscribed on the US Holocaust Memorial in Washington, D.C. "I have issued the command—and I'll have anybody who utters but one word of criticism executed by a firing squad—that our war aim does not consist in reaching certain lines but in the physical destruction of the enemy. Accordingly I have placed my death-head formations in readiness—for the moment only in the east—with orders to them to send to death mercilessly and without compassion men, women and children of Polish derivation and language. Only thus shall we gain the living space (Lebensraum) which we need. Who, after all, speaks today of the annihilation of the Armenians?" Hitler was referring to the systematic murder of one and a half million Armenians by the Ottoman Empire during and after World War I, a slaughter for which the word "genocide" was first coined.

It is clear from this meeting at the Berghof that Hitler knew exactly what he intended to do and that his commanders were fully aware of their roles in it. As he promised them fame and honor, he demanded that they "be hard, be without mercy, act more quickly and brutally than the others. The citizens of Europe must tremble with horror. This is the most humane way of conducting a war, for it scares the others off."

One report says that the speech was received with enthusiasm: "Göring jumped on a table, gave bloodthirsty thanks to the Führer and made bloodthirsty promises. He danced like a wild man."

Iexperienced those poor worms Daladier and Chamberlain in Munich. They will be too cowardly to attack. They won't go beyond a blockade. Against that we have our autarchy and the Russian raw materials.

Poland will be depopulated and settled with Germans. My pact with the Poles was merely conceived of as a gaining of time. As for the rest, gentlemen, the fate of Russia will be exactly the same as I am now going through with in the case of Poland. After Stalin's death—he is a very sick man—we will break the Soviet Union. Then there will begin the dawn of the German rule of the earth.

The little States cannot scare me. After Kemal's death Turkey is governed by cretins and half idiots. Carol of Roumania is through and through the corrupt slave of his sexual instincts. The King of Belgium and the Nordic kings are soft jumping jacks who are dependent upon the good digestions of their over-eating and tired peoples.

We shall have to take into the bargain the defection of Japan. I save Japan a full year's time. The Emperor is a counterpart to the last Czar—weak, cowardly, undecided. May he become a victim of the revolution. My going together with Japan never was popular. We shall continue to create disturbances in the Far East and in Arabia. Let us think as "gentlemen" and let us see in these peoples at best lacquered half-maniacs who are anxious to experience the whip.

The opportunity is as favorable as never before. I have but one worry, namely that Chamberlain or some other such pig of a fellow will come at the last moment with proposals or with ratting. He will fly down the stairs, even if I shall personally have to trample on his belly in the eyes of the photographers.

OBERSALZBERG SPEECH ON GERMANY'S NEED FOR LIVING SPACE ("LEBENSRAUM")

RIGHT: Hitler at the Berghof with his head of the Luftwaffe, Hermann Göring in traditional Bavarian attire.

We are called, with our allies, to meet the challenge of a principle which, if it were to prevail, would be fatal to any civilized order in the world.

It is the principle which permits a state, in the selfish pursuit of power, to disregard its treaties and its solemn pledges; which sanctions the use of force, or threat of force, against the sovereignty and independence of other states.

Such a principle, stripped of all disguise, is surely the mere primitive doctrine that might is right; and if this principle were established throughout the world, the freedom of our own country and of the whole British Commonwealth of Nations would be in danger. But far more than this—the peoples of the world would be kept in the bondage of fear, and all hopes of settled peace and of the security of justice and liberty among nations would be ended.

This is the ultimate issue which confronts us. For the sake of all that we ourselves hold dear, and of the world's order and peace, it is unthinkable that we should refuse to meet the challenge.

It is to this high purpose that I now call my people at home and my peoples across the seas, who will make our cause their own. I ask them to stand calm, firm, and united in this time of trial. The task will be hard. There may be dark days ahead, and war can no longer be confined to the battlefield. But we can only do the right as we see the right, and reverently commit our cause to God.

If one and all we keep resolutely faithful to it, ready for whatever service or sacrifice it may demand, then, with God's help, we shall prevail.

May He bless and keep us all.

KING'S SPEECH, FIRST WARTIME RADIO BROADCAST ON BRITAIN'S DECLARATION OF WAR ON GERMANY

LEFT: King George VI broadcasting from Buckingham Palace.

George VI
Declaration of war against Germany

(September 3, 1939)

King George VI of Great Britain was not raised in the expectation of ascending the throne. He was thrust there by the abdication of his older brother Edward VIII. His reluctant acceptance of the crown, combined with a stammer and indifferent health, made him an unlikely figurehead for a country on the brink of global war.

George VI (born Albert Frederick Arthur George) was known as Albert until his accession. He served in the Royal Navy and the Royal Air Force during World War I. Thereafter he fulfilled his royal duty in public engagements but otherwise led a relatively normal life as a family man with two daughters. His stammer made any public speaking traumatic for him; when he tried to get his words out during his speech at the closing ceremony of the 1925 Empire Exhibition in London, the prolonged silences were a profound embarrassment, not only to Albert himself but to citizens of the British Empire listening around the world.

From 1926 onward, he sought the help of a speech therapist and undertook an unorthodox course of treatment made famous by the 2011 film *The King's Speech*. Although he was never completely free of his stammer, his therapist, Lionel Logue, had considerable success with it. Albert, who at first could not say the letter 'K,' was expected to toast the health of the king, his father, at many functions. He wrote to Logue during a tour in 1927 to say, "You remember my fear of 'The King'. I give it every evening at dinner on board. This does not worry me any more."

As the storm clouds of war gathered over Europe in the late 1930s, less than twenty years after the end of the last world war, Albert and all of Britain revisited memories of the horrific, senseless losses of the 1914–1918 conflict. No one wanted to go through that again, and Albert, now King George VI, supported Prime Minister Neville Chamberlain's efforts to appease Chancellor Hitler's expansionist ambitions. When war became inevitable, it was a king's duty to address his subjects. George was faced "in this grave hour, perhaps the most fateful in our history," with having to make a

live radio broadcast to a waiting nation.

His task was to provide morale-boosting leadership for the population, quite different from the political leadership of his government. From the beginning of his speech he displayed the personal touch that made him so effective in comforting the nation during the war's darkest days. "I send to every household of my peoples this message, spoken with the same depth of feeling as if I were able to cross your threshold and speak to you myself." He did not need to express horror at the prospect of another world war, which everyone knew and felt; he simply included himself in tacit acknowledgement of it. "For the second time in the lives of most of us we are at war."

He spoke not of politics but of the need to stand against "the mere primitive doctrine that 'might is right.'" And he talked repeatedly of "us," sharing the coming burden with his subjects. "It is unthinkable that we should refuse to meet the challenge."

After the broadcast, amid the quiet seriousness of a nation bracing itself for the worst, there was a sense that George VI was the man for the job. The dignity and solemnity with which he overcame his stammer to reassure his audience at a time of trepidation commended him to them. He rejected advice to leave the country for the safety of Canada.

Instead, he and his wife toured the country tirelessly, visiting arms factories and standing with the victims of the Blitz air raids, which destroyed so much of East London and elsewhere. When bombs landed on Buckingham Palace, Elizabeth remarked, "I'm glad we've been bombed. Now we can look the East End in the face." When victory in Europe was declared, six long years after George's radio speech, crowds surged to the Palace chanting, "We want the King! We want the King!"

Charles Lindbergh
"There has never been a greater test for the democratic principle of government"

(October 13, 1939)

Charles Lindbergh was an American hero when he became the first man to fly nonstop and solo from New York to Paris. In the late 1930s he undertook several trips to Germany on behalf of the US. In 1939, Lindbergh used his celebrity to push his fervent view on American neutrality to a public keen not to get involved, unaware of his pro-Nazi sympathies and his anti-Semitic beliefs.

To those who argue that we could make a profit and build up our own industry by selling munitions abroad, I reply that we in America have not yet reached a point where we wish to capitalize on the destruction and death of war. I do not believe that the material welfare of this country needs, or that our spiritual welfare could withstand, such a policy. If our industry depends upon commerce of arms for its strength, then our industrial system should be changed.

It is impossible for me to understand how America can contribute to civilization and humanity by sending offensive instruments of destruction to European battlefields. This would not only implicate us in the war, but it would make us partly responsible for its devastation. The fallacy of helping to defend a political ideology, even though it be somewhat similar to our own, was clearly demonstrated to us in the last war. Through our help that war was won, but neither the democracy nor the justice for which we fought grew in the peace that followed our victory.

Our bond with Europe is a bond of race and not of political ideology. We had to fight a European army to establish democracy in this country. It is the European race we must preserve; political progress will follow. Racial strength is vital—politics, a luxury. If the white race is ever seriously threatened, it may then be time for us to take our part in its protection, to fight side by side with the English, French, and Germans, but not with one against the other for our mutual destruction.

URGING THE US TO STAY NEUTRAL IN WWII

After his flight across the Atlantic in the *Spirit of St. Louis*, Charles Lindbergh used his celebrity to promote US Air Mail and aviation as a modern means of travel. But when his son was kidnapped and killed in 1932, the public attention overwhelmed him, and he fled to France.

From there he visited Germany on many occasions. As a famous pilot he was introduced to leaders of the country's aviation industry, including aircraft designers Heinkel and Messerschmitt and Hitler's air minister Hermann Göring. Göring presented him with the Order of the German Eagle, a medal normally awarded to foreign sympathizers of the Nazi cause. Other recipients of the honor included Japanese prime minister Hideki Tojo, and Italian prime minister Benito Mussolini.

Lindbergh returned to the US in early 1939 when he was asked to assess America's own aerial readiness for combat. When Britain declared war on Germany on September 3, 1939, America was bound to a position of neutrality. But President Roosevelt sought to help Britain by removing restrictions on the use of American shipping to deliver much-needed goods, and by lifting the existing embargo on arms sales to foreign powers. Lindbergh was opposed to any such involvement, and in a radio broadcast given six weeks after Hitler invaded Poland, he explained why.

First, he was at pains to make clear, neutrality was not the same as pacifism. "Let us give no one the impression that America's love of peace means she is afraid of war." The United States should defend not only its own borders but all of the Americas: "from Canada to South America we must allow no invading army to set foot. These are the outposts of the United States."

However, "sooner or later we must demand the freedom of this continent from the dictates of European power." It was, he

reasoned, the spur to the American Revolution. "We had to fight a European army to establish democracy in this country." Although he sidestepped the fact that it was another European country, France, who had made victory possible.

In one significant passage, Lindbergh raised the question of race. "It is the European race we must preserve; political progress will follow. Racial strength is vital—politics, a luxury. If the white race is ever seriously threatened, it may then be time for us to take our part in its protection."

On the matter of arms sales, he was clear: If the US were to supply arms to its European friends now, "then why mislead ourselves by talk of neutrality?" If the motive for selling arms was merely profit, "we in America have not yet reached a point where we wish to capitalize on the destruction and death of war."

On supplying Britain by sea, Lindbergh suggested that German planes might accidentally bomb American merchant ships, which should therefore be banned from entering the theater of war. Although they were plausible arguments, the underlying drive of Lindbergh's remarks could be seen as a desire not to give succor or support to Germany's enemies.

In future speeches Lindbergh became much more explicitly pro-German, and in the matter of race more explicitly anti-Semitic. In 1940 he became the spokesman for America First, a fascist, noninterventionist, anti-Semitic pressure group. Roosevelt publicly rebuked him as an appeaser, and an offended Lindbergh resigned his US army commission. Although Lindbergh did enter the war after the attack on Pearl Harbor, Roosevelt blocked his reinstatement as a military officer, and the former mail pilot was forced to serve his country as a civilian consultant.

I say to the House as I said to ministers who have joined this government, I have nothing to offer but blood, toil, tears and sweat. We have before us an ordeal of the most grievous kind. We have before us many, many months of struggle and suffering.

You ask, what is our policy? I say it is to wage war by land, sea, and air. War with all our might and with all the strength God has given us, and to wage war against a monstrous tyranny never surpassed in the dark and lamentable catalog of human crime. That is our policy.

You ask, what is our aim? I can answer in one word. It is victory. Victory at all costs—Victory in spite of all terrors—Victory, however long and hard the road may be, for without victory there is no survival.

Let that be realized. No survival for the British Empire, no survival for all that the British Empire has stood for, no survival for the urge, the impulse of the ages, that mankind shall move forward toward his goal.

I take up my task in buoyancy and hope. I feel sure that our cause will not be suffered to fail among men.

I feel entitled at this juncture, at this time, to claim the aid of all and to say, 'Come then, let us go forward together with our united strength.'

"BLOOD, TOIL, TEARS AND SWEAT" SPEECH

LEFT: Winston Churchill leaving 10 Downing Street.

Winston Churchill
"Blood, toil, tears and sweat"

(May 13, 1940)

Winston Churchill had been in a political wilderness for a decade. When Chamberlain lost a vote of confidence in Parliament following the fall of Norway, Churchill was asked to lead a coalition government. His first task was to secure the backing of Parliament for his leadership.

Churchill had been a member of Parliament since 1900, a liberal Conservative who in 1929 found himself at odds with his party's policies. For Chamberlain he served as First Lord of the Admiralty, the political head of the Royal Navy, an office he had first held in 1911. Churchill was a keen military historian but a compromise choice to lead Britain's wartime government.

On the day that Churchill was appointed prime minister, Germany invaded Holland and Belgium, and began its assault on France. With that escalation of the war, Churchill had to be sure that he had Parliament's support. Therefore, three days later, he asked his fellow MPs to vote on the motion "that this House welcomes the formation of a Government representing the united and inflexible resolve of the nation to prosecute the war with Germany to a victorious conclusion."

It comes as a surprise to many people that Winston Churchill did not receive a university education. After school he went straight to a military academy and joined the British army. When he entered politics he felt at a disadvantage to his more qualified peers, more so because he stammered and lisped slightly when he spoke. He spent many hours crafting his speeches, choosing words and rhythms that would conceal these handicaps, and in the process developing a distinctive style of rhetoric.

Churchill felt that his long experience as a soldier and politician had prepared him for the job at hand. The same experience helped him to grasp the severity of the situation and the difficulty of the task ahead. "We have before us many, many months of struggle and suffering," he now warned.

He did not offer a detailed action plan—it was too soon for that. "What is our policy? It is to wage war. What is our aim? It is victory. Victory at all costs, victory in spite of all terrors, for without victory there is no survival. No survival for the British Empire, no survival for all that the British Empire has stood for." He made the battle Britain's battle; not France's or Poland's or the Low Countries' battle in which Britain had a mere supporting role.

Of his own abilities he was falsely modest, but in describing them he was encouraging everyone in his audience in Parliament and across the nation to make what contributions they could to the war effort. "I have nothing to offer but blood, toil, tears, and sweat." Well, everyone could contribute those, and—that being the case—he closed with a direct appeal: "I feel entitled at this juncture, at this time, to claim the aid of all and to say, 'Come then, let us go forward together with our united strength.'"

It was, he apologized, a short speech, because there was much to do. And in truth, parliamentary approval was a foregone conclusion at such a time of urgency. But Churchill's carefully chosen words focused on the need for national unity in government and across the country. The motion was carried unanimously.

Winston Churchill
"We shall fight on the beaches"

(June 4, 1940)

Churchill's first month as prime minister was marked by military setbacks. The Netherlands was overrun; Belgium surrendered; France was falling; and the army sent to support them was cut off and trapped at Dunkirk. If Britain was to withstand a German invasion on its own soil, it needed to bring that force home.

The remarkable rescue of 335,000 British and French troops from the beaches of Dunkirk by a flotilla of boats of every shape and size was portrayed as a defiant act of essentially British pluck. But the ongoing evacuation of the British expeditionary force marked a military setback and a significant loss of useful equipment abandoned in flight.

British public morale was badly dented by the defeat, however, many lives had been saved in the course of it. With all of Britain's neighbors across the sea now falling into German hands, the likelihood of Britain being invaded was very real. When Churchill stood up in the House of Commons to report on the military situation, he could not ignore it.

He admitted the very high possibility of fighting on the British mainland, painting a deliberately shocking picture of the forms it might take. Churchill sought to rouse the fighting spirit of a depressed people by showing them what they faced. "When we see the originality of malice, the ingenuity of aggression which our enemy displays, we may certainly prepare ourselves for every kind of novel stratagem and every kind of brutal and treacherous manoeuvre."

Churchill then expressed confidence in Britain's ability "to outlive the menace of tyranny" before summing up, in one of the greatest closing passages ever spoken: "We shall go on to the end. We shall fight in France, we shall fight on the seas and oceans, we shall fight with growing confidence and growing strength in the air, we shall defend our Island, whatever the cost may be. We shall fight on the beaches, we shall fight on the landing grounds, we shall fight in the fields and in the streets, we shall fight in the hills; we shall never surrender."

In his speech less than three weeks earlier Churchill had listed the "blood, toil, tears and sweat" that every man and woman could bring to the fight. Now he listed the places, familiar to all where that fight might happen. In all, the speech drove home the message that "we shall fight" seven times; and in that verbal sea of determination, two other phrases leapt out. "We shall defend our Island"; "we shall never surrender."

The speech was immediately recognized as a masterpiece of the art. Some MPs cried, and one wrote to Churchill afterward that "that was worth a thousand guns and the speeches of a thousand years." Ordinary Britons who heard reports of the speech on radio news

I have, myself, full confidence that if all do their duty, if nothing is neglected, and if the best arrangements are made, as they are being made, we shall prove ourselves once again able to defend our Island home, to ride out the storm of war, and to outlive the menace of tyranny, if necessary for years, if necessary alone. At any rate, that is what we are going to try to do. That is the resolve of His Majesty's Government— every man of them. That is the will of Parliament and the nation.

The British Empire and the French Republic, linked together in their cause and in their need, will defend to the death their native soil, aiding each other like good comrades to the utmost of their strength.

Even though large tracts of Europe and many old and famous States have fallen or may fall into the grip of the Gestapo and all the odious apparatus of Nazi rule, we shall not flag or fail.

We shall go on to the end. We shall fight in France, we shall fight on the seas and oceans, we shall fight with growing confidence and growing strength in the air, we shall defend our Island, whatever the cost may be. We shall fight on the beaches, we shall fight on the landing grounds, we shall fight in the fields and in the streets, we shall fight in the hills; we shall never surrender.

And even if, which I do not for a moment believe, this Island or a large part of it were subjugated and starving, then our Empire beyond the seas, armed and guarded by the British Fleet, would carry on the struggle, until, in God's good time, the New World, with all its power and might, steps forth to the rescue and the liberation of the old.

"WE SHALL FIGHT ON THE BEACHES" SPEECH

bulletins were swept along by Churchill's obvious passion and resolve on behalf of his country. With those qualities, this speech reversed the tide of public opinion, which had begun to question Britain's involvement in the war. Their determination restored, British civilians and troops turned to face the fight to come.

Hitler's rapid advance across northern Europe and the unexpectedly swift capitulation of the French had put him in a strong position for intended peace negotiations with Britain. But Churchill's speech made it quite clear that Britain would not be cowed.

OPPOSITE: The front page of the Daily Mirror *newspaper from June 5, 1940, reprinting the words from Churchill's speech.*

Winston Churchill
"This was their finest hour"

(June 18, 1940)

Although British morale had been boosted by Churchill's insistence "we shall fight on the beaches," the situation in Europe continued to deteriorate over the next two weeks. Italy entered the war on Germany's side, putting further pressure on French borders and persuading the French leader Marshal Pétain to seek peace with Germany at any price.

All of northern Europe now lay under German domination. Nothing stood between Hitler and Britain except the English Channel. "The Battle of France is over," reported Winston Churchill to his fellow MPs on June 18, 1940. "I expect that the Battle of Britain is about to begin."

Churchill had personally flown to France a week earlier to urge its leaders to continue the fight against Germany, but to no avail. Now, from Bordeaux to Gdansk, Hitler controlled the entire European coastline from which he might launch an invasion of Britain. Having observed the relentless German advance over the past nine months, Churchill was under no illusions about the ferocity of any such attack. "The whole fury and might of the enemy," he predicted, "must very soon be turned on us."

In his first speech as prime minister, Churchill had argued that this was a war between Britain and Germany, by declaring that the British Empire was at stake. Now, barely a month later, he found it prudent to stress that Britain was not isolated, despite the defeat or surrender of its allies. "We in this Island . . . will never lose our sense of comradeship with the French people"; "Czechs, Poles, Norwegians, Dutch, Belgians have joined their causes to our own. All these shall be restored."

And not for the first time he reached out to the United States, which had so far been publicly neutral in the conflict. With Britain now in grave peril he suggested that even America was under threat from German aggression in Europe. "Hitler knows that he will have to break us in this Island or lose the war. . . . But if we fail, the whole world, including the United States, including all that we have known and cared for, will sink into the abyss of a new Dark Age." In fact, America had already

promised Britain to support it with arms; and the New World entered the war on December 8, 1941, after the Japanese attack on Pearl Harbor.

Meanwhile, it was Britain on her own resisting Hitler's "perverted science" and seemingly unstoppable advance. After painting such a bleak picture of possibilities, Churchill concluded with a single sentence that defied any red-blooded patriot not to stand up to the Nazi threat. "Let us therefore brace ourselves to our duties, and so bear ourselves, that if the British Empire and its Commonwealth last for a thousand years, men will still say, 'This was their finest hour.'"

"Blood, toil, tears and sweat"; "we shall fight on the beaches"; "this was their finest hour." The three speeches by Winston Churchill given in the month following his appointment as head of Britain's wartime government defined the British character, both for Britons themselves and for the wider world. They inspired British civilians to endure personal discomfort and loss, and British troops not only to fight against an enemy but to fight for a cause.

Fearing Britain's naval power, Hitler chose to launch his inevitable assault on Britain from the air a month after Churchill's speech. The defense of Britain by its fighter pilots proved staunch; and by October, Germany had changed its tactics from aerial combat to blitz bombing of civilian populations. The failure of the Luftwaffe to disable the RAF in the Battle of Britain was Hitler's first major defeat, the first proof that Germany was not invincible. In August 1940, Churchill was moved to remark: "The gratitude of every home in our Island goes out to the British airmen. Never in the field of human conflict was so much owed by so many to so few."

However matters may go in France or with the French Government, or other French Governments, we in this Island and in the British Empire will never lose our sense of comradeship with the French people. If we are now called upon to endure what they have been suffering, we shall emulate their courage, and if final victory rewards our toils they shall share the gains, aye, and freedom shall be restored to all. We abate nothing of our just demands; not one jot or tittle do we recede. Czechs, Poles, Norwegians, Dutch, Belgians have joined their causes to our own. All these shall be restored.

What General Weygand called the Battle of France is over. I expect that the Battle of Britain is about to begin. Upon this battle depends the survival of Christian civilization. Upon it depends our own British life, and the long continuity of our institutions and our Empire. The whole fury and might of the enemy must very soon be turned on us.

Hitler knows that he will have to break us in this Island or lose the war. If we can stand up to him, all Europe may be free and the life of the world may move forward into broad, sunlit uplands. But if we fail, then the whole world, including the United States, including all that we have known and cared for, will sink into the abyss of a new Dark Age made more sinister, and perhaps more protracted, by the lights of perverted science.

Let us therefore brace ourselves to our duties, and so bear ourselves that, if the British Empire and its Commonwealth last for a thousand years, men will still say, 'This was their finest hour.'

"THIS WAS THEIR FINEST HOUR" SPEECH

LEFT: Winston Churchill walking the deck of HMS The Prince of Wales, *during the 1941 Atlantic conference.*

Has the last word been said? Must we abandon all hope? Is our defeat final and irremediable? To those questions I answer—No!

Speaking in full knowledge of the facts, I ask you to believe me when I say that the cause of France is not lost. The very factors that brought about our defeat may one day lead us to victory.

For, remember this, France does not stand alone. She is not isolated. Behind her is a vast empire, and she can make common cause with the British empire, which commands the seas and is continuing the struggle. Like England, she can draw unreservedly on the immense industrial resources of the United States.

This war is not limited to our unfortunate country. The outcome of the struggle has not been decided by the battle of France. This is a world war. Mistakes have been made, there have been delays and untold suffering, but the fact remains that there still exists in the world everything we need to crush our enemies some day.

Today we are crushed by the sheer weight of mechanized force hurled against us, but we can still look to a future in which even greater mechanized force will bring us victory. The destiny of the world is at stake.

I, General de Gaulle, now in London, call on all French officers and men who are at present on British soil, or may be in the future, with or without their arms; I call on all engineers and skilled workmen from the armaments factories who are at present on British soil, or may be in the future, to get in touch with me.

Whatever happens, the flame of French resistance must not and shall not die.

APPEAL OF JUNE 18, 1940

RIGHT: *Relatively unknown before the war, de Gaulle seized the initiative while Marshal Pétain and his cabinet were organizing collaboration with the Germans.*

General de Gaulle
"The flame of French resistance must not and shall not die"

(June 18, 1940)

In a little over a month during May and June 1940, the German army overran northern France, and on June 17, Marshal Pétain agreed a ceasefire. In return he was allowed to lead a puppet government in southern France while Germany occupied the north. For some French soldiers, however, the battle was not over.

Before the fall of France, Charles de Gaulle was commander of an armored division of the French army. After the German invasion he was promoted to brigadier general and appointed a junior war minister with responsibility for liaising with Britain. In the last days before Pétain surrendered, de Gaulle flew back and forth between France and London, finally making his escape on the day of the French armistice with Germany.

A hundred thousand French troops had been evacuated to various centers in Britain from Dunkirk. With the French army scattered both at home and abroad, and the senior chain of command disrupted, de Gaulle was effectively the senior officer in exile. He was a relatively unknown figure, but he went straight to Prime Minister Winston Churchill and asked to broadcast an appeal to France on BBC radio. The two leaders had met during de Gaulle's earlier visits and Churchill agreed.

De Gaulle opposed Pétain's surrender and his willingness to cooperate with Germany afterward. His armored troops had fought one of the few successful engagements in the battle for France. He conceded that France had been caught by surprise by the suddenness and the ferocity of the German attack by tank and plane. But, he asked Frenchmen on both sides of the English Channel from a microphone in Broadcasting House, "must we abandon all hope? Is our defeat final and irremediable? I answer—No!"

Addressing an audience at its lowest ebb, de Gaulle sought to comfort them with some perspective on their dire situation. "For remember this," he told them. "France does not stand alone. She is not isolated. Behind her is a vast empire, and she can make common cause with the British empire. Like England, she can draw unreservedly on the immense industrial resources of the United States."

At the end of this short broadcast, de Gaulle issued a rallying cry. "I, General de Gaulle, now in London, call on all French officers and men who are at present on British soil, or may be in the future, with or without their arms; I call on all engineers and skilled workmen from the armaments factories who are at present on British soil, or may be in the future, to get in touch with me. Whatever happens, the flame of French resistance must not and shall not die."

De Gaulle's broadcast, made at short notice and almost unannounced, was heard by relatively few of his intended audience that night. But word spread that someone still spoke for France. When de Gaulle issued a similar call to arms in another transmission four nights later, many more were tuned in. Transcripts of it were posted all over the French-speaking world. Coming at precisely the time when French men and women needed to believe that all was not lost, de Gaulle's speech is today considered the moment at which the guerrilla war of the French Resistance was launched.

With support from London and at the cost of many lives, the Resistance was a constant thorn in the occupying power's side. De Gaulle found himself at the head of both the Resistance and the Free French government in exile, and after France's liberation in 1944, he led its provisional government in Paris. His policies yielded a remarkable period of economic growth for the country, and its grateful citizens elected him as their president from 1959 to 1969.

Vyacheslav Molotov
Nazi invasion of the Soviet Union

(June 22, 1941)

The fascism of Adolf Hitler and the Marxism of Joseph Stalin were ideological opposites. In an act of mutual appeasement, the pair signed a nonaggression agreement that gave Hitler the peace of mind to invade Poland, and Stalin the confidence to let him.

Vyacheslav Molotov was Joseph Stalin's most loyal ally in the Soviet government. Although the nonaggression pact was directly between the leaders of Russia and Germany, the Molotov-Ribbentrop Pact was named after their foreign ministers. It partitioned Finland, the Baltic states, and Poland, the countries that lay between Russia and Germany. Stalin, doubting that capitalist Western Europe would be reliable allies against Hitler, thought an agreement with Germany would be the better course to ensure the security of his borders.

For Hitler, the pact neutralized the threat of any Russian counterattack following an invasion of Poland. But he made clear to his officers at the time that the pact was no more than a marriage of convenience until he was ready to strike at Russia too. In 1941, having swept through Western Europe meeting little resistance except from Britain, he felt that the time was right; and in the early hours of June 22 he tore up the agreement with attacks along the Russian border and bombing raids deep into Soviet territory.

It cannot have come as a complete surprise to Stalin. Hitler's antipathy to Marxism was no secret, and, in fact, Soviet troops were already stationed along the new border with Germany. Nevertheless, Hitler's full-scale assault seems to have caught Stalin on the hop. It was a full hour and a half after the first bombs were dropped that the German ambassador in Moscow delivered a formal declaration of war.

Stalin dispatched Molotov to break the news to the Soviet peoples on the radio. The foreign minister presented the German attack as the completely unprovoked invasion of a Soviet Union, which had innocently abided by the terms of the pact. "This unheard of attack upon our country," he told Russians, "is perfidy unparalleled in the history of civilized nations."

Molotov made it an ideological dispute as much as a military one. "This war has been forced on us not by the German people but by the clique of bloodthirsty Fascist rules of Germany who have enslaved the French, Czechs, Poles, Serbs, Norway, Belgium, Denmark, Holland, Greece and other nations."

Hitler for his part, in a radio broadcast made the same day as Molotov's, claimed that there had been border violations by Russian troops and blamed the escalation on a "plot by Jewish-Anglo-Saxon warmongers and the Jewish rulers of Moscow's Bolshevist headquarters." Like Molotov he claimed to be the innocent victim of enemy aggression and to have done everything in his power to maintain peace before being forced to go to war.

Molotov evoked memories of an earlier "arrogant foe. At the time of Napoléon's invasion . . . our people's reply was war for the fatherland, and Napoléon suffered defeat and met his doom." It was a prescient analogy. Hitler's Russian campaign, although it inflicted unimaginable losses on the Soviets, ultimately foundered on the same rocks as Napoléon's—a lack of resources to sustain such a vast military operation so far from home.

German defeat at the Battle of Stalingrad marked a turning point, which eventually resulted in the advance of Russian troops deep into German territory and the capture of Berlin. Hitler's ill-considered betrayal of the Molotov-Ribbentrop Pact therefore sowed the seeds for the postwar shape of Europe and its division by the Iron Curtain.

Molotov's unquestioning support for Stalin, and his involvement of some of the worst excesses of Stalin's brutal regime, saw him sidelined after Stalin's death. He died in relative obscurity at the age of ninety-six.

The government of the Soviet Union expresses its unshakable confidence that our valiant army and navy and brave falcons of the Soviet Air Force will acquit themselves with honor in performing their duty to the fatherland and to the Soviet people, and will inflict a crushing blow upon the aggressor.

This is not the first time that our people have had to deal with an attack of an arrogant foe. At the time of Napoléon's invasion of Russia our people's reply was war for the fatherland, and Napoléon suffered defeat and met his doom.

It will be the same with Hitler, who in his arrogance has proclaimed a new crusade against our country. The Red Army and our whole people will again wage victorious war for the fatherland, for our country, for honor, for liberty.

The government of the Soviet Union expresses the firm conviction that the whole population of our country, all workers, peasants and intellectuals, men and women, will conscientiously perform their duties and do their work. Our entire people must now stand solid and united as never before.

Each one of us must demand of himself and of others discipline, organization and self-denial worthy of real Soviet patriots, in order to provide for all the needs of the Red Army, Navy and Air Force, to insure victory over the enemy.

The government calls upon you, citizens of the Soviet Union, to rally still more closely around our glorious Bolshevist party, around our Soviet Government, around our great leader and comrade, Stalin. Ours is a righteous cause. The enemy shall be defeated. Victory will be ours.

RADIO SPEECH ON NAZI INVASION OF RUSSIA

LEFT: Molotov stands far right, with Joseph Stalin and von Ribbentrop to his left. The Molotov cocktail was a derogatory name for the petrol bomb used by the Finns against Russian tanks after the signing of the Molotov-Ribbentrop Pact.

Franklin D. Roosevelt
"A date which will live in infamy"

(December 8, 1941)

The day after the Japanese attack on Pearl Harbor, US president Franklin D. Roosevelt addressed a joint session of Congress. The nation was in a state of shock, but Roosevelt's prompt response and powerful oratory united and galvanized the population, both inside and beyond the walls of Washington, D.C.

Yesterday, December 7th, 1941—a date which will live in infamy—the United States of America was suddenly and deliberately attacked by naval and air forces of the Empire of Japan. The United States was at peace with that nation and, at the solicitation of Japan, was still in conversation with its government and its emperor looking toward the maintenance of peace in the Pacific. . . .

Yesterday, the Japanese government also launched an attack against Malaya. Last night, Japanese forces attacked Hong Kong. Last night, Japanese forces attacked Guam. Last night, Japanese forces attacked the Philippine Islands. Last night, the Japanese attacked Wake Island. And this morning, the Japanese attacked Midway Island. Japan has, therefore, undertaken a surprise offensive extending throughout the Pacific area. The facts of yesterday and today speak for themselves.

As Commander in Chief of the Army and Navy, I have directed that all measures be taken for our defense. But always will our whole nation remember the character of the onslaught against us. No matter how long it may take us to overcome this premeditated invasion, the American people in their righteous might will win through to absolute victory.

I believe that I interpret the will of the Congress and of the people when I assert that we will not only defend ourselves to the uttermost, but will make it very certain that this form of treachery shall never again endanger us. Hostilities exist. There is no blinking at the fact that our people, our territory, and our interests are in grave danger.

With confidence in our armed forces, with the unbounding determination of our people, we will gain the inevitable triumph—so help us God.

"A DATE WHICH WILL LIVE IN INFAMY"—PEARL HARBOR SPEECH

Japan's surprise bombing of the US fleet stationed at Pearl Harbor in Hawaii resulted in the greatest single loss of life in US history at the time—2,335 were killed, 188 aircraft destroyed on the ground, and six navy ships sunk. Tensions had risen between the two countries as Japan expanded its occupation of Indo-Chinese territories in the 1930s. Diplomatic efforts to settle their differences had so far proved unsuccessful, but were still underway at the time of the attack. Since Japan had not declared war on the United States, it was later deemed to be a war crime.

Roosevelt had been quietly preparing to enter World War II for some months, and his speech the following day was an astute political display to that end. The promptness with which he called the joint session showed him to be a decisive leader of a traumatized nation. He made a symbolic link with World War I by arriving at the House of Representatives in the company of Edith Wilson, the widow of Woodrow Wilson who took the US into the earlier conflict. While he spoke, his son James stood by his side in the uniform of the Marine

Corps, illustrating the readiness of an American father to see his boy go to war.

Roosevelt was well aware that the speech would be broadcast live to every home in America. He made extensive use of the passive voice to describe the day—"America was suddenly and deliberately attacked," "it will be recorded that the attack was deliberately planned," "very many American lives have been lost," "American ships have been reported torpedoed."

He then switched to the active voice to depict Japan. "Last night, Japanese forces attacked Hong Kong. Last night, Japanese forces attacked Guam. Last night, Japanese forces attacked the Philippine Islands. Last night, the Japanese attacked Wake Island." The length of the list and the repetitive rhythm of the words were like the bombs that rained down on Pearl Harbor.

The final section of the speech was a rallying cry to the American people. First, Roosevelt made the desire to go to war theirs and not his: "the people of the United States have already formed their opinions," "the American people in their righteous might will win," "I believe that I interpret the will of the people when I assert that we will defend ourselves."

He then abandoned the first person singular altogether, and for the rest of the speech used a unifying plural: "There is no blinking at the fact that our people, our territory, and our interests are in grave danger. With confidence in our armed forces, with the unbounding determination of our people, we will gain the inevitable triumph—so help us God."

The speech had the desired effect. Half an hour after Roosevelt sat down, Congress declared war on Japan. When three days later Germany and Italy declared war on the US, America was drawn into a fully global conflict. When Roosevelt described the assault as "a date which will live in infamy," he was claiming it to be a historic moment, and so it proved, though drafts of the speech show that "infamy" was only inserted later, but made it all the more powerful.

LEFT: Roosevelt delivers his landmark speech to a joint session of Congress, with his son James at his side. James Roosevelt served in the Marine Corps in the Pacific and saw action at Midway.

Dwight D. Eisenhower
"The free men of the world are marching together to victory!"

(June 6, 1944)

General Eisenhower, Supreme Allied Commander for the Allies' counterinvasion of Europe, felt confident enough of its success to broadcast a message to Western Europe at the end of the first day—D-Day. But Operation Overlord, as the invasion was known, was by no means a sure thing. It did not go as smoothly as planned, and nearly didn't go at all.

People of Western Europe:

A landing was made this morning on the coast of France by troops of the Allied Expeditionary Force. This landing is part of the concerted United Nations' plan for the liberation of Europe, made in conjunction with our great Russian allies. I have this message for all of you. Although the initial assault may not have been made in your own country, the hour of your liberation is approaching.

All patriots, men and women, young and old, have a part to play in the achievement of final victory. To members of resistance movements, I say, 'Follow the instructions you have received.' To patriots who are not members of organized resistance groups, I say, 'Continue your passive resistance, but do not needlessly endanger your lives until I give you the signal to rise and strike the enemy.' The day will come when I shall need your united strength. Until that day, I call on you for the hard task of discipline and restraint.

ANNOUNCING THE ALLIES HAD LANDED IN FRANCE

OPPOSITE: General Eisenhower talking with American paratroopers on the evening of June 5, 1944, as they prepared for the Battle of Normandy. The men were part of Company E, 502nd Parachute Infantry Regiment of the 101st Airborne Division based at Greenham Common in England.

Overlord finally got underway on June 6, 1944, after power struggles and disagreements among the Allied leaders De Gaulle, Churchill, and Eisenhower, and between Eisenhower and his commanders. General Patton in particular was hard to control; and another, Admiral King, refused to lend Eisenhower the extra landing craft he wanted. Churchill only reluctantly yielded control of the Royal Air Force to Eisenhower, and de Gaulle had to be forced to let Eisenhower use the resources of the French Resistance.

On June 5, the original date for D-Day, Eisenhower issued an Order of the Day on BBC radio to the "Soldiers, Sailors and Airmen of the Allied Expeditionary Force," telling them that "you are about to embark upon the Great Crusade" for "the elimination of Nazi tyranny over the oppressed peoples of Europe." The fighting would be savage, but the troops would have superior support in the air and from the Home Fronts. "The tide has turned! The free men of the world are marching together to victory!"

But the weather that day was too poor for an amphibious landing in Normandy. Since there were only a few days a month when tides and moonlight were in the Allies' favor, the delay was nerve-racking. Luckily, the forecast for the following day improved, and Eisenhower gave the go-ahead. But the largest invasion by sea in history was not an unqualified success. Few of its Day One objectives were achieved, though Pegasus Bridge was successfully captured. Despite a successful decoy operation to convince the Germans the attack was going to be made farther north, near Calais, Allied casualties were high—4,400 dead. Privately, army commanders estimated it would be double that figure. Full communication between the five beachheads was finally established on June 12.

Nevertheless, Eisenhower, whose experience included the command of the war in North Africa and the Allied invasion of Italy, felt sufficiently encouraged to issue a message of hope to the beleaguered citizens of Nazi-occupied Europe. He announced the landings as "part of the United Nations' plan for the liberation of Europe made in conjunction with our great Russian allies." Although the invasion would not reach most of Europe for many weeks and months, "the hour of your liberation is approaching."

Aware of how desperate many people would be for this news, Eisenhower was careful to urge caution. Eisenhower hoped to forestall unauthorized civilian activity, which might even jeopardize the Allied campaign, with the promise of patience now, revenge later. Organized resistance groups had already received their orders in support of Operation Overlord, but to ordinary citizens he advised, "Continue your passive resistance but do not needlessly endanger your lives until I give you the signal to rise and strike the enemy."

The result of Operation Overlord was indeed the eventual surrender of Germany, not in the summer months of 1944 as hoped, but in May, 1945, eleven months later. German troops beat a vindictive, vengeful retreat through Europe, which took the lives of civilians both in occupied countries and in concentration camps. Much of the credit went to Eisenhower's shrewd judgment and the handling of his sometimes fractious generals. He never had to issue a short statement, which he had prepared on June 5, 1944. It read, in part, "Our landings have failed to gain a satisfactory foothold. The troops, the air and the navy did all that bravery and devotion to duty could do. If any blame or fault attaches to the attempt, it is mine alone."

How different things might have been. But admiration for Eisenhower's successful conduct of the closing stages of World War II carried him in 1953 to the first of two terms in the White House, both won by landslides.

Emperor Hirohito
Humanity Declaration

(January 1, 1946)

Traditionally, the emperors of Japan were descended from the sun goddess Amaterasu and were therefore gods themselves. The Japanese people revered them as deities, gods in human form and not the same as other men. Emperor Hirohito was a twentieth-century god confronted with earthly problems.

Following its attack on Pearl Harbor, Japan experienced considerable military success for six months. The tide turned at the Battle of Midway, after which a series of bitterly fought engagements and outright defeats gradually brought the country to its knees. Hirohito repeatedly refused to surrender until the cataclysmic atomic bombing of Hiroshima and Nagasaki on August 6 and 9, 1945, forced him to reconsider.

The formalities of Japanese society separated the aristocracy from the peasants, and the imperial court from almost everyone. When a recording of Hirohito was played on the radio on August 15, 1945, announcing that "the enemy has begun to employ a new and most cruel bomb," it was the first time that most Japanese citizens had heard his voice. That was almost more shocking than his surrender to Allied demands: "Should we continue to fight, it would not only result in an ultimate collapse and obliteration of the Japanese nation, but also it would lead to the total extinction of human civilization."

Japan became a country under American occupation and control, overseen by General MacArthur. As blame for Japanese war crimes was apportioned, many felt that Hirohito was as complicit in them as his prime minister General Tojo. Tojo was executed for his sins, but the Emperor was not. MacArthur was planning a gradual transformation of Japanese society into a constitutional, democratic monarchy. He believed that the survival of its figurehead would be an important thread of continuity for the defeated nation.

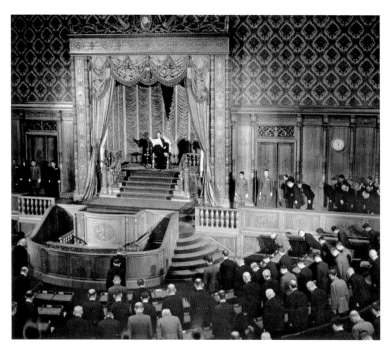

Hirohito's imperial remoteness made it possible to construct an alternative history in which he was the innocent stooge of manipulative warmongers. The two men met many times, and MacArthur was active behind the scenes in persuading witnesses to amend their testimonies and not to testify against the emperor. On January 1, 1946, Hirohito made a statement about the Meiji oath of 1868, Japan's first attempt to modernize with a tentative constitution. His speech was intended to bolster Japanese support for its postwar future by showing that Japan had always had democracy. But it was far more remarkable for one very short section in it.

"We stand by the people," Hirohito promised, "and we wish always to share with them in their moments of joy and sorrow. The ties between us and our people have always stood upon mutual trust and affection. They do not depend upon mere legends and myths. They are not predicated on the false conception that the Emperor is divine and that the Japanese people are superior to other races, and fated to rule the world."

Hidden in a declaration of solidarity with his defeated subjects was a shocking assertion from their god-emperor: he was not a god. Although MacArthur denied it, it was widely assumed that Hirohito's renunciation of divinity was the price MacArthur demanded for remaining at the head of his country. But Hirohito may indeed have seized the opportunity to admit his mortality. He was the first emperor born in the twentieth century and received a twentieth-century education. As a young man he had dared to question imperial descent from divinity on the grounds of biological impossibility. And later in 1946, he claimed that "I have never considered myself a god. Nor have I ever attempted to arrogate to myself the powers of a divine being."

The news came like an earthquake to the people of Japan. Accustomed to bowing automatically as they passed the Imperial Palace, they now prostrated themselves before it as if praying to their fallen idol. But Hirohito set about transforming himself into an ordinary man in a gray flannel suit, meeting his subjects in their places of work, asking and answering questions, having an interest in marine biology—in short, being human, and neither a war criminal nor a god.

OPPOSITE: Hirohito delivering a speech to the 89th parliament in front of his gold-and-red imperial throne.

BELOW: The no-longer divine Hirohito in 1946, visiting the agricultural community of Saitama.

We welcome Russia to her rightful place among the leading nations of the world. We welcome her flag upon the seas. Above all, we welcome constant, frequent and growing contacts between the Russian people and our own people on both sides of the Atlantic. It is my duty however, for I am sure you would wish me to state the facts as I see them to you, to place before you certain facts about the present position in Europe.

From Stettin in the Baltic to Trieste in the Adriatic, an iron curtain has descended across the Continent. Behind that line lie all the capitals of the ancient states of Central and Eastern Europe: Warsaw, Berlin, Prague, Vienna, Budapest, Belgrade, Bucharest and Sofia, all these famous cities and the populations around them lie in what I must call the Soviet sphere, and all are subject in one form or another, not only to Soviet influence but to a very high and, in many cases, increasing measure of control from Moscow.

Athens alone—Greece with its immortal glories—is free to decide its future at an election under British, American and French observation. The Russian-dominated Polish Government has been encouraged to make enormous and wrongful inroads upon Germany, and mass expulsions of millions of Germans on a scale grievous and undreamed-of are now taking place.

The Communist parties, which were very small in all these Eastern States of Europe, have been raised to pre-eminence and power far beyond their numbers and are seeking everywhere to obtain totalitarian control. Police governments are prevailing in nearly every case, and so far, except in Czechoslovakia, there is no true democracy.

"The Sinews of Peace" Iron Curtain speech

Winston Churchill
"An iron curtain has descended"

(March 5, 1946)

The surprise defeat of Winston Churchill's Conservative party after the end of World War II had the benefit of releasing him from the need to be diplomatic. When Harry S. Truman invited him to speak at a college in the president's home state of Missouri, Churchill took full advantage of the occasion to speak frankly about the future of Europe.

From his dealings with his Russian allies during the war, Churchill could see which way the wind was blowing in a postwar Europe. The spread of communist totalitarianism was, he believed, no less dangerous to peace than Hitler's national socialism. The only way to avert a third world war was to maintain preparedness in peace. But after punishing conflicts in Europe and Asia, war-weary military and civilian populations in both Britain and America were reluctant to confront the possibility of a new threat from "good old Uncle Joe" Stalin.

Churchill knew that his view would be unwelcome, and crafted his speech with even greater care than usual. It was said that every minute of a Churchill speech took an hour to write, and this one took the best part of two weeks, including the five days spent on a liner crossing the Atlantic Ocean to the States. He showed it to Truman in advance, and to members of Truman's administration, who recommended minor changes.

But it was only on the eve of his address, in search of evocative imagery for his ideas, that he hit upon the metaphor of an iron curtain marking the boundary between enlightened Europe and the darkness of the Soviet sphere of influence. The following afternoon at Westminster College, Fulton, Missouri, he was introduced by the US president, whose own intelligence services now backed the British statesman's analysis. "Mr. Churchill and I believe in freedom of speech," Truman said. "I understand Mr. Churchill might have something useful and constructive to say."

Churchill's primary purpose was to affirm the special relationship between America and Britain that exemplified state democracy and which, along with the recently created United Nations, must form the basis of any lasting peace. This thought led naturally on to the threat to that peace and democracy: "war and tyranny. Prevention," he said bluntly, "is better than cure."

He welcomed their wartime ally Russia's emergence onto the world stage, but added: "It is my duty however . . . to place before you certain facts about the present position in Europe. From Stettin in the Baltic to Trieste in the Adriatic, an iron curtain has descended across the Continent. Behind that line lie all the capitals of the ancient states of Central and Eastern Europe."

He spoke in terms of light—"The dark ages may return," "A shadow has fallen over the scenes so lately lighted by the Allied victory," "War can find any nation, wherever it may dwell between dusk and dawn." And he argued that a balance of power was not enough—that there must be superiority and preparedness even in peacetime, to hold the expansion of communist influence at bay.

Besides his great oratory, what gave Churchill's speech such power was his insightful overview of an international stage, partly instinctive and partly the product of a long life in global politics. He knew that, although he was the bearer of bad news, his views would be received with respect.

In Russia, however, politicians blamed the speech for introducing suspicion into the USSR's relationship with the West. It therefore marked the start of the Cold War, a struggle of espionage and counterespionage that continues to this day.

OPPOSITE: *Freed from the diplomatic constraints of government, and counselled by his hosts, Churchill was able to deliver a speech that was chillingly prescient.*

Albert Speer
Nuremberg Trial Testimony
(August 31, 1946)

Albert Speer was one of the twenty-one defendants in the first Nuremberg trial, accused of crimes against peace and humanity. Eleven of them were sentenced to death but Speer, who became known in later years as "the Nazi who said sorry," escaped with his life.

Albert Speer joined Germany's National Socialist Party in 1931, before Adolf Hitler rose to power in the organization; but from 1934 onward the pair became close friends. Speer was an architect by profession and designed several iconic Nazi buildings for Hitler, including the Nuremberg Zeppelinfeld, the auditorium in which Hitler staged his vast rabble-rousing rallies.

During World War II, Hitler appointed Speer as Minister of the War Economy, and in that post Speer had remarkable success in increasing Germany's manufacture of armaments. This was achieved partly through Speer's knowledge of the production line innovations of Henry Ford, the American car manufacturer and Nazi sympathizer. But the increase in output was also managed by the use of slave labor, including prisoners, abducted workers, and the inmates of concentration camps.

Speer's guilt of war crimes depended on the extent of his knowledge. Did he know about the use of prisoners? Did he know about the mass extermination of the Jews?

He denied knowing about either. On the question of slavery, he insisted that "neither I nor my Ministry was responsible for this recruitment." His role had been merely to record the labor requirements of the industries and pass them on to the task force responsible for manpower "without specification as to whether the laborers be German, foreign workers or prisoners."

As for the Holocaust, there was evidence that Speer had been at the conference during which Heinrich Himmler announced it with the words "the grave decision had to be taken to cause this people to vanish from the earth. In the lands we occupy, the Jewish question will be dealt with by the end of the year." Speer claimed, as other politicians have done in similar circumstances, that he left before Himmler spoke.

He did, however, admit that the Nazis were anti-Semitic and that German Jews were being deported from their homes and their country. And having learned after the end of the war about the genocide, he said from the Nuremberg witness stand, "This war has brought an inconceivable catastrophe. Therefore it is my unquestionable duty to assume my share of responsibility for the disaster of the German people." It was not a full apology, but it did show some remorse, in marked contrast to most of his codefendants.

On August 31, each defendant was allowed to make a closing statement before judgment was passed. Speer, who had toward the end of the war urged Hitler to end it and surrender, damned his former friend for the suffering that he had brought on the German people.

Speer was given a twenty-year prison sentence, which he served in full. On his release in 1966, he wrote three revealing books about Germany's operation of the war, all bestsellers, which kept him comfortable until his death. His guilt, he always insisted, was in not having

As a former minister of a highly developed armament system, it is my last duty to say the following:

A new large-scale war will end with the destruction of human culture and civilization. Nothing prevents unconfined technique and science from completing the work of destroying human beings, which it has begun in so dreadful a way in this war.

Therefore, this Trial must contribute towards preventing such degenerate wars in the future and towards establishing rules whereby human beings can live together. Of what importance is my own fate after everything that has happened in comparison with this high goal?

During the past centuries the German people have contributed much towards the creation of human civilization. Often they have made these contributions in times when they were just as powerless and helpless as they are today. Worthwhile human beings will not let themselves be driven to despair. They will create new, lasting values and, under the tremendous pressure brought to bear upon everyone today, these new works will be of particular greatness.

But if the German people create new cultural values in the unavoidable period of their poverty and weakness—but at the same time in the period of their reconstruction—then they will, in that way, make the most valuable contribution to world events which their position allows them to.

It is not war alone which shapes the history of humanity, but also, in a higher sense, the cultural achievements which one day will become the common property of all humanity. But a nation which believes in its future will never perish. May God protect Germany and the culture of the West.

TESTIMONY AT THE NUREMBERG TRIALS

asked questions about the fate of the Jews to which he feared the answers. For example, a colleague once advised him never to accept an invitation to inspect a concentration camp because: "I saw something there which I am not permitted to describe and moreover could not describe." Speer knew that this was Auschwitz but had not pursued the matter. "I had closed my eyes. Because I failed at that time, I still feel, to this day, responsible for Auschwitz in a wholly personal sense." Only in 2007 did some private correspondence come to light in which he admitted that he had, in fact, heard Himmler's conference announcement of the coming extermination of the Jews.

It seems unimaginable that such a close confidant of the führer should not have known what was going on. Speer's relatively light sentence is attributed to his quiet, repentant performance in court. It lost him the respect of his Nazi colleagues, but it won him his life.

LEFT: Albert Speer in the Nuremberg witness box.

Jawaharlal Nehru
"Tryst with Destiny"

(August 14, 1947)

After centuries of rule by Britain and decades of resistance in various forms by the population of India, the independence of the subcontinent was settled quickly, in only a few months, in the wake of World War II. The Indian National Congress elected Jawaharlal Nehru as the new country's first Prime Minister.

Agitation to shake off British rule increased with the return of Mahatma Gandhi to India in the early twentieth century. His campaigns of civil disobedience were a focus for mass action. Nehru met Gandhi in 1916 at the annual conference of the Indian National Congress (INC) and Gandhi, recognizing the young man's potential and spirit, took him under his wing. Nehru, guided by his mentor, emerged as the figurehead of the growing independence movement.

Both men were imprisoned on several occasions for their involvement, and when Gandhi launched his Quit India campaign in 1942, Britain responded with a heavier hand than usual to suppress it. Embroiled in war with Japan from its bases in India, the British army now had to deal with insurrection from within. Sir Maurice Hallett, British governor of the United Provinces, described Gandhi as "cunning as a cartload of monkeys." The INC was banned, and 100,000 protesters, including Gandhi and Nehru, arrested.

After the war, Britain's military strength and economy were greatly depleted, and it was clear that it could no longer run India in the way to which it had become accustomed. The viceroy Lord Mountbatten was instructed to prepare to leave India as soon as possible and made plans over a few months in 1946 and 1947. Nehru, on his release from prison, was elected as leader of India's provisional government, and Independence Day was set for August 15, 1947.

On the eve of the transition, Nehru addressed the Constituent Assembly of India in New Delhi about the historic day ahead, which he referred to as a "tryst with destiny." "At the stroke of the midnight hour, when the world sleeps, India will awake to life and freedom." He spoke with poetry and wisdom about the moment for which he had worked for thirty years.

Nehru spoke of the challenges ahead and appealed for unity and trust in his new government. "To the people of India, whose representatives we are, we make an appeal to join us with faith and confidence in this great adventure. We have to build the noble mansion of India where all her children may dwell." This touched on a sore point. Under pressure from India's Muslim League, and despite opposition from Nehru, the independence plan included the partition of Hindu India and Muslim Pakistan. Nehru described in his speech: "Our brothers and sisters who have been cut off from us by political boundaries and cannot share in the freedom that has come. They are of us and will remain of us whatever may happen."

Gandhi's part in winning that freedom was so well known by Nehru's audience that he did not need to name him. He merely referred to "the greatest man of our generation" and "the architect of this freedom, the father of our nation, this great son of India, magnificent in his faith and strength and courage and humility."

It was an inspirational speech that sought to bind the disparate religious and social groups of Indians together in the work of shaping the new country. He presented the new nation with its first icon, Mahatma Gandhi, but he also reminded India and the world of that nation's long, rich history, in which this new freedom was a new chapter. "We end today a period of ill fortune as India discovers herself again." The whole speech was encapsulated in its final sentence: "And to India, our much-loved motherland, the ancient, the eternal and the ever-new, we pay our reverent homage and we bind ourselves afresh to her service."

There were troubles ahead. The separation of Hindu and Muslim was to blame; it was ill-advised and led to war and tension between India and Pakistan that

Long years ago we made a tryst with destiny, and now the time comes when we shall redeem our pledge, not wholly or in full measure, but very substantially.

At the stroke of the midnight hour, when the world sleeps, India will awake to life and freedom. A moment comes, which comes but rarely in history, when we step out from the old to the new, when an age ends, and when the soul of a nation, long suppressed, finds utterance.

It is fitting that at this solemn moment we take the pledge of dedication to the service of India and her people and to the still larger cause of humanity.

At the dawn of history India started on her unending quest, and trackless centuries are filled with her striving and the grandeur of her success and her failures. Through good and ill fortune alike she has never lost sight of that quest or forgotten the ideals which gave her strength. We end today a period of ill fortune as India discovers herself again.

We are citizens of a great country, on the verge of bold advance, and we have to live up to that high standard. All of us, to whatever religion we may belong, are equally the children of India with equal rights, privileges and obligations. We cannot encourage communalism or narrow-mindedness, for no nation can be great whose people are narrow in thought or in action.

To the nations and peoples of the world we send greetings and pledge ourselves to cooperate with them in furthering peace, freedom and democracy.

And to India, our much-loved motherland, the ancient, the eternal and the ever-new, we pay our reverent homage and we bind ourselves afresh to her service. Jai Hind [Victory to India].

OPENING AND CLOSING SECTIONS OF THE "TRYST WITH DESTINY" SPEECH, DECLARING INDIAN INDEPENDENCE

continues to this day. A Hindu extremist assassinated Gandhi less than six months after independence. Nehru, his pupil, was shaken to the core, and he reported the terrible news on the radio with these words: "Friends and comrades, the light has gone out of our lives, and there is darkness everywhere, and I do not quite know what to tell you or how to say it. Our beloved leader, Bapu as we called him, the father of the nation, is no more." Nehru led the country until his own death in 1964.

RIGHT: *Nehru (far left) speaking in August 1947 at the Constituent Assembly in Delhi.*

We hereby declare the establishment of a Jewish state in Eretz-Israel, to be known as the State of Israel.

The State of Israel will be open for Jewish immigration and for the Ingathering of the Exiles; it will foster the development of the country for the benefit of all its inhabitants; it will be based on freedom, justice and peace as envisaged by the prophets of Israel; it will ensure complete equality of social and political rights to all its inhabitants irrespective of religion, race or sex; it will guarantee freedom of religion, conscience, language, education and culture; it will safeguard the Holy Places of all religions. . . .

The State of Israel is prepared to cooperate with the agencies and representatives of the United Nations in implementing the resolution of the General Assembly of the 29th November, 1947, and will take steps to bring about the economic union of the whole of Eretz-Israel.

We appeal to the United Nations to assist the Jewish people in the building-up of its State and to receive the State of Israel into the comity of nations.

We appeal—in the very midst of the onslaught launched against us now for months— to the Arab inhabitants of the State of Israel to preserve peace and participate in the upbuilding of the State on the basis of full and equal citizenship and due representation in all its provisional and permanent institutions.

We extend our hand to all neighboring states and their peoples in an offer of peace and good neighborliness, and appeal to them to establish bonds of cooperation and mutual help with the sovereign Jewish people settled in its own land. The State of Israel is prepared to do its share in a common effort for the advancement of the entire Middle East.

ISRAELI DECLARATION OF INDEPENDENCE

LEFT: David Ben-Gurion in May 1948, declaring the independent State of Israel at Tel Aviv Museum.

David Ben-Gurion
Israeli Declaration of Independence
(May 14, 1948)

David Ben-Gurion's proclamation of the new State of Israel was both the culmination of decades of wrangling by the international community and the beginning of decades of tension in the region. For Jews around the world who had survived World War II, it was a moment of profound emotion.

Calls for a separate Jewish state rose in volume toward the end of the nineteenth century when a wave of Russian Jewish émigrés returned to their ancient lands in Palestine. After the Ottoman Empire was defeated in World War I, Britain became the ruling authority in the region. Prime Minister Arthur Balfour supported Zionist calls, but opposition from the majority Arab population prevented progress during the interwar years.

Hitler's rise to power and his persecution of German Jews encouraged a further wave of immigration to the area. The discovery of the scale of his genocide after World War II prompted further international support for a Jewish homeland, now boosted by the United States. A proposed partition of Palestine left the Arab majority with only 46 percent of the land. When the newly created United Nations ruled in favor of the division, Britain, whose authority in the region was to expire on May 15, 1948, refused to be party to it.

Jewish settlers took matters into their own hands, forming militias that took control of the areas assigned to them. They were led by David Ben-Gurion, head of the pressure group the Zionist Organisation and of the Jewish Agency, a body that facilitated the migration of Jews to Palestine. As the British prepared to leave the area, it fell to Ben-Gurion to proclaim a new, permanent home for the Jews. Born amid continuing war with its neighbors, its future was by no means secure. But its birth was a precious moment for the Jewish diaspora reeling from the Holocaust.

"The land of Israel," he began, "was the birthplace of the Jewish people. Here their spiritual, religious and political identity was shaped." He spoke of the hope since their dispersal of a return to the region, and praised the pioneer settlers who had "made the desert bloom, revived the Hebrew language, created a thriving community controlling its own economy and culture, loving peace but knowing how to defend itself."

He summed up the legal justifications for the new state—the Balfour Declaration of 1917, the subsequent rulings of both the League of Nations and the United Nations, which recognized the right of Jews to establish their country. "Accordingly we representatives of the Jewish community and of the Zionist movement . . . hereby declare the establishment of a Jewish state in Eretz-Israel to be known as the State of Israel."

Ben-Gurion used the proclamation to appeal for recognition of Israel—from Arab neighbors and from the United Nations. He outlined the high moral principles on which the country was founded: "it will be based on freedom, justice and peace as envisaged by the prophets of Israel; it will ensure complete equality of social and political rights to all its inhabitants irrespective of religion, race or sex; it will guarantee freedom of religion, conscience, language, education and culture; it will safeguard the Holy Places of all religions."

President Truman recognized the new state of Israel within minutes of Ben-Gurion's proclamation. But even as the British army withdrew from the area, Egypt, Jordan, Syria, and Lebanon attacked in support of displaced Palestinians. Ben-Gurion's Israel Defense Forces were drawn into the first of many wars through which it not only defended but expanded its borders. Today, Israel is a thoroughly modern, thriving country supported by international goodwill. It nevertheless lives under constant threat from neighbors upon whom Israel was imposed without consent. Ben-Gurion's appeal to them "in an offer of peace and good neighborliness to establish bonds of cooperation and mutual help" remains a forlorn hope seventy years after his declaration.

Aneurin Bevan
"The eyes of the world are turning to Great Britain"

(July 4, 1948)

The British Labour Party's vision of a system of universal healthcare was a response to the chaotic network of health provision that existed before World War II. It met with staunch opposition from doctors and the Conservative Party, about whom Health Minister Aneurin Bevan spoke in scathing terms.

Aneurin Bevan (pronounced An-eye-rin and usually shortened to Nye) grew up in poverty, the son of a Welsh coal miner. A lifelong Labour Party supporter, he served on the committee of the medical aid society formed by local miners and ironworkers in Tredegar, which ran the local hospital. He never forgot his working-class background and its grassroots approach to mutual support. When he was working to introduce the National Health Service (NHS) after the war, he said, "All I am doing is extending to the entire population of Britain the benefits which we had in Tredegar."

Nye Bevan's politics were driven by anger at the abuse and neglect of working-class communities, and the belief that the nation as a whole benefited from the good education and health of the whole population. The state therefore should make provision for these advantages, particularly to those least able to provide them for themselves—as his leader Clement Attlee put it: "The weak first, the strong next."

All parties supported the Conservative government's Education Act in 1944, which reformed schooling in Britain after the war ended. But although there was general support for a similar reform of healthcare provision, there were different views on exactly how. Doctors wanted to retain control of medical facilities and argued for the introduction of a medical insurance scheme. Bevan and his Conservative predecessor, Henry Willink wanted a system centrally funded by general taxation and free at the point of access. When Labour came to power in 1945, the Conservatives voted against their plans; but in 1946, the National Health Services Act was passed.

Nye Bevan worked hard to win the support of the medical profession, and the NHS was officially launched in Manchester on July 5, 1948. At a prelaunch rally in the Gorton area of the city, Bevan addressed an audience of Labour supporters. Unforgiving of his opponents' free-market capitalist approach to social welfare, he attacked the willingness of Conservative "spivs" to put business profit before public welfare. After recalling his own early life experiences of hunger and unemployment, he declared that nothing could "eradicate from my heart a deep burning hatred for the Tory Party that inflicted those bitter experiences on me. So far as I am concerned they are lower than vermin."

At a time when politics was still a game played by gentlemanly rules, not the undignified roughhouse that it so often appears today, this was a shocking remark. It was seized on by the Conservatives as a slur not on the party but on its voters. Conservative supporters took to wearing badges declaring themselves to be "Vermin;" "Vile Vermin" if they recruited ten other badge wearers; "Very Vile Vermin" if they recruited twenty. Future prime minister Margaret Thatcher was an enthusiastic member of this new Vermin Club and became its official Chief Rat.

More importantly, the furor that the remark caused was an unwelcome distraction from the implementation of the new NHS. Attlee was privately angry with Bevan and advised him to "be a bit more careful." At first the NHS included free dentistry and glasses; and when Labour introduced charges for these services in 1951, Bevan resigned as health minister. Labour lost a general election the same year, and the incoming Conservative government introduced charges for prescriptions.

That is why no amount of cajolery, and no attempts at ethical or social seduction, can eradicate from my heart a deep burning hatred for the Tory Party that inflicted those bitter experiences [of childhood] on me. So far as I am concerned they are lower than vermin. They condemned millions of first-class people to semi-starvation. Now the Tories are pouring out money in propaganda of all sorts and are hoping by this organized sustained mass suggestion to eradicate from our minds all memory of what we went through. But, I warn you young men and women, do not listen to what they are saying now. Do not listen to the seductions of Lord Woolton. He is a very good salesman. If you are selling shoddy stuff you have to be a good salesman. But I warn you they have not changed, or if they have they are slightly worse than they were.

But after today the weak will be entitled to clamour. After a while the newspapers in the hands of our enemies will give the impression that everything is going wrong. Don't be deceived, it is then that they will start going right. We are the people to whom the people can complain. I shall be unmoved by the newspapers, but moved by the distress.

In 1950 we shall face you again with all our program carried out. And when I say all, I mean all. I mean steel is going to be added, we are going to establish a new record: that of being the only British Government that ever carried out all its election promises.

SPEECH TO THE HOUSE OF COMMONS ON THE FOUNDING OF THE NHS

The costs of the National Health Service have exceeded expectations almost from the day it was introduced. Despite its consistent popularity with the electorate it is still the unfortunate football kicked between ideologically opposed politicians, all determined to shape its funding. Nevertheless, its survival and level of provision are the envy of many countries, as Nye Bevan predicted on July 4, 1948: "The eyes of the world are turning to Great Britain. We now have the moral leadership of the world, and we shall have people coming here as to a modern Mecca, learning from us."

RIGHT: Aneurin Bevan, the Labour Health Minister, in 1948, pictured at work in his office.

Chairman Mao Zedong
"The Chinese People Have Stood Up!"

(September 21, 1949)

For much of the first half of the twentieth century, China was a country torn apart by civil war between the Chinese Nationalist and Communist Parties, and by Japanese invasion. Having repelled Japan and overcome the Nationalists, Mao Zedong was ready to declare the People's Republic of China on October 1, 1949.

From his earliest days as a leader of student protest at the beginning of the twentieth century, Mao Zedong had distinguished himself by word and deed in the communist cause. In 1921 he attended the inaugural session of the Chinese Communist Party's National Congress and in 1927 he became commander in chief of the Red Army. In 1935, during the Long March of the Red Army's retreat northward, Mao was elected as leader of the party as well as the army, and he held the chairmanship of the party from 1943 onward.

At a conference ten days before the declaration of the Republic, Mao addressed delegates who were about to decide on the form of the new country's laws, government and flag. He had defined the communists' journey to this point, and now he set about defining the next stage—statehood. Although those present needed no reminding, Mao began by trumpeting the Red Army's success and demonising their defeated Nationalist opponent Chiang Kai-shek and "the reactionary government backed by US imperialism."

"There is," he insisted, "absolutely no room for compromise with Chiang Kai-shek's Kuomintang ['National People's Party'], the running dog of imperialism and its accomplices." Although America had supported the Kuomintang with arms deliveries during the civil war with the Red Army, it had latterly suspended them and made friendly diplomatic advances to Mao's headquarters in Yan'an—the so-called Dixie Mission from 1944 to 1947. During that time US military and political personnel were impressed by Mao's organization and considered him a potential postwar ally. For his part, anti-imperialist Mao had once described the US as "the most murderous of hangmen."

Now triumphant at the head of an unimaginably large army, population, and landscape, he told delegates,

"we are all convinced that our work will go down in the history of mankind, demonstrating that the Chinese people, comprising one quarter of humanity, have now stood up." It was an empowering image—an entire population, then of 475 million, rising as one and pitching in with the economic reconstruction of their country. What a resource, what potential!

Like earlier revolutionary leaders in America, France, and Russia, Mao was anxious to stress that the revolution was by no means over, that difficult times lay ahead, with counterrevolutionary opposition both at home and from abroad. Military and economic strength were the keys to success. "As long as we keep to our style of plain living and hard struggle we shall be able to win speedy victory on the economic front." He paved the way for a continuing alliance with fellow communist dictator Joseph Stalin. "Internationally, we must unite with the Soviet Union, so that we shall not stand alone in our struggle to safeguard these fruits of victory and to thwart the plots of domestic and foreign enemies for restoration."

From the man who would in 1966 launch China's brutal Cultural Revolution came these closing remarks: "An upsurge in economic construction is bound to be followed by an upsurge of construction in the cultural sphere. The era in which the Chinese people were regarded as uncivilized is now ended. We shall emerge in the world as a nation with an advanced culture." After Mao's death, the Chinese government announced the Cultural Revolution to be "responsible for the most severe setback and the heaviest losses suffered by the Party, the country, and the people since the founding of the People's Republic."

Since then the People's Republic has recovered, and its population, now approaching 1.4 billion, has stood

Fellow delegates, we are all convinced that our work will go down in the history of mankind, demonstrating that the Chinese people, comprising one quarter of humanity, have now stood up. The Chinese have always been a great, courageous and industrious nation; it is only in modern times that they have fallen behind. And that was due entirely to oppression and exploitation by foreign imperialism and domestic reactionary governments.

For over a century our forefathers never stopped waging unyielding struggles against domestic and foreign oppressors, including the Revolution of 1911 led by Dr. Sun Yat-sen, our great forerunner in the Chinese revolution. Our forefathers enjoined us to carry out their unfulfilled will. And we have acted accordingly. We have closed our ranks and defeated both domestic and foreign oppressors through the People's War of Liberation and the great people's revolution, and now we are proclaiming the founding of the People's Republic of China.

From now on our nation will belong to the community of the peace-loving and freedom-loving nations of the world and work courageously and industriously to foster its own civilization and well-being and at the same time to promote world peace and freedom. Ours will no longer be a nation subject to insult and humiliation. We have stood up. Our revolution has won the sympathy and acclaim of the people of all countries. We have friends all over the world. . . .

Let the domestic and foreign reactionaries tremble before us! Let them say we are no good at this and no good at that. By our own indomitable efforts we the Chinese people will unswervingly reach our goal.

Hail the victory of the People's War of Liberation and the people's revolution!
Hail the founding of the People's Republic of China!
Hail the triumph of the Chinese People's Political Consultative Conference!

SECTIONS FROM "THE CHINESE PEOPLE HAVE STOOD UP!" SPEECH

up again to become a major force in the world economy, skillfully, and pragmatically balancing capitalism and communism. As Mao concluded in 1949: "By our own indomitable efforts we the Chinese people will unswervingly reach our goal."

RIGHT: Although the US considered Mao a potential ally, they had backed his opponent in the civil war.

Eva Perón
"I have always believed in my beloved descamisados"

(October 17, 1951)

Under Juan Perón's presidency, October 17 was Loyalty Day, an annual celebration of the mass protest that forced Perón's release after he was arrested in 1946 by the army. At a rally five years later the president's wife, Eva, addressed an adoring million-strong crowd. She knew, and they did not, that it would be her farewell.

Eva Duarte's fairy-tale rise from poverty to power as the wife of Argentine president Juan Perón is as divisive as it is familiar. Reviled by her detractors, revered by the working-class men and women for whom she spoke, the truth of her life is obscured by the myths spun on all sides. Whatever her complicity in the corrupt schemes of her husband, she introduced radical improvements in the rights of women and the poor of her country. She touched the hearts of her people, where she is still held in devoted affection.

In 1950, after four years as the First Lady of Argentina, Eva Perón's health began to deteriorate rapidly. She fainted in public and was diagnosed with an aggressive cervical cancer. Although Juan kept the truth from her, it was clear to Eva that something was seriously wrong. She was in intense pain, which may have been responsible for the increasingly angry note of dissent expressed in her public speeches. She was certainly losing weight and strength at an alarming rate.

A hysterectomy in the summer of 1951 was unsuccessful in eliminating the cancer. When she spoke to her supporters on Loyalty Day that year, she was painfully aware of her physical decline. "No one or nothing could ever prevent me from coming, because I have a sacred debt to Perón and all of you, to the workers, to the boys of the CGT [General Labor Confederation], to the descamisados and the people. And it doesn't matter to me if I have to leave shreds of my life along the way in order to repay it."

Descamisado (literally "shirtless") was originally a derogatory term for someone so poor that he or she couldn't afford shirts, but it had become a badge of honor for the working classes whose hopes and realities Evita represented. If she could pull herself up from village poverty to glamorous leadership, so could they.

Evita's appeal to the masses was a powerful weapon for her campaigning husband as well as for her own ambition, and much of her speech was in support of his 1952 campaign for reelection. "I'm not important for what I am or have," she told the descamisados. "I have only one thing that matters, and I have it in my heart. It's love for this people and for Perón."

But mortality was on her mind. "The enemies of the people have long known that Perón and Eva Perón are ready to die for this people. Now they also know that the people are ready to die for Perón. I ask that all of us publicly vow to defend Perón and to fight for him until death." And the longer she spoke, the closer to home that mortality came. She thanked them all for their prayers for her health, "and though I leave shreds of my life along the road, I know that you will pick up my name and will carry it to victory as a banner."

Finally, she told them, "my wish is that I will soon be back in the struggle with more strength and love, but if for health reasons I am not, take care of the General. And to all the descamisados, I hold them so very closely to my heart, and want them to know how much I love them."

It was a remarkable, moving, valedictory declaration of love for the people. In 1952, Juan Perón won a second presidential term. By then Evita was too weak to stand. At a rally in May, Perón supported her discreetly by her hips, and for a parade in June, she stood in a presidential cavalcade only with the aid of a plaster cast around her body, reinforced with a wire frame and concealed beneath a huge fur coat. She died on July 26, 1952, aged thirty-three.

Let the enemies of the people, of Perón and the Fatherland come. I have never been afraid of them because I have always believed in the people. I have always believed in my beloved descamisados because I have never forgotten that without them October 17 would have been a date of pain and bitterness, for this date was supposed to be one of ignominy and treason, but the courage of this people turned it into a day of glory and happiness. Finally, compañeros, I thank you for all your prayers for my health; I thank you with all my heart. . . . I don't ask or want anything for myself. My glory is and always will be to be Perón's shield and the flag of my people, and though I leave shreds of my life along the road, I know that you will pick up my name and will carry it to victory as a banner. I know that God is with us because he is with the humble and despises the arrogance of the oligarchy. This is why victory will be ours. We will achieve it sooner or later, whatever the cost, whoever may fall.

My descamisados: . . . I ask you just one thing: it's certain I will soon be with you, but if for health reasons I am not, take care of the general. Remain faithful to Perón as you've been until today, because this means being loyal to the Fatherland and loyal to yourselves. And to all the descamisados of the interior, I hold them closely, so very closely to my heart, and want them to know how much I love them.

SPEECH TO THE DESCAMISADOS

RIGHT: Eva Perón in August 1951, speaking to an assembly of the General Federation of Labour.

Queen Elizabeth II
"My experience is so short and my task so new"

(June 2, 1953)

When Britain's King Edward VIII abdicated in 1936, his brother Albert assumed the crown as George VI. His daughter Princess Elizabeth, suddenly found herself thrust into the public spotlight as the heir presumptive to the British Empire at ten years old.

Throughout this memorable day I have been uplifted and sustained by the knowledge that your thoughts and prayers were with me. I have been aware all the time that my peoples, spread far and wide throughout every continent and ocean in the world, were united to support me in the task to which I have now been dedicated with such solemnity. . . .

The ceremonies you have seen today are ancient, and some of their origins are veiled in the mists of the past. But their spirit and their meaning shine through the ages never, perhaps, more brightly than now. I have in sincerity pledged myself to your service, as so many of you are pledged to mine. Throughout all my life and with all my heart I shall strive to be worthy of your trust.

In this resolve I have my husband to support me. He shares all my ideals and all my affection for you. Then, although my experience is so short and my task so new, I have in my parents and grandparents an example which I can follow with certainty and with confidence.

There is also this. I have behind me not only the splendid traditions and the annals of more than a thousand years but the living strength and majesty of the Commonwealth and Empire; of societies old and new; of lands and races different in history and origins but all, by God's Will, united in spirit and in aim.

Therefore I am sure that this, my Coronation, is not the symbol of a power and a splendor that are gone but a declaration of our hopes for the future, and for the years I may, by God's Grace and Mercy, be given to reign and serve you as your Queen.

CORONATION SPEECH

OPPOSITE: The coronation of Elizabeth II in Westminster Abbey.

George VI and his wife, Queen Elizabeth, led the country through World War II by example, refusing to be flown to Canada for their safety. From George, as from all those involved, the war took a heavy toll on his health. His final years were beset with illness, including lung cancer and the thrombosis that finally took his life in 1952.

His daughter Elizabeth, now a woman of twenty-five, had increasingly undertaken royal duties in his place, accompanied by her husband, Prince Philip. She was in Kenya on February 6, 1952, on another royal tour when she got news of her father's death. It was a moment of personal loss, but with fifteen years to prepare for the moment, she was as ready to be a monarch as she could be. She became queen immediately, but the preparations for her coronation would take fourteen months, and she was not formally crowned in Westminster Abbey until June 2, 1953.

That evening she spoke as the crowned head of the United Kingdom and six other Commonwealth countries, and head of state of many other members of the British Empire. Millions of people tuned in to her address. Although the monarchy was popular, she was stepping into very big shoes. Her father and grandfather had both been good kings, and the most recent British

queen was the long-reigning sovereign who gave her name to an entire age, Queen Victoria. Her namesake had once made a speech defining the very nature of Englishness. Elizabeth II met her subjects' expectations head-on.

With a few words she claimed her legitimacy to rule, by adding herself to the long direct line of British kings and queens. "Although my experience is so short and my task so new," she said, "I have in my parents and grandparents an example which I can follow with certainty." She appealed to Britain's sense of history and empire. "The ceremonies you have seen today are ancient . . . I have behind me not only the splendid traditions and the annals of more than a thousand years but the living strength and majesty of the Commonwealth and Empire; of lands and races different in history . . . but all, by God's Will, united in spirit and in aim."

Having invoked the past, she conjured the future too. "This, my Coronation is not the symbol of a power and a splendor that are gone but a declaration of our hopes for the future, and for the years I may, by God's Grace and Mercy, be given to reign and serve you as your Queen."

Elizabeth next touched on the qualities that made modern Britain great: "free speech and respect for the rights of minorities, and the inspiration of a broad tolerance in thought and expression," which she suggested had been encouraged by the countries of the Empire and Commonwealth. Although this was a rose-tinted view of Britain's colonial history, it was a welcome gesture of inclusivity and the most personal indication of her hopes for her reign.

The Commonwealth, the royal family, and the British nation have been through much trauma and transformation since that day in 1952, often straining the credibility of young Elizabeth's vision of her realm. But she has risen to the challenges of many occasions. And today she is the oldest and longest-reigning monarch in British history, and the oldest and longest-reigning living monarch in the world. Outlasting even the great Queen Victoria's sixty-four-year reign, Elizabeth II is the only British sovereign to celebrate silver, golden, diamond, and sapphire jubilees of her accession to the throne. No longer is her experience short or her task new.

Earl Warren
"In the field of public education, the doctrine of 'separate but equal' has no place"

(May 17, 1954)

A US court ruling in 1896 about segregated railcars supported the argument that racial segregation in schools was legal as long as the educational facilities were of equal standard. In 1954, some seventeen Southern states enforced compulsory segregation, while sixteen Northern states made it illegal.

The reality of schooling in the segregated states was far from equal. Black schools were housed in poor buildings with fewer resources, often farther away than their white counterparts and with worse transport provisions. The National Association for the Advancement of Colored People (NAACP) sponsored a group of parents in Topeka, Kansas, to mount a class action suit against their local board of education as a means of drawing attention to the inequality.

Of the thirteen plaintiffs, twelve were women and only one—Oliver Brown—a man. Brown was made the named plaintiff because it was felt that a male would carry more weight. The battle for equality between the sexes was one for another day.

The NAACP's first move was to encourage the parents to apply for a place at their nearest white school. All their applications were rejected. For Oliver Brown's daughter this meant a six-block walk to her school bus stop followed by a one-mile journey to the black school, while the white school was only seven blocks away from the Brown home. The district court ruled in favor of the school board on the grounds that the schools were substantially equal in provision and therefore upheld the Fourteenth Amendment, that all citizens should be treated equally in law.

The NAACP took its challenge to the 1896 doctrine of "separate but equal" to the Supreme Court, where it was heard by recently appointed Chief Justice Earl Warren. Warren, best remembered today for heading the commission that investigated the 1963 assassination

of John F. Kennedy, also ruled in 1966 that a suspect's statements were only admissible if he or she had been read his rights on arrest. His ruling in the case of *Brown vs. Board of Education*, delivered on May 17, 1954, was his first landmark decision in office.

Warren reviewed the history of the Fourteenth Amendment with regard to education and observed that equality of provision had come a long way since its adoption in 1868. "We must look instead," he said, "to the effect of segregation itself on public education." Education, said Warren, was "the very foundation of good citizenship. Does segregation . . . deprive the children of the minority group of equal educational opportunities? We believe that it does."

Modern thinking confirmed that "to separate them from others of similar age and qualifications solely because of their race generates a feeling of inferiority as to their status in the community . . . in a way unlikely ever to be undone," and therefore, Warren rejected any argument to the contrary in the 1896 ruling. That sense of inferiority meant that "separate educational facilities [were] inherently unequal," and violated the Fourteenth Amendment. "We conclude that, in the field of public education, the doctrine of 'separate but equal' has no place."

The court's unanimous ruling of this fact was hailed as a victory for the civil rights movement. However, it made no provision or timetable for the dismantling of education apartheid in America. Many Southern states continued to resist integration, although by 1956, Topeka integrated its schools at every level. A further

We come then to the question presented: does segregation of children in public schools solely on the basis of race, even though the physical facilities and other 'tangible' factors may be equal, deprive the children of the minority group of equal educational opportunities? We believe that it does.

Such considerations apply with added force to children in grade and high schools. To separate them from others of similar age and qualifications solely because of their race generates a feeling of inferiority as to their status in the community that may affect their hearts and minds in a way unlikely ever to be undone. The effect of this separation on their educational opportunities was well stated by a finding in the Kansas case by a court which nevertheless felt compelled to rule against the negro plaintiffs:

Segregation of white and colored children in public schools has a detrimental effect upon the colored children. The impact is greater when it has the sanction of the law, for the policy of separating the races is usually interpreted as denoting the inferiority of the negro group. A sense of inferiority affects the motivation of a child to learn. Segregation with the sanction of law, therefore, has a tendency to retard the educational and mental development of negro children and to deprive them of some of the benefits they would receive in a racially integrated school system.

We conclude that, in the field of public education, the doctrine of 'separate but equal' has no place. Separate educational facilities are inherently unequal. Therefore, we hold that the plaintiffs and others similarly situated for whom the actions have been brought are, by reason of the segregation complained of, deprived of the equal protection of the laws guaranteed by the Fourteenth Amendment.

RACIAL SEGREGATION IN US SCHOOLS

case known as Brown II ruled only that desegregation of schools should be pursued "with all deliberate speed," an ambiguous and noncommittal statement. But Warren's ruling gave heart and strength to the civil rights campaign. A year later Rosa Parks refused to give up her seat on a bus in Montgomery, Alabama, and it became clear that the chief justice's demolition of "separate but equal" could be applied to many other forms of public segregation in the United States.

RIGHT: Chief Justice Earl Warren's landmark judgment as it was reported in the local press.

Stalin tried to inculcate the notion that the victories gained by the Soviet nation were all due to the courage, daring, and genius of Stalin and of no one else. Let us take our military films. They make us feel sick. Let us recall The Fall of Berlin. Here only Stalin acts. He issues orders in a hall in which there are many empty chairs. And where is the military command? Where is the politburo? Where is the government? What are they doing, and with what are they engaged? There is nothing about them in the film.

Comrades! The cult of the individual acquired such monstrous size chiefly because Stalin himself supported the glorification of his own person. The edition of his short biography, which was published in 1948, is an expression of the most dissolute flattery, approved and edited by Stalin personally. He marked the very places where he thought that the praise of his services was insufficient. Here are some examples characterizing Stalin's activity, added in Stalin's own hand, 'The guiding force of the party and the state was comrade Stalin.' Thus writes Stalin himself! Then he adds: 'Although he performed his tasks as leader of the people with consummate skill, Stalin never allowed his work to be marred by the slightest hint of vanity, conceit or self-adulation.' Where and when could a leader so praise himself?

Comrades! The cult of the individual brought about rude violation of party democracy, sterile administration, deviations of all sorts, cover-ups of shortcomings, and varnishings of reality. Our nation bore forth many flatterers and specialists in false optimism and deceit.

LEFT: Khrushchev was careful to portray the party as a victim of Stalin's dictatorship, not an accessory to it. To blame the party would be to undermine communism and the entire Russian Revolution. The speech was delivered in private because "we cannot let this matter get out of the party, especially not to the press. We should not wash our dirty linen before their eyes."

Nikita Khrushchev
"Cult of the individual"

(February 25, 1956)

The Twentieth Congress of the Communist Party of the Soviet Union concluded on February 24, 1956. But an unexpected extra session was convened on the following day, from which the press and observers were excluded. Khrushchev, victor in the power struggle that followed Stalin's death in 1953, had something to say.

Stalin's murderous purges of the 1930s and the Robespierrian atmosphere of fear and suspicion that he engendered, were no secret. But no one dared criticize them because of the overpowering "cult of the individual" that he encouraged. He was, he convinced everyone, supremely wise; every abuse he perpetrated must be good because he was single-handedly acting in the interests of the Soviet Union and the Communist Party.

It was three years after Stalin's death before anyone dared to speak out about his outrages. Khrushchev's closed-session speech to the Twentieth Congress was prompted by a report into Stalin's suppression of collective decision-making after the Seventeenth Congress in 1934. As Khrushchev reminded the 1956 delegates, "of the 139 members of the central committee who were elected [in 1934], 98 persons—70 percent— were arrested and shot." Stalin had invented the notion of an "enemy of the people," which made possible the cruelest repression against anyone who disagreed with him. The cult of the individual encouraged "cover-ups of shortcomings, and varnishings of reality. Our nation bore forth many flatterers and specialists in false optimism and deceit."

The 1956 delegates had been issued a copy of the Lenin Testament, a view of the future of the revolution written when its first leader knew he was dying. Khrushchev quoted Lenin on Stalin: "I am not certain whether he will always be able to use this power with the required care." He invoked memories of Lenin in contrast to Stalin, as a modest, quiet man who wished Stalin could be replaced by "a man who would differ from Stalin in only one quality, namely greater tolerance, greater loyalty, greater kindness."

Khrushchev attacked Stalin's vanity. He mocked Soviet propaganda films about World War II, known in the Soviet Union as the Great Patriotic War, in which "Stalin tried to inculcate the notion that the victories gained by the Soviet nation were all due to the courage, daring, and genius of Stalin and no one else." Concerning Stalin's merits, he joked, "an entirely sufficient number of books, pamphlets and studies had already been written in his lifetime."

Referring to the 1948 biography of Stalin, "approved and edited by Stalin personally," Khrushchev quoted some of the corrections and insertions that Stalin had suggested, including this self-effacing statement: "'Stalin never allowed his work to be marred by the slightest hint of vanity, conceit or self-adulation.' Where and when," Khrushchev asked rhetorically, "could a leader so praise himself?" The remark drew nervous laughter from some sections of his audience.

But not everyone was relieved to feel the blanket of oppression being lifted. In Georgia, land of Stalin's birth, reports of Khrushchev's attack on their greatest son provoked riots that the Red Army had to quell. Some Congress delegates were so shocked at this overturning of doctrine that they had heart attacks. Some committed suicide, faced with the destruction of their idol or the fear of revenge.

Hard-line Stalinist leaders in Poland and Albania were critical of Khrushchev's revisionism. The Polish leader at the time died in Moscow under mysterious circumstances a few days after the Congress, and uprisings later in 1956 in both Poland and Hungary were blamed on Khrushchev's undermining of Stalinist authoritarianism. China and Russia, two great powers that had hitherto supported each other's Marxist revolutions, now diverged because China retained its faith in Stalinism.

Harold Macmillan
"The wind of change is blowing through this continent"

(February 3, 1960)

At the start of 1960 Britain's prime minister Harold Macmillan began a tour of the British Empire's African colonies. He wanted to take the political temperature of the countries for which Britain had made itself responsible. When at the end of his trip he addressed the South African parliament, his conclusions shocked his audience and presaged great change for the continent.

The Union of South Africa came into being in 1910 with the unification of four British colonies—the Cape, Natal, Transvaal, and Orange River—and was technically a dominion of the Empire, ruled independently of Britain under the watchful but detached eye of a British governor-general. In 1960, it celebrated its golden jubilee, and Macmillan's address to its parliament was anticipated as part of the celebrations. Instead, Macmillan used the occasion to confront the reality of postwar imperialism. "A wind of change is blowing through this continent," he told his audience. "We must all accept it as a fact, and our national policies must take account of it."

Britain still ruled in sixteen African countries at the start of 1960, but faced increasing agitation within them. Macmillan gave credit to western civilization for "this tide of national consciousness"—the spread of science, improvements in economic production, communication, and above all education. Africans who had served in Britain's forces during World War II wanted their contributions to be recognized. And a new breed of African leader was emerging, educated in British universities and both interested in and capable of home rule.

From Britain's point of view, the war had strained its resources and it lacked the wealth and energy to administer a large empire. India had been given its independence in 1947; and in Africa, Ghana, Somalia, and Eritrea had all been granted control of their own affairs in the 1950s. Unrest was spreading in other countries, notably Kenya, where the Mau Mau uprising had become a permanent and costly drain on Britain's military strength.

Of great political concern was the spread of communism, which was taking advantage of discontent and uncertainty in the wake of World War II to influence emerging independence movements. To delay granting nationhood might be to allow communist influence to gain the upper hand. "The great issue . . . is whether the uncommitted peoples of Asia and Africa will swing to the East or to the West," Macmillan warned. "The struggle is joined, and it is a struggle for the minds of men."

The minority white rulers of South Africa received Macmillan's speech in stunned silence. The prime minister of the mother country was effectively abandoning the principles on which their country was based—white supremacy and apartheid. "I hope you won't mind my saying frankly," he told them, "that there are some aspects of your policies which make it impossible for us [to give South Africa our support] without being false to our deep convictions about the political destinies of free men."

By convention, the South African prime minister Hendrik Verwoerd rose to reply to Macmillan's speech but was rather lost for words. "I am pleased you were frank, even if we differ." But, he added, "there must not only be justice to the black man in Africa but also to the white man. We are whites but we are in Africa. We believe that places on us a special duty." Within a year South Africa had declared itself a republic and withdrawn from the British Commonwealth, followed in 1965 by Kenya. Apartheid attitudes became more entrenched, and the suppression of African nationalism in those countries increasingly violent.

The world today is divided into three main groups. First there are what we call the Western Powers. You in South Africa and we in Britain belong to this group, together with our friends and allies in other parts of the Commonwealth. In the United States of America and in Europe we call it the Free World.

Secondly there are the Communists—Russia and her satellites in Europe and China whose population will rise by the end of the next ten years to the staggering total of 800 million.

Thirdly, there are those parts of the world whose people are at present uncommitted either to Communism or to our Western ideas.

In this context we think first of Asia and then of Africa. As I see it the great issue in this second half of the twentieth century is whether the uncommitted peoples of Asia and Africa will swing to the East or to the West. Will they be drawn into the Communist camp? Or will the great experiments in self-government that are now being made in Asia and Africa, especially within the Commonwealth, prove so successful, and by their example so compelling, that the balance will come down in favor of freedom and order and justice?

The struggle is joined, and it is a struggle for the minds of men. What is now on trial is much more than our military strength or our diplomatic and administrative skill. It is our way of life. The uncommitted nations want to see before they choose.

THE "WIND OF CHANGE" SPEECH DELIVERED IN SOUTH AFRICA, SIGNALING THAT THE DAYS OF EMPIRE WERE OVER

In Britain there was substantial opposition to the shift in policy from the right wing of Macmillan's own Conservative party, who wished to see the British Empire continue. But its days were numbered, and by the end of the decade twelve British colonies in Africa ruled their own destinies. Although the British Empire was never formally dismantled, it gradually divested itself of its possessions over the next four decades. The handover of Hong Kong to China in 1997 was a fitting conclusion to the century—a timely end of an Empire.

RIGHT: Harold Macmillan raising his hat to a crowd as he stands alongside South African prime minister Hendrik Verwoerd, in February 1960. Macmillan's words proved so inflammatory that within a year, South Africa had declared itself a republic.

Elvis Presley
"You'll never know how happy
I am to be here"

(March 7, 1960)

He was the biggest name in show business when he went into the army. On discharge, Elvis Presley returned to his home Graceland in Memphis and held a press conference. The world was anxious to hear what he proposed to do next.

Like most American men, Elvis Presley faced conscription into military service—the draft—the day he turned twenty-one. Unlike other American men Elvis was the biggest name in showbiz at the time, something of which he, his screaming fans and the military were all well aware. The fans were horrified that he would not be available to them for the duration of his service, and both the army and the navy offered him special treatment in return for entertaining the troops.

Elvis's manager Colonel Tom Parker, who controlled every aspect of his client's career, persuaded him to decline their offers and instead enlist as an ordinary guy like everyone else. It would, Parker insisted, be better for the Presley image in the long run. Certainly during his two years of service, Elvis won the admiration of his fellow soldiers for this approach. He was proud to have got through it as one of the boys. When asked to name the most important thing to happen during his service, he replied, "The biggest thing of all is the fact that I made it just like everybody, I mean I tried to play it straight you

know like everybody else."

The death of his beloved mother at the age of only forty-six, two months before he set sail for Germany, cast a long shadow over his time abroad. He was, for much of the time, desperately homesick. "You'll never know how happy I am to be here," he told reporters at Graceland on his return. "Someone asked me this morning what did I miss about Memphis and I said 'everything.'"

Of great concern to Presley and Parker was the potential impact on Elvis's career of a two-year absence from the stage and the recording studio. By 1960, radio stations were playing less rock 'n' roll in favor of bubblegum pop, and reporters were asking with some glee whether Elvis would keep his sideburns and continue to use the swiveling hips that had been so shocking before he signed up. It's likely that Parker was already proposing a change of style, and at Graceland, Elvis commented, "[I] f [music] has changed, well, I would be foolish not to try and change with it." His first scheduled performance was to be a

Elvis, you were asked about Nancy Sinatra. How about any romance? Did you leave any hearts, shall we say, in Germany?

ELVIS: Not any special ones. There was a little girl that I was seeing quite often over there, her father was in the air force. Actually they only got over there about two months before I left. I was seeing her and she was at the train, at the airport when I left and there were some pictures made of her. But it was no big romance. The stories came out, 'the girl he left behind' and all that. It wasn't like that. I mean, I have to be careful when I answer questions like that!

"HOME FROM THE ARMY" PRESS CONFERENCE

guest appearance on *The Frank Sinatra Show.*

Within two weeks of his return Elvis was back in the studio, recording six songs for RCA in Nashville including "Stuck on You," his polished rock 'n' roll comeback; its follow-up "Fame and Fortune" and the ballad "Soldier Boy." Parker had made many plans for Elvis's return to musical duty. Besides the Sinatra TV show, he was committed to making three more movies between March and the end of 1960, starting appropriately with *GI Blues.* Elvis's last assignment before starting his basic training had been to complete shooting on *Kid Creole,* and he was thoroughly bitten by the acting bug. Was that his ultimate ambition? "As of the present time," he confirmed in Graceland, "it really is, that's what I want to do."

Elvis's military service was a turning point in his career. Before he went he was a rock 'n' roll rebel. Now, aged twenty-five, he was an established star. The music became gentler, and as Colonel Parker had predicted, military service had broadened his appeal to older listeners who had been turned off by the overtly sexual performances of the King. Las Vegas could already be heard calling in the distance.

Meanwhile, the reporters at Graceland were hoping for hot gossip. Sinatra had sent his daughter Nancy to deliver a gift to Elvis at Fort Bix a few days earlier. Was there romance in the air? "Uh, no sir, I'm afraid not. I think she's engaged to Tommy Sand, I don't think he would appreciate that!" But then had he left any broken hearts in Germany? "Not any special ones. There was a

little girl that I was seeing quite often over there. . . . But it was no big romance. The stories came out, 'the girl he left behind' and all that. It wasn't like that."

But it was. The little girl was fourteen-year-old Priscilla Beaulieu whom Elvis had met six months earlier and would marry seven years later. He was inseparable from her in Germany, but at the Graceland press conference he gave nothing away. "I mean," he joked with the reporters, "I have to be careful when I answer questions like that!"

ABOVE: Elvis's only appearance in the UK was a short press conference at Prestwick Airport, Scotland, on his way home.

OPPOSITE: Elvis at an earlier army press conference in Germany.

Fidel Castro
"No embassy rules our country; our country is ruled by its people!"

(September 26, 1960)

"You may rest assured that we shall endeavor to be brief," Fidel Castro told the assembled world leaders at the United Nations. Four and a half hours later he sat down, having delivered the longest speech ever given there. The US delegate, already wary of Cuba's new prime minister, left the chamber implacably opposed.

By 1959, 70 percent of Cuba's land, and nearly all of its principal industry of sugar production, was in foreign, American ownership. After Castro helped to overthrow the US-backed military dictatorship of Cuba's President Batista, he set about redistributing the country's natural wealth by nationalizing land and industries, including Shell and Esso oil refineries. America rejected his offer to compensate former owners with a bond maturing in twenty years.

In a war of tit-for-tat diplomacy America introduced a series of economic sanctions, culminating in the suspension of sugar imports from Cuba, a bitter blow to the island's economy. But Castro was less concerned with the economy than with social reform. He leveled pay, halved rents, improved education facilities, and passed out parcels of confiscated land to Cuba's poorest citizens. At the same time he spent heavily on improving the island's transport infrastructure and—"to arm our workers against imperialist attacks"—expanded Cuba's army and civic militia. A suspicious explosion in an arms shipment that had come to Cuba from Belgium via Miami, for which Castro blamed the US, only added to tensions between the two countries.

Arriving in New York for the UN General Assembly, the Cuban delegation chose to stay not in the fancy midtown Shelburne Hotel as arranged, but in downtown Harlem at the Hotel Theresa. There, Castro held court with representatives of America's counterculture, including black leader Malcolm X and beat poet Allen Ginsberg. He was visited there by several heads of state who were also in town for the assembly, including the Soviet premier Nikita Khrushchev, who saw in Castro a potentially useful ally in the Cold War.

If all of this was irritating to the American government, Castro's speech to the United Nations pulled no punches in a prolonged accusation of US interference in Cuban political and economic affairs. He stated flatly "that revolutions do not ruin countries, and that imperialist governments do try to ruin countries." He described the ways in which the revolutionary government had dismantled the US-owned monopolies that ran so much of Cuba—mines, banks, oil, sugar, telephone, and electricity—and whose profits had been drained from the island to the tune of a billion dollars over the previous ten years, "and not the slightest contribution to the economic development of our country."

The United Nations did not escape Castro's scathing tongue. He accused it of using its role in international affairs to crush the revolutions of smaller countries that dared to disrupt the status quo. Of its refusal to admit China to the organization, he said, "It is simply an absurdity, when we have here"—he pointed to the Spanish delegation—"representatives of Franco, for example."

Despite its length, Castro's speech drew many ovations—often led by Khrushchev, but also by the Egyptian representatives whose country had recently annoyed the major powers by nationalizing the Suez Canal. Castro won the admiration of many smaller nations, particularly in South America, for his refusal to kowtow to American dominance. America's immediate response was to impound the Cuban delegation's planes at Idlewild Airport in lieu of debts to American businesses. The move backfired politically when Krushchev immediately lent his. "The Soviets are our

It is well, I think, for countries just entering this Organization, countries just beginning their independent life, to bear in mind our history and to note any similar conditions which they may find waiting for them along their own road. And if it is not they, then those who came after them, or their children, or grandchildren, although it seems to us that we will not have to wait that long.

Then began the new colonization of our country, the acquisition of the best agricultural lands by United States firms, concessions of Cuban natural resources and mines, concessions of public utilities for exploitation purposes, commercial concessions of all types. These concessions, when linked with the constitutional right—constitutional by force—of intervention in our country, turned it from a Spanish colony into an American colony.

Colonies do not speak. Colonies are not known until they have the opportunity to express themselves. That is why our colony and its problems were unknown to the rest of the world. In geography books reference was made to a flag and a coat of arms. There was an island with another color on the maps, but it was not an independent republic. Let us not deceive ourselves, since by doing so we only make ourselves ridiculous. Let no one be mistaken. There was no independent republic; there was only a colony where orders were given by the Ambassador of the United States.

We are not ashamed to have to declare this. On the contrary: we are proud to say that today no embassy rules our country; our country is ruled by its people!

UNITED NATIONS'S LONGEST SPEECH AT 4.5 HRS

friends," Castro announced from the steps of the aircraft. "Here you took our planes. Soviet gave us planes."

In the wake of the General Assembly the United States severed all relations with Cuba, imposing an economic blockade and mounting a series of ill-considered subversive campaigns to destabilize or overthrow Castro's government, including the disastrous Bay of Pigs invasion. Castro's bodyguard once estimated that there had been 638 attempts to assassinate the leader. Fidel Castro died of old age in 2016, one year after President Obama declared the intended normalization of relations between America and Cuba.

RIGHT: *Fidel Castro would prove to be a thorn in the side of US foreign policy for many years to come.*

ABOVE: *Mervyn Griffith-Jones photographed during the 1963 Profumo scandal trial. Despite bungling the Lady Chatterly prosecution, he was given the job of prosecuting Dr. Stephen Ward in the case that rocked the British establishment.*

LEFT: *Londoners were prepared to stand in line for hours for admission to the public gallery during the trial.*

Mervyn Griffith-Jones
Lady Chatterley's Lover Obscenity Trial
(October 20, 1960)

D. H. Lawrence's final work, *Lady Chatterley's Lover*, was first published in 1928, in Italy—despite being written in English. It faced censorship under Britain's Obscene Publications Act of 1857. Legislation was revised by a new Act of 1959, and Penguin Books decided to publish the book in paperback.

The new Act allowed sexually explicit material to be published if the overall literary merit of the book justified it. Previously, any erotic content was automatically illegal if a judge ruled that it could corrupt any reader susceptible to corruption. *Lady Chatterley's Lover* received a heavily censored British publication in 1932; and in America the novel was first banned in 1929 and then allowed in 1959. Uncensored versions in the English language were published in Europe by German and Swedish publishers, and literary travelers could smuggle copies into Britain if they were not seized by customs officials. King George V is said to have confiscated a copy that found its way to his wife, Queen Mary.

Penguin's decision to publish its paperback 1960 edition was a calculated move to test the boundaries of the new Act. On August 25, nine days after the company delivered copies to a police officer on the day of publication, it received a summons, and the case went to court at the Old Bailey on October 20. The court's eventual verdict was the result of both shrewd defense and thoroughly inept prosecution. The defense called thirty-eight witnesses from the literary, religious, and academic worlds to testify to the book's moral and literary values. The prosecution called no witnesses at all; and the book's greatest asset in the courtroom was the counsel for the prosecution, Mervyn Griffith-Jones.

Griffith-Jones was a decorated war hero who had distinguished himself as part of the British prosecution team at the Nuremberg trials of captured Nazis. In 1955, he had successfully prosecuted Ruth Ellis, the last woman to be hanged in Britain. But in the matter of obscene publications he had no understanding of literature, sex, or the common man and woman.

All this was encapsulated in his opening remarks on the first day of the trial. After asking the jury to assess the book's obscenity and literary merit, he continued: "Would you approve of your young sons, young daughters—because girls can read as well as boys— reading this book? Is it a book that you would have lying around in your own house? Is it a book that you would even wish your wife or your servants to read?"

Laughter filled the court. Servants, a common enough presence in the middle-class English household before World War II, were a thing of the past now. And women, whether wives or daughters, had provided such support during the war that patronizing remarks about them were entirely inappropriate.

Later in his opening remarks, he reeled off a list of the expletives used in the book, with the frequency of their use, as if reciting rather shocking football results. In the course of the trial, he struggled to understand Lawrence's description of one particular sexual act—"Not very easy, sometimes, not very easy, you know, to know what in fact he is driving at in that passage"—which gave rise to jokes about precisely which passage was being driven at.

It was clear that the Establishment as represented by Griffith-Jones was completely out of touch with postwar society, and the jury of three women and nine men voted unanimously to acquit Penguin Books. The trial attracted great public interest, and its result pushed sales of the book through the roof.

Sales were also boosted by its low price of 3/6d (17½p, then the price of a packet of ten cigarettes), which gave thousands of ordinary citizens affordable access to *Lady Chatterley's Lover* and other great works of literature published in paperback. Whether or not the novel corrupted the morals of its readers, its trial marked the start of the sixties and the decade's Permissive Society.

John F. Kennedy
"Ask not what your country can do for you; ask what you can do for your country"

(January 20, 1961)

Widely considered the best inaugural speech by an American president, John Fitzgerald Kennedy's address was daringly idealistic. He was the first president born in the twentieth century, and the youngest man ever elected to the office. He spoke with the vigor of youth, and his words held an optimistic, poetic energy.

It was a thrilling time in American politics; a pivotal moment. As an Irish Catholic who supported civil rights, Kennedy overcame religious opposition from many quarters in a narrow victory. His election was the first to benefit from television coverage, notably a winning performance in a televised debate with his rival Richard Nixon. His inauguration was the first to be televised in color.

With his youth he embraced modern America—"I do not believe any of us would exchange places with any other people of any other generation," he said at his inauguration—and that included popular culture. On the eve of the big day, singer Frank Sinatra hosted a ball in his honor, attended by stars of all races from stage and screen (although Sammy Davis Jr., about to enter into a mixed-race marriage, was excluded). Kennedy was the first of only three presidents to date, with Clinton and Obama, to invite poets to read at their inauguration.

The great international issues of the day were Fidel Castro's Cuba and the spread of communism. In the wake of World War II, the rush to independence of former colonies of the world's empires was making the world an uncertain place. America and Russia vied for influence and allegiance, and the early part of Kennedy's first speech as president was devoted to preserving old alliances and encouraging new ones through offers of aid: "If a free society cannot help the many who are poor, it cannot save the few who are rich."

Kennedy had served with distinction in the South Pacific during the war, and his idealism did not extend to pacifism or disarmament. "Only when our arms are sufficient beyond doubt," he said, "can we be certain beyond doubt that they will never be employed?" But he sought peaceful negotiation if the alternative was atomic warfare. "Civility is not a sign of weakness. Let us never negotiate out of fear, but let us never fear to negotiate. Let both sides seek to invoke the wonders of science instead of its terrors." To that end, he called for cooperation, not conflict: "together let us explore the stars, conquer the deserts, eradicate disease, tap the ocean depths and encourage the arts and commerce."

Having raised the specter of war and the battle of ideologies between the United States and the Soviet Union, Kennedy was clear about America's spirit—"this hemisphere intends to remain the master of its own house." After a speech that confronted the hopes and fears of the world that his presidency was inheriting, he summed up: "Now the trumpet summons us again—not as a call to bear arms, though arms we need—not as a call to battle, though embattled we are—but a call to bear the burden of a long twilight struggle, year in and year out, 'rejoicing in hope, patient in tribulation'—a struggle against the common enemies of man: tyranny, poverty, disease and war itself."

Finally, he asked for the unity and active participation of the American people. "And so, my fellow Americans: ask not what your country can do for you—ask what you can do for your country." And, he added, aware of his global television audience east and west: "My fellow citizens of the world: ask not what America will do for you, but what together we can do for the freedom of man."

Now the trumpet summons us again—not as a call to bear arms, though arms we need; not as a call to battle, though embattled we are—but a call to bear the burden of a long twilight struggle, year in and year out, 'rejoicing in hope, patient in tribulation'—a struggle against the common enemies of man: tyranny, poverty, disease, and war itself. Can we forge against these enemies a grand and global alliance, North and South, East and West, that can assure a more fruitful life for all mankind? Will you join in that historic effort?

In the long history of the world, only a few generations have been granted the role of defending freedom in its hour of maximum danger. I do not shrink from this responsibility—I welcome it. I do not believe that any of us would exchange places with any other people or any other generation. The energy, the faith, the devotion which we bring to this endeavor will light our country and all who serve it—and the glow from that fire can truly light the world.

And so, my fellow Americans: ask not what your country can do for you; ask what you can do for your country. My fellow citizens of the world: ask not what America will do for you, but what together we can do for the freedom of man.

Finally, whether you are citizens of America or citizens of the world, ask of us the same high standards of strength and sacrifice which we ask of you. With a good conscience our only sure reward, with history the final judge of our deeds, let us go forth to lead the land we love, asking His blessing and His help, but knowing that here on earth God's work must truly be our own.

INAUGURAL ADDRESS

Kennedy was as good as his word in standing up to Soviet belligerence in Cuba, although unsuccessful in turning back the tide of communism there. His backing for civil rights confirmed the idealistic promise of his inaugural speech. We will never know how his presidency might be remembered if he had not been assassinated less than three years into his first term. Few idealists are allowed the luxury of uncompromising adherence to their ideals, but Kennedy's rhetoric of hope still encourages us all to compromise a little less on the things that really matter.

RIGHT: John F. Kennedy delivering his vision for America.

Space science, like nuclear science and all technology, has no conscience of its own. Whether it will become a force for good or ill depends on man, and only if the United States occupies a position of pre-eminence can we help decide whether this new ocean will be a sea of peace or a new terrifying theater of war. I do not say that we should or will go unprotected against the hostile misuse of space any more than we go unprotected against the hostile use of land or sea, but I do say that space can be explored and mastered without feeding the fires of war, without repeating the mistakes that man has made in extending his writ around this globe of ours.

There is no strife, no prejudice, no national conflict in outer space as yet. Its hazards are hostile to us all. Its conquest deserves the best of all mankind, and its opportunity for peaceful cooperation many never come again. But why, some say, the moon? Why choose this as our goal? And they may well ask why climb the highest mountain? Why, 35 years ago, fly the Atlantic? Why does Rice play Texas?

We choose to go to the moon. We choose to go to the moon in this decade and do the other things, not because they are easy, but because they are hard, because that goal will serve to organize and measure the best of our energies and skills, because that challenge is one that we are willing to accept, one we are unwilling to postpone, and one which we intend to win, and the others, too.

"WE CHOOSE TO GO TO THE MOON" SPEECH

LEFT: John F. Kennedy speaking at Rice University in Houston.

John F. Kennedy
"We choose to go to the moon"

(September 12, 1962)

In his inaugural speech, President Kennedy had invited the Soviet Union to work with the United States for the benefit of mankind. "Together let us explore the stars." Nevertheless, the so-called Space Race was a race between competing ideologies, which the Soviets were winning. In 1961, Kennedy raised the stakes.

Russia launched the first satellite, Sputnik. It sent the first animal into space, Laika the dog. Soviet cosmonaut Yuri Gagarin was the first man in space. America passed all these milestones too, but always came second. In 1959, Russia had even landed an unmanned spacecraft, Luna 2, on the moon.

American national morale was at stake, especially when only five days after Gagarin's achievement, the US invasion of Cuba at the Bay of Pigs proved to be an embarrassing failure. The next stage of the race was to put a human being on the moon, and in a speech to Congress on May 25, 1961, Kennedy announced that "this nation should commit itself to achieving the goal, before this decade is out, of landing a man on the Moon and returning him safely to the Earth."

This ambition required a major expansion of NASA resources at Houston, Texas, and it was on a visit to Houston in 1962 that Kennedy made a more public speech about America's intentions in space. "To be sure, we are behind, and will be behind for some time in manned flight," he admitted. "We have had our failures, but so have others, even if they do not admit them." But, quoting William Bradford about the 1630 founding of the Plymouth Bay colony, "all great and honorable actions are accompanied with great difficulties, and both must be enterprised and overcome with answerable courage."

This was a speech to win hearts and answer objections to the high cost and unknown returns of such a huge undertaking. Kennedy fought on two fronts—the benefits to mankind of new science, and the importance of getting there before the Russians. "We have vowed," he said, "that we shall not see space filled with weapons of mass destruction, but with instruments of knowledge and understanding."

The enormous cost of the space program—the 1962 budget was over five billion dollars—was a hard sell. Kennedy shrewdly broke it down on a per capita basis. Space expenditures will soon rise, he admitted, "from 40 cents per person per week to more than 50 cents a week for every man, woman and child in the United States." It almost seemed affordable, "even though I realize that this is in some measure an act of faith and vision, for we do not now know what benefits await us."

It was that very uncertainty of what mankind would learn from space, the fact that "the vast stretches of the unknown and the unanswered and the unfinished still far outstrip our collective comprehension," which made the space program worth pursuing. Kennedy infused his speech with idealism and the nobility of human striving for progress.

If any hearts remained to be won, surely President Kennedy's closing thought clinched them. Quoting the climber George Mallory on why he wanted to climb Mount Everest—"because it is there"—Kennedy paused and looked out over his audience. "Well, space is there, and we're going to climb it, and the moon and the planets are there, and new hopes for knowledge and peace are there. And, therefore, as we set sail we ask God's blessing on the most hazardous and dangerous and greatest adventure on which man has ever embarked."

Kennedy regarded the decision to go to the moon as one of the most important of his presidency. When Neil Armstrong set foot on its surface in 1969, it was not only an assertion of the boldness of human endeavor but confirmation of America's preeminence in the field of space exploration. Although the USSR rejected Kennedy's offer to collaborate during the 1960s, the International Space Station now demonstrates the spirit of cooperation that he hoped for.

John F. Kennedy
"Ich bin ein Berliner"

(June 26, 1963)

In the Cold War struggle between Western democracy and communism, Berlin was an isolated jewel to be fought over. President Kennedy's show of support in visiting the city and declaring his sense of oneness with their predicament was a turning point in the fortunes of the former German capital.

At the end of World War II, control of Germany was divided among the occupying powers: France, Britain, America, and Russia. The German capital, Berlin—carved up into Russian, British, French, and American sectors—was surrounded by Russian-controlled East Germany. West Berlin—made of the US, French, and British areas of the city—was a capitalist island in a communist sea.

Russia tried to take control of West Berlin in the late 1940s by blocking all its rail, road, and canal connections with the west. The attempt failed, thanks to an international airlift of supplies into the city. But Nikita Krushchev, the Russian premier, described West Berlin as a bone in his throat and determined to reunite it with the east.

He threatened another blockade in 1961, and Kennedy responded by increasing the presence of American forces in Europe. East Germany in turn closed the border between East and West Berlin with a line of barbed wire, which by 1963 had become the notorious Berlin Wall. As Cold War tensions escalated, there was a genuine fear that Berlin could be the spark to ignite a third world war.

When Kennedy came to Berlin, his mission was to encourage the Berliners without angering the Russians. But when he saw the grim reality of the wall, and the drab view of East Berlin from Checkpoint Charlie, he knew that more must be said—as Churchill had spelled out in his Iron Curtain speech seventeen years earlier, a balanced approach was not possible. He must speak out about the value of freedom.

A few moments before he was due to speak from the steps of the Rathaus Schöneberg, Kennedy made some notes at the beginning and end of his written text. When he stood up, and after his opening paragraph of thanks,

he briefly went off-script: "Two thousand years ago the proudest boast was 'civis Romanus sum' [I am a Roman citizen]. Today, in the world of freedom, the proudest boast is 'Ich bin ein Berliner [I am a citizen of Berlin].'"

The assembled crowd, which had given him a standing ovation before he began to speak, did so again now. In the rest of the speech he praised the resilience of Berliners, under siege for eighteen years since the end of the war, and through them he praised Western values. "Freedom has many difficulties and democracy is not perfect, but we have never had to put a wall up to keep our people in, to prevent them from leaving us. Freedom is indivisible, and when one man is enslaved, all are not free."

Kennedy was at the time preparing his Civil Rights Bill in America, and that last sentence would have resonated in the US as much as it did in Berlin. In the German city that day, he made Berlin indivisibly part of the free world. The boost to the morale of Berliners was incalculable; but the speech also sent a clear message to Russia that Berlin's freedom would be defended. There never was another attempt to blockade the city; and although the wall, a concrete symbol of the iron curtain, persisted for another twenty-six years, its toppling in 1989 also symbolized the tearing down of the curtain. Berlin, and all of Germany, were reunited the following year.

OPPOSITE: It has been suggested that by using the article "ein" before the word "Berliner," Kennedy mistakenly called himself a doughnut. In fact, Kennedy was correct, and his audience fully understood his show of solidarity.

I am proud to come to this city as the guest of your distinguished Mayor, who has symbolized throughout the world the fighting spirit of West Berlin.

And I am proud to visit the Federal Republic with your distinguished chancellor who for so many years has committed Germany to democracy and freedom and progress, and to come here in the company of my fellow American, General Clay, who has been in this city during its great moments of crisis and will come again if ever needed.

Two thousand years ago the proudest boast was 'civis Romanus sum.' Today, in the world of freedom, the proudest boast is 'Ich bin ein Berliner.'

There are many people in the world who really don't understand, or say they don't, what is the great issue between the free world and the Communist world. Let them come to Berlin.

There are some who say that Communism is the wave of the future. Let them come to Berlin.

And there are some who say in Europe and elsewhere we can work with the Communists. Let them come to Berlin.

And there are even a few who say that it is true that Communism is an evil system, but it permits us to make economic progress. Lass' sie nach Berlin kommen. Let them come to Berlin.

Freedom has many difficulties and democracy is not perfect, but we have never had to put a wall up to keep our people in, to prevent them from leaving us.

"ICH BIN EIN BERLINER" SPEECH

And so even though we face the difficulties of today and tomorrow, I still have a dream. It is a dream deeply rooted in the American dream.

I have a dream that one day this nation will rise up and live out the true meaning of its creed: 'We hold these truths to be self-evident, that all men are created equal.'

I have a dream that one day on the red hills of Georgia, the sons of former slaves and the sons of former slave owners will be able to sit down together at the table of brotherhood.

I have a dream that one day even the state of Mississippi, a state sweltering with the heat of injustice, sweltering with the heat of oppression, will be transformed into an oasis of freedom and justice.

I have a dream that my four little children will one day live in a nation where they will not be judged by the color of their skin but by the content of their character. I have a dream today!

I have a dream that one day, down in Alabama, with its vicious racists, with its governor having his lips dripping with the words of 'interposition' and 'nullification'—one day right there in Alabama little black boys and black girls will be able to join hands with little white boys and white girls as sisters and brothers. I have a dream today!

"I Have a Dream" speech

LEFT: A crowd estimated at 250,000 packed into the National Mall in front of the Lincoln Memorial to listen to Dr. King and other speakers.

Martin Luther King Jr.
"I have a dream"

(August 28, 1963)

If ever a speech changed the world, it is the address that Martin Luther King Jr. gave in 1963 at the end of the March on Washington for Jobs and Freedom. At the time it paved the way for President Kennedy's equal rights legislation. It still resonates over fifty years later.

A quarter of a million people marched through Washington on August 28, 1963. The occasion was the March on Washington for Jobs and Freedom, and the jobs and freedom being called for were those of black Americans. The civil rights movement was growing in strength. When nonviolent protests were brutally suppressed in Alabama, TV news pictures brought many more Americans out in support of change. President Kennedy proposed a new Civil Rights Act in June 1963, and the Washington march was intended as a show of support for his ideas.

The march finished at the Lincoln Memorial, from which the vast crowd stretched all the way back to the Washington Monument. Dr. King was the last of many campaigners for civil rights to address the sea of faces. He had given the speech in different forms on several previous occasions, but in structure, passion, and effect, it struck a chord in Washington as never before.

King was an astute politician, and his highly literate speech contained powerful references to Lincoln's Emancipation Proclamation issued a hundred years earlier, to the national anthem, and to the US Constitution, whose promises of equality he told the audience had not been fulfilled. This was a speech not only for those present, but for President Kennedy, who with millions of other Americans was watching the event on television.

But King was also a preacher, and for the assembled masses he spoke simply: with sorrow of their shared suffering and with hope of the possibility of change. He spoke musically, with rhythm and repetition, like the leader of a gospel choir. "There are those who are asking the devotees of civil rights, 'When will you be satisfied?'" he asked. And he answered, "We can never be satisfied

as long as the Negro is the victim of the unspeakable horrors of police brutality. We can never be satisfied as long as our children are stripped of their self-hood and robbed of their dignity by signs stating: 'For Whites Only.' We will not be satisfied until justice rolls down like waters, and righteousness like a mighty stream."

Turning from dissatisfaction to hope, he spoke of the American dream in words that became a song of optimism with a recurring chorus: "I have a dream." King painted a vivid picture of unity and equality, especially for future generations: "I have a dream that my four little children will one day live in a nation where they will not be judged by the color of their skin but by the content of their character. I have a dream today! I have a dream that one day . . . right there in Alabama little black boys and black girls will be able to join hands with little white boys and white girls as sisters and brothers. I have a dream today!"

In all, he declared "I have a dream" eight times. He used other phrases in a similar way. "With this faith" punctuated one section four times. Quoting the national anthem, he named mountains in eight states from which, he implored after each one, "let freedom ring!" He used this rhythmic litany to build to a climax, his final wish: to be able to sing, in the words of a Negro spiritual familiar to all who heard him that day: "Free at last! Free at last! Thank God Almighty, we are free at last!"

Although Kennedy was assassinated only three months later, his Civil Rights Act was signed into law by Lyndon B. Johnson the following year. Dr. King's speech was hailed as the finest of the day at the time, and in 1999, voted the best speech of the century. More importantly, it became an inspiration for millions of black Americans, including a young Barack Obama.

Harold Wilson
The White Heat of Technology

(October 1, 1963)

By 1963 the Labour Party had been out of power for twelve years in Britain. Harold Wilson had just been elected its leader following the sudden death of Hugh Gaitskell. His priority was the next general election, the third since 1951, when Labour was voted out. In the Swinging Sixties, change was the order of the day, and Wilson sensed an opportunity.

If there is one theme running through this Conference this week, it is the theme of change, the overdue need for this country to adapt itself to different conditions. It is the theme and the challenge which faces the Labour party, which faces every one of us.

It is of course a cliché that we are living at a time of such rapid scientific change that our children are accepting, as part of their everyday life, things which would have been dismissed as science fiction a few years ago. We are living perhaps in a more rapid revolution that some of us realise. . . . When you reckon, as it is calculated, that 97% of all the scientists who have ever lived in the history of the world, since the days of Euclid, Pythagoras and Archimedes, are alive and at work today, you get some idea of the rate of progress we have to face.

It is only a few years since we first in this Conference debated automation, when almost every word uttered in that debate is already as out of date today as if we had been talking about the advent of the spinning jenny. Automation is beginning to make its impact felt in quarters of British industry, as many delegates here know—the engineers, the technical workers, the chemical workers, the scientific workers, and not least the Post Office workers and the Post Office engineers, who have pioneered some of the developments in automation and who, thanks to the combination of our trade union skill and of public ownership in the Post Office, lead the world in these developments.

THE WHITE HEAT OF TECHNOLOGY, A RALLYING CRY FOR THE TECHNOLOGICAL AND SCIENTIFIC REVOLUTION OF THE SIXTIES

OPPOSITE: Harold Wilson in 1963, speaking at the Labour Party Conference in Scarborough.

Harold Wilson inherited a party divided by internal debate about its future. Public desire for change, which had swept it to power after the collective trauma of World War II, had now relapsed into traditional British conservatism. But as society began to recover from the rigors of war and postwar austerity, changes were again afoot—in fashion, in social attitudes, in popular culture, and in technology.

Benefiting from the wartime need for efficient mass-production of everything from food to bullets, British industry—and, from Labour's point of view, the working man whom it employed—was being transformed by science and technology. New better-paid jobs were being created that required technical expertise, not just manual labor, and the Labour Party feared that the working-class core of its electorate was being eroded.

Science represented modernity, and new products were being advertised for their scientific benefits, often endorsed by the presence of a white-coated, bespectacled scientist. British governments of all colors had often been deaf to the advice of scientists, believing that civil servants knew best how to run a country, and a scientist's place was in an industrial research laboratory. Harold Wilson saw in science an opportunity to make Labour the party of modernity, of progress, of the future, especially in comparison to the aging and self-evidently traditional leadership of the Conservatives. His opponent, the prime minister, was the Eton-educated Alec Douglas-Home, fourteenth Earl of Home.

In his first speech to the Labour Party conference as leader, Wilson embraced science and promised to apply it to all areas of party policy. "There is no room for Luddites in the Socialist Party," he declared to delegates in Scarborough. "We must harness socialism to science, and science to socialism." He extolled, as President Kennedy was doing in America, the potential of science to defeat poverty and sickness; to advance communication, learning, and living standards. A socialist government would ensure these benefits for the many, not the few.

"In all our plans for the future," he announced, "we are re-defining and we are re-stating our socialism in terms of the scientific revolution." He outlined campaign pledges for the coming election, including the transformation of education to promote scientific and engineering skills, efforts to halt the so-called brain drain of British scientists out of the country, a new Ministry of Science, and a new post of Government Chief Scientist.

So far so good; but Wilson also recognized the threat to traditional working practices that science would bring in this second Age of the Machine, as it had during the first wave of the Industrial Revolution two centuries earlier. He sought to forestall the objections of trade unions. "The Britain that is going to be forged in the white heat of this revolution will be no place for restrictive practices or for outdated methods on either side of industry."

Wilson's "white heat" speech succeeded in "capturing science for the Labour Party" as one trade union leader put it. Labour were returned to power in 1964, and Wilson began the first of four terms as prime minister. But despite his pledges and changes, his governments failed to forge the new Britain that he promised and to harness the power of the trade unions. His vision never became a reality, and concerns about the impact of technology on levels of employment are as loud today as they were over fifty years ago.

RIGHT: Before the advent of cable, the fight was screened live in cinemas across the US.

BELOW: Ali predicted victory in the eighth round, but was happy to see Liston fail to emerge from his corner in the seventh. Ali's eyes had been stung during the opening rounds, and he had been struggling to see.

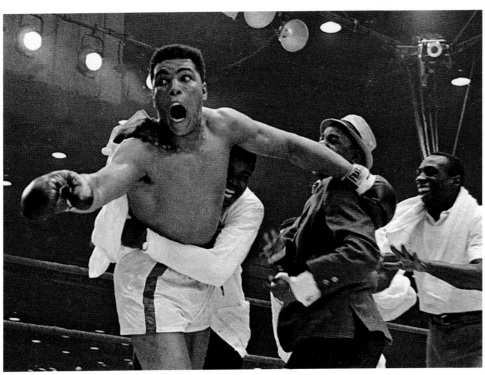

Muhammad Ali
"I am the greatest!"

(February 25, 1964)

Born Cassius Marcellus Clay, Muhammad Ali's record was an impressive 100 wins and five losses. He turned professional after taking the light heavyweight gold medal at the Rome Olympics of 1960. His professional rise was steady; but by 1964 he was the clear challenger for the world title held by Sonny Liston.

Clay was developing a reputation for brash prematch trash talk in which he talked himself up and belittled his opponent, sometimes in rhyming couplets. He modeled himself on the professional wrestler Gorgeous George Wagner, whom he met in 1961 and whose flamboyant, larger-than-life persona brought him popularity far beyond the wrestling arena. Wagner told Clay, "A lot of people will pay to see someone shut your mouth. So keep on bragging."

Once Clay had defeated all Liston's other rivals, a date was set of February 25, 1964, for his world heavyweight championship challenge. His wins so far had not been convincing, and the odds were very much against him defeating Liston. In interviews before the fight, Liston boasted that he would probably be arrested after it, for murder. Liston's nickname was The Big Bear, and Clay taunted him: "Liston even smells like a bear. After I beat him I'm going to donate him to the zoo."

One of the highlights of the prematch hype was an extraordinary performance by Clay in front of an audience of 200 fans in which he delivered eight comic monologues in his trademark trash-talk style. The show was recorded and released as an LP and contained tracks such as "Will the Real Sonny Liston Please Fall Down." The tracks were labeled Round One, Round Two, and so on; and Round Eight was called "The Knockout."

Round One, the title track, took the form of a poem. Clay declaimed it after announcing its title: "'I am the Greatest!' by Cassius Clay." It began: "This is the legend of Cassius Clay, The most beautiful fighter in the world today." He boasted—"He talks a great deal, and brags indeed-y, Of a muscular punch that's incredibly speed-y." He mocked—"The fistic world was dull and weary, But with a champ like Liston, things had to be dreary." And he predicted—"I am the man this poem's

about, I'll be champ of the world, there isn't a doubt. Here I predict Mr. Liston's dismemberment, I'll hit him so hard; he'll wonder where October and November went. I am the greatest!"

The album climbed to number 61 in the charts and was nominated for a Best Comedy Record at the Grammy Awards. "I am the greatest!" became something of a catchphrase for Clay, and before the Liston fight he repeated it. "He'll fall in [Round] Eight, To prove that I'm great. And if he keeps talking jive, I'm going to cut it to Five." After his surprise victory in the seventh round, at odds of 7 to 1, he shouted from the ring, "I am the greatest! I'm the greatest thing that ever lived. I don't have a mark on my face. I must be the greatest. I showed the world. I shook up the world, I'm the king of the world. You must listen to me. I am the greatest! I can't be beat!"

No one would argue with him. To mark the victory CBS released a single from "I Am the Greatest!" the title track with a musical backing. The B-side was "Will the Real Sonny Liston Please Fall Down." Later in the year the single was rereleased, this time with a cover version of Ben E. King's "Stand by Me" on the B-side.

Within a week of the fight, Cassius Clay changed his name to Muhammad Ali, having already converted to Islam before the fight. Cassius Clay, Ali said, was his slave name. In the course of his career, which coincided with the golden age of heavyweight boxing, he defeated every challenger and thereby proved his claim. "I am the greatest!" He would say, "I said I was the greatest even before I knew I was!" His success gave him the power to fight outside the ring, too, whether against the draft, or racism, or Parkinson's disease. Toward the end of his life he clarified one thing: "Allah is the Greatest; I'm just the greatest boxer."

Malcolm X
"The Ballot or the Bullet"
(April 3, 1964)

Broadly speaking, campaigners for civil rights for black Americans fell into one of two camps—the nonviolent constitutional approach of men like Martin Luther King Jr., or the violent, separatist rhetoric typified by the Nation of Islam, whose figurehead was Malcolm X. The latter rejected democratic processes, which, they believed, served only the ruling white population.

Malcolm X's more aggressive pursuit of civil rights divided black Americans and frightened whites. He urged his followers to arm themselves in defense against white supremacists—his father had shot at white arsonists who burned the family home down in 1929, and he believed racists were responsible for his father's "accidental" death in 1931.

As a young man Malcolm turned to crime. He was radicalized and converted to Islam in 1948, while serving a prison term for theft. Malcolm rose quickly through the ranks of the militant group Nation of Islam (NOI), which advocated separatism rather than integrated equal rights. NOI believed that blacks could only rely on other blacks and should reject all interaction with whites, who would only abuse them as they had always done in the past.

But in the early 1960s, the situation was changing. President Kennedy's Civil Rights Act, supported by Martin Luther King Jr.'s March on Washington for Jobs and Freedom, had been passed into law by President Johnson after Kennedy's assassination. Malcolm X began to doubt the wisdom of NOI's isolationist stance, and he clashed with the group's leader Elijah Muhammad over ideology. When he spoke to an audience of thousands in Cleveland, Ohio, it became clear that he had shifted his position.

Although he began by insisting that he was still a Muslim, he pointed out that many civil rights leaders were also religious. What was important was not religion but unity of purpose. "Whether we are Christians or Muslims or nationalists or agnostics or atheists, we must first learn to forget our differences. If we have differences, let us differ in the closet."

The year 1964 was a presidential election year, "the

year when all of the white political crooks will be right back in your community with their trickery and their treachery, with their false promises which they don't intend to keep." And here Malcolm X decisively broke ranks with NOI, which banned its members from voting. He noted how close past elections had been, including the last between Kennedy and Nixon. "When white people are evenly divided and black people have a bloc of votes of their own, it is left up to them to determine who's going to sit in the White House and who's going to be in the dog house." In a significant volte-face, Malcolm X was telling his audience to register and vote in their own interests.

He still preached the black man's right to defend himself with arms against racism. "I hope you understand. Don't go out shooting people; but any time you read where they bomb a church and murder in cold blood four little girls while they were praying, and you see the government can't find who did it . . . . I mean, you'd be justified, but it would be illegal and we don't do anything illegal." A knowing wink was implicit in his remarks.

His message was clear. Use the ballot; and if that doesn't work, use the bullet. He was scathing about Martin Luther King Jr.'s march and the singing of "We Shall Overcome" in Washington the year before. Nevertheless, it represented a significant softening of his stance and was seen as a bid to unite with the mainstream of civil rights activism, something else that the separatist NOI had banned along with voting. "We need new friends," he said, "new allies. We need to expand the civil rights struggle to a higher level, to the level of human rights."

Like Martin Luther King Jr., Malcolm X used the rhetoric of rhythm. He repeated the phrase "the ballot or

Whether you're educated or illiterate, whether you live on the boulevard or in the alley, you're going to catch hell just like I am. We're all in the same boat and we all are going to catch the same hell from the same man. He just happens to be a white man. All of us have suffered here, in this country, political oppression at the hands of the white man, economic exploitation at the hands of the white man, and social degradation at the hands of the white man.

Now in speaking like this, it doesn't mean that we're anti-white, but it does mean we're anti-exploitation, we're anti-degradation, we're anti-oppression. And if the white man doesn't want us to be anti-him, let him stop oppressing and exploiting and degrading us. Whether we are Christians or Muslims or nationalists or agnostics or atheists, we must first learn to forget our differences. If we have differences, let us differ in the closet; when we come out in front, let us not have anything to argue about until we get finished arguing with the man. If the late President Kennedy could get together with Khrushchev and exchange some wheat, we certainly have more in common with each other than Kennedy and Khrushchev had with each other.

If we don't do something real soon, I think you'll have to agree that we're going to be forced either to use the ballot or the bullet. It's one or the other in 1964. It isn't that time is running out—time has run out!

"THE BALLOT OR THE BULLET" SPEECH

the bullet" eight times in the course of his speech. They were its last words, and in his closing remarks he said, "If I die in the morning, I'll die saying one thing: the ballot or the bullet."

For his rejection of NOI principles, Malcolm X was assassinated by three gunmen from the Nation of Islam less than a year later. Although he was seen as a divisive figure during his lifetime, he is now recognized as an important voice of the black community. Streets, schools, and libraries bear the name of the man who told his people: "It'll be ballots, or it'll be bullets. It'll be liberty, or it will be death."

RIGHT: Malcolm Little adopted the name Malcolm X in 1950, stating, "For me, my 'X' replaced the white slavemaster name of 'Little' which some blue-eyed devil named Little had imposed upon my paternal forebears."

"**A**fricans want to be allowed out after eleven o'clock at night and not to be confined to their rooms like little children. Africans want to be allowed to travel in their own country and to seek work where they want to and not where the Labour Bureau tells them to. Africans want a just share in the whole of South Africa; they want security and a stake in society.

Above all, we want equal political rights, because without them our disabilities will be permanent. I know this sounds revolutionary to the whites in this country, because the majority of voters will be Africans. This makes the white man fear democracy.

But this fear cannot be allowed to stand in the way of the only solution which will guarantee racial harmony and freedom for all. It is not true that the enfranchisement of all will result in racial domination. Political division, based on colour, is entirely artificial and, when it disappears, so will the domination of one colour group by another. The ANC has spent half a century fighting against racialism. When it triumphs it will not change that policy.

This then is what the ANC is fighting. Their struggle is a truly national one. It is a struggle of the African people, inspired by their own suffering and their own experience. It is a struggle for the right to live.

During my lifetime I have dedicated myself to this struggle of the African people. I have fought against white domination, and I have fought against black domination. I have cherished the ideal of a democratic and free society in which all persons live together in harmony and with equal opportunities. It is an ideal which I hope to live for and to achieve. But if needs be, it is an ideal for which I am prepared to die."

"AN IDEAL FOR WHICH I AM PREPARED TO DIE" SPEECH

RIGHT: Nelson Mandela survived his years of imprisonment under successive South African regimes. Activist Steve Biko was beaten by police and died in detention in 1977, the 46th person to die under South Africa's 1963 law that allowed imprisonment without trial.

...I am prepared to die

This is virtually the complete text of the now famous speech in his defence by Nelson Mandela at the Rivonia Trial which ended in June 1964. Certain brief passages relating to the technical details of the defence have been omitted

Nelson Mandela
"An ideal for which I am prepared to die"

(April 20, 1964)

Convicted in 1962 of inciting workers to strike, Nelson Mandela was already serving a five-year sentence when he faced further charges. He had little prospect of being found innocent and admitted his guilt on some counts. Rather than defend himself, he delivered a speech that put the South African legal system on trial.

A raid by police on a house in suburban Johannesburg in July 1963 netted several senior leaders of the African National Congress (ANC) and uncovered papers that implicated them and Nelson Mandela in planned acts of sabotage against the state. The charges carried the death penalty, and it was assumed that the state would press for that punishment.

The defendants, caught in possession of such incriminating evidence, decided therefore not to defend themselves. Instead, aware of international interest in the trial, it was agreed that Mandela should make a political speech from the dock. Its aim was to challenge the moral authority of the policy of white supremacy and contrast it with the aims and methods of the ANC.

Mandela knew that the speech might make the difference between life and death. He modeled it on the long speech given by Fidel Castro when he was on trial in 1953 for attacking Cuban barracks. In the days leading up to his trial, Mandela spent weeks choosing his words with the help of two white supporters of the ANC, the writers Anthony Sampson and Nadine Gordimer.

What followed when he stood up to address the court on April 20, 1964, was an irrefutably logical critique of apartheid. Speaking directly but dispassionately, Mandela began by setting out his own position as a prisoner and as a member of the ANC. The ANC had been forced to abandon its principle of nonviolent opposition to apartheid, he argued, because the government had violently suppressed all peaceful means. The disenfranchisement of the majority black population meant that 70 percent of the country had no say in their government. "The government which uses force to support its rule teaches the oppressed to use

force to oppose it." The ANC was left with no peaceful way to pursue its aims, and sabotage presented the least danger to human life.

Refuting claims that the Communist Party (CP) and the ANC were inseparable, Mandela was at pains to highlight the clear differences between them. He noted that he had never been a member of the CP, yet had been imprisoned under laws banning the CP. And he pointed out that the Communist Party was the only group that recognized black South Africans as fully human beings. "White supremacy implies black inferiority." Mandela described black poverty in detail, contrasting it with the country's wealth and resources. And he argued that black citizens remained in an inferior condition only because of the scarcity of opportunities and education provided for them by the white minority in power.

After speaking for three hours, he summed up: "I have fought against white domination, and I have fought against black domination. I have cherished the ideal of a democratic and free society in which all persons live together in harmony and with equal opportunities. It is an ideal which I hope to live for and to achieve. But if needs be," he turned to the presiding judge, Quartus de Wet, and looked him straight in the eye, "it is an ideal for which I am prepared to die."

Mandela was sentenced to life imprisonment, and has said that he believes he only escaped the death penalty because in that last stare he dared the judge to impose it. The measured but heartfelt speech galvanized the ANC, and pressure from them and the international anti-apartheid movement eventually secured Mandela's release twenty-six years later. In 1994, he was elected President of South Africa.

John Lennon
"We're more popular than Jesus"

(August 12, 1966)

No voices were raised in objection when a British newspaper ran the interview in which John Lennon claimed that the Beatles were more popular than Jesus. At a time of shrinking congregations in Britain and rising adulation for the Fab Four, it was probably true. But when American pop-culture magazine *Datebook* reprinted the article and brought it to the attention of an Alabama radio station, it was a different story.

A series of lifestyle pieces on each Beatle for the *London Evening Standard* newspaper in March 1966 began with John Lennon, whom the journalist Maureen Cleave visited at his Surrey home. Cleave was impressed by Lennon's large and well-ordered library and told her readers that John was "reading extensively about religion." She saw a large old Bible that he had bought in Chester, and a volume of reminiscences of colonial life in India. The Beatles would travel to India later in search of spiritual satisfaction. "Don't the Indians appear cool to you?" Lennon asked Cleave as he played her a recording of sitar music that George Harrison had introduced him to.

By comparison, British religious life seemed dull

and in decline. "Christianity will go," John said. "It will vanish and shrink. We're more popular than Jesus now. I don't know which will go first—rock 'n' roll or Christianity." It was just one remark in a lengthy interview about all aspects of his daily life and his responses to fame and wealth. He said more about his beloved gorilla suit than he did about Christianity, and except among adoring Beatles fans, nothing about the ensuing *Evening Standard* article aroused any comment.

Beatles press officer Tony Barrow offered the series of articles to *Datebook* magazine in the US in a move to generate publicity in advance of the Beatles' third US tour of North America in August. *Datebook*'s July 1966 edition splashed Lennon's "I don't know which will go first—rock 'n' roll or Christianity" on its front cover. Out of context, the remark was enough to incense Tommy Charles, a Birmingham, Alabama, DJ who heard about it from a colleague at Top 40 radio station WAQY. Charles at once declared, "That does it for me. I'm not going to play the Beatles any more."

His protest spread to churches and other stations in the Bible Belt, and to other countries. In the Southern states, there were organized bonfires of Beatles records and memorabilia. When a preemptive press conference by Beatles manager Brian Epstein failed to smooth things over, Tony Barrow persuaded John Lennon to talk to reporters before their first concert in Chicago.

Lennon tried to explain the British religious context of his remarks, and insisted, "I'm not anti-Christ or anti-religion or anti-God. I'm not saying we're better or greater, or comparing us with Jesus Christ as a person, or God as a thing or whatever it is." The controversy surrounding his comments had shaken him badly; he and the rest of the group were now dreading the tour ahead.

I wasn't saying the Beatles are better than Jesus or God or Christianity. I was using the name Beatles because I can use them easier, 'cos I can talk about Beatles as a separate thing and use them as an example, especially to a close friend. But I could have said TV, or cinema, or anything else that's popular . . . or motor cars are bigger than Jesus.

Q: What's your reaction to the repercussions?

LENNON: Well when I first heard it, I thought 'It can't be true.' It's just like one of those things like 'Bad Eggs In Adelaide' and things. And then when I realized it was serious I was worried stiff, you know, because I knew sort of how it'd go on. And the more things that'd get said about it, and all those miserable looking pictures of me looking like a cynic, and that. And they'd go on and on and it'd get out of hand, and I couldn't control it, you know. I can't answer for it when it gets that big 'cos it's nothing to do with me then.

Q: A disc jockey in Birmingham Alabama, who really started most of the repercussions, has demanded an apology from you.

LENNON: He can have it, you know. I apologize to him if he's upset and he really means it, you know, I'm sorry. I'm sorry I said it for the mess it's made. But I never meant it as a lousy or anti-religious thing, or anything. You know, and I can't say any more than that. There's nothing else to say really, you know—no more words. But if an apology—if he wants one, you know, he can have it. I apologize to him.

PRESS CONFERENCE APOLOGY FOR SAYING THE BEATLES WERE MORE POPULAR THAN JESUS

"I just said what I said and was wrong, or was taken wrong, and now it's all this," he pleaded, before joking, "if I had said television was more popular than Jesus, I might have got away with it."

Pressed about the possibility of a formal apology, Lennon said, "If you want me to apologize, if that will make you happy, then okay, I'm sorry." He was obviously contrite, and the apology was enough for many. But the tour was dogged by death threats; protests by the religious right and pickets by the Ku Klux Klan, who nailed a Beatles album to a cross. Ticket sales were down and not all venues sold out. The group felt besieged by the threatening atmosphere surrounding the tour, and by the time of the final concert in San Francisco's Candlestick Park, they had decided never to tour again.

The Beatles were from then on a studio band. They finally broke up in 1970, the year a certain Mark Chapman became a born-again Christian. Ten years later Chapman, incensed by the ex-Beatle's misunderstood remark about being more popular than Jesus, killed John Lennon with four shots in the back.

OPPOSITE: American protests about the Beatles weren't confined to the Bible Belt. Here, teenagers from Sunnyvale, California, make their objections known.

ABOVE: *Two posters promoting the free event in Golden Gate Park.*

LEFT: *Timothy Leary preaching the "gospel" to his 30,000-strong audience, at a time when LSD was a legal drug.*

Timothy Leary
"Turn on, tune in, drop out"

(January 14, 1967)

Timothy Leary said that he was given his catchphrase "turn on, tune in, drop out" by Marshall Macluhan, the controversial media theorist who came up with the idea that "the medium is the message." Leary began to popularize the phrase during 1966, and in early 1967, it became the theme of his lecture at the Human Be-In.

After being sacked from his post as lecturer in clinical psychology at Harvard University in 1963, Leary became a full-time advocate of the controlled use of the psychedelic drug lysergic acid diethylamide (LSD) for spiritual purposes. At the time LSD was legal and widely available. With the help of a wealthy family, he bought a mansion in Millbrook, New York, where he and his adherents took LSD in group sessions and ran weekend retreats for the paying public.

By 1966, the widespread use of LSD was causing concern for the moral, physical, and mental well-being of America's youth. Leary testified to a Senate subcommittee in defense of the drug, warning that its use would only spread in a new Prohibition era. When challenged by Ted Kennedy about the dangers of its use, Leary famously replied, "Sir, the motor car is dangerous if used improperly." Despite his testimony, LSD was banned in California in October that year, and throughout the US in 1968.

In an effort to circumvent the ban on religious grounds, Leary established the League for Spiritual Discovery (also LSD), which claimed that LSD the drug was its holy sacrament. The league's mantra was "Drop Out, Turn On, Tune In," which Leary explained thus: "Drop Out—detach yourself from the external social drama which is as dehydrated and ersatz as TV. Turn On—find a sacrament which returns you to the temple of God, your own body. Go out of your mind. Get high. Tune In—be reborn. Drop back in to express it. Start a new sequence of behavior that reflects your vision."

Despite that sequence of commands in the league's practice, it was under the title of "Turn On, Tune In, Drop Out" that Leary released an album of guided meditation in 1966. Later in the year he began to perform in student venues with: "The Death of the Mind," a mixed-media happening that tried to recreate the sensations of an LSD trip; and in early 1967 he was invited to give a lecture at the Human Be-In in San Francisco.

The Human Be-In, "a gathering of the tribes," was attended by 30,000 hippies, six times more than any such event in the past. They were entertained by speakers and local musicians such as Jefferson Airplane and the Grateful Dead. There was free LSD and turkey sandwiches. The Hells Angels ran a crèche for lost children. Leary's "Turn On, Tune In, Drop Out" became the keynote of the event, despite the reservations of poet Allen Ginsberg, who saw that "Drop Out" could be misinterpreted. Ginsberg recited mantras to get the Be-In underway.

It was an extraordinary assembly of all the different strands of counterculture that had been fermenting in San Francisco's Haight-Ashbury district and elsewhere, and its sheer scale marked the moment when hippies became a national cultural phenomenon. The summer of that year became the Summer of Love, and Leary's catchphrase was its slogan.

By the end of the year, hippies had already become parodies of themselves, their love-ins spawning TV comedy revue *Rowan & Martin's Laugh-In*.

Leary, whom President Nixon had called "the most dangerous man in America" because of his subversive advocacy, was frequently arrested and imprisoned for drugs offenses. He continued to develop his transcendental spiritual philosophy, and in the 1980s became interested in computers and a virtual reality, which was digital rather than pharmaceutical. Declaring that "the PC is the LSD of the 1990s," he reinvented his catchphrase for a new generation: "Turn on, boot up, jack in."

Earl Warren
Loving vs. Virginia

(June 12, 1967)

Richard Loving and his wife, Mildred Jeter Loving, were arrested in their bed in Central Point, Virginia, in 1958 and imprisoned solely because one was "white" and the other "colored." Nine years later, the case of *Loving vs. Virginia* became a landmark ruling by the Supreme Court.

Richard and Mildred were friends and lovers. He was white and she was of mixed African and Native American heritages. When Mildred became pregnant in 1958, they traveled to Washington, D.C., where interracial marriage was legal. The newlyweds returned to Virginia, where it was not. Local law officers, tipped off about their cohabitation, broke into their home at 2 a.m. and arrested them. In 1959, they were found guilty by the Caroline County circuit court in Virginia of living together and of marrying out of state with intent to return.

Their prison sentence was suspended on condition that they leave the state and not return in each other's company for twenty-five years. The couple moved to the District of Columbia, but grew weary of not being able to visit their Virginia relatives together. The American Civil Liberties Union (ACLU) took up their case, first by asking the court to declare its decision void. "Almighty God created the races white, black, yellow, Malay and red," the Virginian judge Leon Bazile replied, "and He placed them on separate continents. And but for the interference with His arrangement there would be no cause for such marriages. The fact that He separated the races shows that He did not intend for the races to mix."

An appeal to the Supreme Court of Virginia on the grounds that the state's anti-miscegenation laws contravened the Fourteenth Amendment of the US Constitution was also rejected. The court ruled that the laws did not violate equal protection rights because both parties had received equal punishment for their "crimes." The ACLU turned finally to the Supreme Court of the United States.

The Supreme Court noted that Virginia didn't care about interracial relationships if they were between two nonwhite races, the "black, yellow, Malay and red" of Judge Bazile's worldview. "The fact that Virginia prohibits only interracial marriages involving white persons," Chief Justice Earl Warren recorded, "demonstrates that the racial classifications must stand on their own justification, as measures designed to maintain White Supremacy.

"Marriage is one of the 'basic civil rights of man,'" said Warren, "fundamental to our very existence and survival. . . . To deny this fundamental freedom on so unsupportable a basis as the racial classifications so directly subversive of the principle of equality at the heart of the Fourteenth Amendment, is surely to deprive all the State's citizens of liberty without due process of law."

The Supreme Court voted unanimously in favor of the Lovings. Earl Warren concluded, "Under our Constitution, the freedom to marry, or not marry, a person of another race resides with the individual and cannot be infringed by the State." Although the sixteen states that still had anti-miscegenation legislation were slow to repeal them in the wake of the decision, they could no longer enforce such laws. Alabama was the last to remove them from the statute books, in 2000.

Richard and Mildred Loving returned to Central Point, Caroline County, Virginia, where in 1975 a drunk driver rammed Richard's car, killing him. Mildred, who never remarried, lived until 2008. The decision that made their marriage legitimate was cited in 2015 in the Supreme Court's ruling in favor of same-sex marriage.

There can be no question but that Virginia's miscegenation statutes rest solely upon distinctions drawn according to race. The statutes proscribe generally accepted conduct if engaged in by members of different races. Over the years, this Court has consistently repudiated 'distinctions between citizens solely because of their ancestry' as being 'odious to a free people whose institutions are founded upon the doctrine of equality.' Indeed, two members of this Court have already stated that they 'cannot conceive of a valid legislative purpose which makes the color of a person's skin the test of whether his conduct is a criminal offense.'

The fact that Virginia prohibits only interracial marriages involving white persons demonstrates that the racial classifications must stand on their own justification, as measures designed to maintain White Supremacy. There can be no doubt that restricting the freedom to marry solely because of racial classifications violates the central meaning of the Equal Protection Clause.

These statutes also deprive the Lovings of liberty without due process of law in violation of the Due Process Clause of the Fourteenth Amendment. The freedom to marry has long been recognized as one of the vital personal rights essential to the orderly pursuit of happiness by free men.—Marriage is one of the 'basic civil rights of man,' fundamental to our very existence and survival. The Fourteenth Amendment requires that the freedom of choice to marry not be restricted by invidious racial discriminations. Under our Constitution, the freedom to marry, or not marry, a person of another race resides with the individual, and cannot be infringed by the State.

· Extract of earl warren's ruling in *Loving vs. Virginia*

RIGHT: *Richard and Mildred Loving with their three childen, Sidney, Donald, and Peggy. Ironically, Virginia's second governor, Thomas Jefferson, not only slept regularly with his mixed-race mistress, Sally Hemmings, but fathered five children by her.*

"**All the world looked to the United States with new hope, for here was youth** and confidence and an openness to the future. Here was a country not being held by the dead hand of the past, nor frightened by the violent hand of the future which was grasping at the world. This was the spirit of 1963.

What is the spirit of 1967? What is the mood of America and of the world toward America today? It is a joyless spirit—a mood of frustration, of anxiety, of uncertainty.

In place of the enthusiasm of the Peace Corps among the young people of America, we have protests and demonstrations. In place of the enthusiasm of the Alliance for Progress, we have distrust and disappointment.

Instead of the language of promise and of hope, we have in politics today a new vocabulary in which the critical word is 'war': war on poverty, war on ignorance, war on crime, war on pollution. None of these problems can be solved by war but only by persistent, dedicated, and thoughtful attention.

But we do have one war which is properly called a war—the war in Vietnam, which is central to all of the problems of America. A war of questionable legality and questionable constitutionality.

A war which is diplomatically indefensible; the first war in this century in which the United States, which at its founding made an appeal to the decent opinion of mankind in the Declaration of Independence, finds itself without the support of the decent opinion of mankind."

DENOUNCING THE VIETNAM WAR

RIGHT: Senator Eugene McCarthy who campaigned for the 1968 Democratic nomination on an anti-war platform.

Eugene McCarthy
"The decent opinion of mankind"

(December 2, 1967)

President Johnson knew that the war in Vietnam could never be won, but felt politically obliged to engage in it. His fellow Democrat, Senator Eugene McCarthy of Minnesota, strongly opposed America's military involvement in the region and decided to stand against Johnson in 1968.

America's involvement in Vietnam, a French colony, stemmed from its fear of the spread of communism. After World War II, American advisers helped to train the Vietnamese Army that was fighting a civil war against the communist Vietcong. The country was partitioned into North and South Vietnam in 1954, and France withdrew.

America remained to stem the communist tide, supporting the South Vietnamese government financially to the tune of $100 million in what was now a guerrilla war with the Chinese-backed Vietcong. America began to bomb North Vietnam in 1964, and the first quarter of a million American troops were sent to the region in the course of 1965.

By the time Senator McCarthy threw his hat into the presidential ring at the end of 1967, half a million GIs were stationed in Vietnam. In a speech on December 2 announcing his candidacy, he challenged Lyndon B. Johnson by invoking the memory of his predecessor John F. Kennedy. "Here was youth and confidence and an openness to the future. . . . This was the spirit of 1963. What is the spirit of 1967? . . . Instead of the language of promise and of hope," McCarthy said, "we have in politics today a new vocabulary in which the critical word is 'war': war on poverty, war on ignorance, war on crime, war on pollution. None of these problems can be solved by war."

Nor, he implied, could the real war in Vietnam, a war in which "the United States . . . finds itself without the support of the decent opinion of mankind." He questioned its legality and its morality. "Our role is not to police the planet but to use military strength with restraint and within limits while we make available our knowledge and our goodwill."

He complained of mission creep. "Estimate after estimate as to the time of success has had to be revised, always upward. More troops, more bombing, a widening and intensification of the war; an overleaping of objectives from protecting South Vietnam to nation-building in Vietnam, to protecting all of Southeast Asia."

The benefits were no longer proportionate to the loss of life and property, and history would judge America badly. McCarthy had previously said privately that the sight of coffins returning from Vietnam would soon turn public opinion against the war and mobilize support for his candidacy. "We are willing to pay a high price for peace—for an honorable, rational and political solution," he said, but "I see little evidence that the administration has set any limits on the price which it will pay for a military victory which becomes less and less sure and more hollow and empty in promise."

Although insiders had doubted the wisdom of challenging an incumbent president for their party's nomination, McCarthy won the support of the growing anti-war movement. But he lost the New Hampshire primary to Johnson in a surprisingly close vote: 42 to 49 percent. Although it was enough to scare Johnson who pulled out of the race, Robert Kennedy now entered it, and after his assassination, Johnson's vice president Hubert Humphrey joined the fray. It was Humphrey who secured the Democratic nomination while anti-war riots raged on the streets of Chicago outside the convention. And it was Humphrey who lost the election to Republican Richard Nixon.

Nixon perpetuated the war, unwilling to be "the President Who Retreated." But he did progressively withdraw troops from the war zone. By the time of the ceasefire in 1973, 150,000 Americans had been injured in Vietnam and 58,000 killed. The partitioned halves of Vietnam were reunited in 1976 as the Socialist Republic of Vietnam.

Martin Luther King Jr.
"I've been to the mountaintop"

(April 3, 1968)

In February 1968, two men were crushed to death in a garbage compactor in Memphis, Tennessee. It was the last straw after years of low-paid, hazardous conditions for the city's mostly black sanitation workers. They declared a strike, which became as much about racial discrimination as about health and safety standards. Martin Luther King Jr. lent his considerable support.

It really doesn't matter what happens now. I left Atlanta this morning, and as we got started on the plane there were six of us. The pilot said over the public address system, 'We are sorry for the delay, but we have Dr. Martin Luther King on the plane. And to be sure that all the bags were checked, and to be sure that nothing would be wrong with the plane, we had to check out everything carefully. And we've had the plane protected and guarded all night.'

And then I got into Memphis. And some began to say the threats, or talk about the threats that were out. What would happen to me from some of our sick white brothers? Well I don't know what will happen now. We've got some difficult days ahead. But it really doesn't matter with me now, because I've been to the mountaintop. And I don't mind.

Like anybody, I would like to live a long life. Longevity has its place. But I'm not concerned about that now. I just want to do God's will. And he's allowed me to go up to the mountain. And I've looked over. And I've seen the Promised Land. I may not get there with you. But I want you to know tonight that we, as a people, will get to the Promised Land! And I'm so happy tonight. I'm not worried about anything. I'm not fearing any man! Mine eyes have seen the glory of the coming of the Lord!

"I'VE BEEN TO THE MOUNTAINTOP" SPEECH

LEFT: *Despite fervent calls for a nonviolent protest, Memphis still called out the National Guard.*

OPPOSITE: *Martin Luther King was well aware he was a target for extremists.*

Memphis in the mid-twentieth century was a notoriously racist town with a police force recruited in part from the ranks of the Ku Klux Klan. African Americans were either barred from joining unions or feared to do so, particularly after thirty-three of them were fired in 1963 immediately after attending a union meeting.

The 1968 strike took as its slogan "I AM a man," derived from the antislavery campaigns that asked, "Am I not a man and a brother?" One of the strikers' leaders, the Reverend James Lawson, reminded them that "at the heart of racism is the idea that a man is not a man. You are human beings. You are men."

Dr. King visited Memphis three times in support of the strikers. He addressed an assembly of thousands on March 18; and on March 28 he took part in a protest where the frustration of the workers boiled over into violence. Windows were broken and one sixteen-year-old African American high school student was shot dead by a policeman. King returned to the city for another, more peaceful demonstration on April 3.

Speaking to the large crowd at Mason Temple, he urged nonviolence so that no other news story could distract from the issues of race that concerned the strikers. "Let us keep the issues where they are. The issue is injustice." Seven weeks into the strike, he called for unity and persistence in the face of police brutality. The strikers' daily marches were met with tear gas and clubs, and King recalled his own protests in Birmingham where the police used dogs, mace, and water hoses against rebellious blacks.

King called on his audience to strengthen black institutions, build a black economy, and boycott banks and manufacturing companies that were racist in their hiring policies. "Tell your neighbors not to buy Coca Cola in Memphis, not to buy Sealtest milk, not to buy Wonder bread. Up to now, only the garbage men have been feeling the pain. Now we must kind of redistribute the pain." And he asked everyone to support the garbage workers in an analogy with the story of the Good Samaritan. "The question is

not, 'if I stop to help this man, what will happen to me?' The question is, 'If I do not stop to help the sanitation workers, what will happen to them?' That's the question."

It was as always from Dr. King a fine display of oratory, passionately, and skillfully delivered. But his speech is mostly remembered today for the way in which he framed it—at the start with a summary of the history of black mankind, which led him to declare that now was the best time to be alive; and at the end with a review of the African American's struggles in the 1960s. His conclusion was a very personal declaration of happiness and peace with the world. He told them there had been death threats since he arrived in Memphis.

"But it really doesn't matter with me now, because I've been to the mountaintop." He was referring to Moses, who led the children of Israel to the Promised Land, but whom God only allowed to see the land from a mountaintop and not to enter. "I've looked over. And I've seen the Promised Land," he assured his people. "I may not get there with you. But I want you to know tonight that we, as a people, will get to the Promised Land! And so I'm happy tonight. I'm not worried about anything. I'm not fearing any man. Mine eyes have seen the glory of the coming of the Lord!"

Did he know what was going to happen next? Martin Luther King was assassinated on his motel balcony in Memphis the following day, April 4, 1968, by James Earl Ray, a prisoner who had been on the run from Missouri State Prison since 1967. It was a heart-stopping moment for the entire civil rights movement.

The Memphis mayor refused to be moved, but four days later a march was conducted by the strikers in complete silence, with King's widow at its head. It was a powerful statement of endurance, which, a week later, resulted in the settlement of the strike with wage increases and recognition of unions. King's death was an unbearably high price to pay, but it was a turning point in race relations in Memphis. Twenty-three years later the city elected its first black mayor, and did not elect another white one for another fourteen years.

Enoch Powell
Rivers of Blood
(April 20, 1968)

Enoch Powell's speech to Conservative Party members in the West Midlands of England was one of the first to discuss publicly the impact of immigration. Delivered with the express intention of "going up 'fizz' like a rocket and staying up" as he told a friend, the speech received wide publicity and exposed deep divisions.

When Britain began to grant independence to its former imperial colonies in Africa and Asia, their citizens had rights of settlement in the UK as members of its Commonwealth of Nations. Some chose to take advantage of those rights, whether in hope of economic benefits there or in fear of instability in their native countries.

It was a very visible influx of "foreigners" that disturbed the more insular of Britain's overwhelmingly white population. Immigration particularly affected poor working-class areas of the country like the West Midlands, a traditional, densely populated manufacturing region where an immigrant might hope to find work.

Signs in the windows of rented accommodation reading "No Blacks" were a common sight in parts of Britain in the mid-1960s. Job vacancies were often advertised with the same stipulation. In response to a rise in verbal and physical displays of discrimination, the Labour government of Harold Wilson proposed a new Race Relations Bill, intended to ban selection made solely on the basis of color, ethnicity, race or nationality. The Conservative Party opposed discrimination of course, but called for restrictions to immigration and incentives to repatriation, and Powell defended those policies in his speech.

Powell began with the wise observation that politics will tend to focus on immediate, present problems rather than on potential future ones. "People are disposed to mistake predicting troubles for causing troubles," he said, identifying the elected politician's need above all to be popular. You are apt to get the blame when things go wrong the way you predicted.

Commenting on a constituent's fear that in twenty years "the black man will have the whip hand over the white man," Powell painted a picture of unstoppable growth of the immigrant population. Immigrants were allowed to bring their relatives—"twenty or thirty additional immigrant children are arriving in [Powell's constituency] Wolverhampton alone every week, an annual flow of some 50,000 dependants who are for the most part the material of the future growth of the immigrant-descended population."

He defended anyone's right "to discriminate in the management of his own affairs between one fellow-citizen and another" and argued that the new bill would not end discrimination against blacks but increase discrimination against the white man as the immigrant population began to occupy hospital beds, school places, homes, and jobs.

Powell also questioned the extent to which integration was possible, especially with immigrant communities large enough to pursue their own customs without it. "We are seeing the growth of vested interests in the preservation and sharpening of racial and religious differences, with a view to the exercise of actual domination, first over fellow immigrants and then over the rest of the population."

Throughout the speech Powell used frightening imagery—"a nation busily engaged in heaping up its own funeral pyre"; "to enact legislation of this kind is to risk throwing a match onto gunpowder"; he described white Englishmen as "a persecuted minority"; and finished with the dire and colorful warning that gave the speech its popular name, "Rivers of Blood." Classical scholar Powell cannot have forgotten that waves of immigration in the past—Romans, Danes, Angles, Saxons, and Normans—shaped the national character of which Britons like him were so proud.

It was a brave speech from a man who insisted for

The Sikh communities' campaign to maintain customs inappropriate to Britain is much to be regretted. Working in Britain, particularly in the public services, they should be prepared to accept the terms and conditions of their employment. To claim special communal rights (or should one say rites?) leads to a dangerous fragmentation within society. This communalism is a canker; whether practiced by one color or another, it is to be strongly condemned.

For these dangerous and divisive elements the legislation proposed in the Race Relations Bill is the very pabulum they need to flourish. Here is the means of showing that immigrant communities can organize to consolidate their members, to agitate and campaign against their fellow citizens, and to overawe and dominate the rest with the legal weapons which the ignorant and the ill-informed have provided. As I look ahead, I am filled with foreboding; like the Roman, I seem to see 'the River Tiber foaming with much blood.'

That tragic and intractable phenomenon which we watch with horror on the other side of the Atlantic but which there is interwoven with the history and existence of the States itself, is coming upon us here by our own volition and our own neglect. Indeed it has all but come. In numerical terms, it will be of American proportions long before the end of the century.

Only resolute and urgent action will avert it even now. Whether there will be the public will to demand and obtain that action, I do not know. All I know is that to see, and not to speak, would be the great betrayal.

"Rivers of Blood" speech

the rest of his career that he was not a racist, merely a concerned native Briton. But its outspoken and apocalyptic vision of a Britain overrun with incomers shocked one half of the population and gave voice to the other half. Although his party leader, Edward Heath, immediately sacked him from his ministerial post, those opposed to immigration rallied around the Conservative flag, giving the party an unexpected win in the 1970 general election. To this day, extreme right-wing racist hate groups look back on Powell as an inspiration. "Enoch was right" is a popular slogan on their T-shirts and button badges.

RIGHT: Controversial and strident, Powell was also an astute political observer who coined the truism "every political career ends in failure."

> # **O**kay, I'm going to step off the LM now.
>
> That's one small step for [a] man; one giant leap for mankind.

LEFT: How the event was reported in the American press. It may not have been a long speech, but it will dominate history books for millennia as the first spoken on another planet.

Neil Armstrong

"One small step for [a] man, one giant leap for mankind"

(July 21, 1969)

An estimated 530 million people watched as Neil Armstrong became the first man to set foot on the moon. The Apollo 11 mission, which carried Armstrong and his colleague Buzz Aldrin to the Sea of Tranquility, was the greatest single technical challenge that mankind had ever set itself.

It's easy to forget what an extraordinary achievement it was in 1969 to carry a man beyond our planet's atmosphere and land him on another object in space. Much of the technology required for the flight had been developed from scratch, and although most of it had been tested in earlier missions, a lot of it was rudimentary by today's standards. The Apollo guidance computer for example had a memory of just sixty-four kilobytes. Little wonder that it overloaded as Armstrong steered the Landing Module to a safe stop on the surface of the moon.

In 1962, President Kennedy declared: "We choose to go to the moon." A monumental creative effort was directed into fulfilling that lofty ambition, that single flight that transformed science fiction into science fact. Although it was a bold idealistic plan, it was also driven by pragmatic concerns. Russia began the 1960s well ahead in the space race. American pride was at stake. The benefits from technologies developed for space travel were not entirely humanitarian. But the achievement—of Armstrong, Aldrin, and their colleague Michael Collins in the Command Module—was for the entire human race, not just for America.

Neil Armstrong emerged from the Landing Module and descended the nine rungs of the ladder on its side. "Okay, I'm going to step off the LM now," said Armstrong. He lifted his left foot from the craft, nicknamed the Eagle, and placed it on the ground.

"That's one small step for [a] man; one giant leap for mankind."

Considering the enormity of the moment and its significance for humanity—no longer earthbound after 400,000 years—those twelve words have received almost as much attention as the step itself. The one-letter word "a" within them is inaudible in recordings of the day, and without it, the sentence is confusing. "Man" and "mankind" are synonymous without the definite or indefinite article. How could man be taking both a small step and a giant leap? Was Armstrong talking nonsense?

Of course not. Audio analysis of the original tapes has been inconclusive, and the most likely explanation is that he formed the "a" with his mouth but did not vocalize it. What matters is what he meant to say; his intended contrast between a single human being and the whole of mankind sums up the moment perfectly.

There is disagreement about when he decided to say it too. He said he composed it while waiting to leave the Landing Module on the moon. His brother Dean Armstrong claimed after Neil's death that the astronaut drafted it several months before the mission took place. Some imagine that it was NASA publicists who gave him the suitably inspiring phrase to say. Whatever the source, the true inspiration was the deed itself: the courage of the crew of Apollo 11; the support of those three men by thousands of others back at Mission Control; and the boldness of vision with which Kennedy committed America to the adventure.

Only ten more men have walked on the moon since Armstrong and Aldrin. In 1972 Apollo 17 was the last mission to carry men there. The Space Shuttle program and the International Space Station have preoccupied NASA since then, and made Kennedy's hope of extraterrestrial cooperation between nations a reality. It is fifty years since Armstrong's giant leap. Those four years of lunar landings are little more than a moment in humanity's 400,000 years of history. But what a moment.

Max B. Yasgur
"This is America, and they are going to have their festival"

(July 21, 1969)

The Woodstock Festival almost didn't happen. With less than a month to go its planners still had not found a venue for the event. Residents of three other towns in New York State raised objections; one even passed a new law to prevent it. Then the organizers were introduced to a dairy farmer called Max Yasgur.

Max Yasgur was forty-nine years old, not at all part of the counterculture of the decade. His farm supplied milk and butter to the store of his local town Bethel. His fields, however, formed a perfect amphitheater in a sloping fold of hillside. On July 20 Woodstock's organizers rented them for a fee of $10,000. The festival had already been advertised as the Woodstock Music and Art Fair and kept that name.

Yasgur seems to have taken a liking to the long-haired festival team. He joked with one of them, Mike Lang, that if it went badly, he would give Mike a crew cut; and if it went well, the balding Max would let his hair grow long.

Dairy farmer Yasgur's relationship with Bethel, however, quickly soured. Some of the townsfolk were strongly opposed to a hippy invasion of their community and plotted to change the zoning law to prevent it taking place. On July 21, the town's zoning board met to discuss the proposal. Max Yasgur was allowed to address the meeting.

"I hear you don't like the look of the kids who are working at the site," he said. "I hear you don't like their lifestyle. I hear you don't like they are against the war and that they say so very loudly." There were loud murmurs of agreement as Yasgur continued: "I don't particularly like the looks of some of those kids either. I don't particularly like their lifestyle, especially the drugs and free love. And I don't like what some of them are saying about our government." Hippy opposition to American involvement in the Vietnam War was growing with every month, and the generation who had fought with pride in World War II did not approve of the way their children were turning out.

Then Max turned the tables on them. "If I know my American history," he continued, "tens of thousands of Americans in uniform gave their lives in war after war just so those kids would have the freedom to do exactly what they are doing. That's what this country is all about and I am not going to let you throw them out of our town just because you don't like their dress or their hair or the way they live or what they believe." Before he sat down, he fired one last shot. "This is America, and they are going to have their festival."

The zoning board gave the festival the green light, which the organizers assured them would attract no more than 50,000 people. Yasgur's words swayed them, but some Bethel citizens were unimpressed. They put up signs calling for a boycott of Yasgur Farm milk to "Stop Max's Hippy Music Festival." He received phone calls threatening arson to his farm buildings. Two days before the first performance, Bethel's concerned citizens attempted to form a human chain across the route into the area as the first of the half a million hippies began to arrive.

The opposition only strengthened Yasgur's support for the festival. "If the generation gap is to be closed, we older people have to do more than we have done." The festival's infrastructure, planned for 50,000, was completely inadequate for ten times that number. When local people started charging hippies for water, a disgusted Yasgur gave it away in milk bottles and supplied food at cost or for free.

He spoke to the crowd on August 17, just before Joe Cocker took to the stage to sing "With a Little Help from My Friends." Max was nervous. "I'm a farmer," he reminded them. "I don't know how to speak to

I hear you are considering changing the zoning law to prevent the festival. I hear you don't like the look of the kids who are working at the site. I hear you don't like their lifestyle. I hear you don't like they are against the war and that they say so very loudly. . . . I don't particularly like the looks of some of those kids either. I don't particularly like their lifestyle, especially the drugs and free love. And I don't like what some of them are saying about our government.

However, if I know my American history, tens of thousands of Americans in uniform gave their lives in war after war just so those kids would have the freedom to do exactly what they are doing. That's what this country is all about and I am not going to let you throw them out of our town just because you don't like their dress or their hair or the way they live or what they believe. This is America and they are going to have their festival.

SPEECH TO THE BETHEL TOWN BOARD PRIOR TO THE WOODSTOCK FESTIVAL

twenty people at one time, let alone a crowd like this. [Y]ou've proven to the world that a half a million kids . . . can get together and have three days of fun and music and have nothing but fun and music. God bless you for it!"

Woodstock, an affirmative coming-together of all the strands of 1960s idealism, was the greatest landmark in popular culture before 1985's Live Aid. In 1970, another dairy farmer, Michael Eavis of Somerset, England, was inspired to host a similar gathering on his Worthy Farm near Glastonbury. Max Yasgur declined to hold a repeat event in 1970, however. His farm had suffered extensive damage under the feet of the Woodstock crowd, and although the organizers paid him an additional $50,000 in compensation, he announced, "I'm going back to running a dairy farm."

RIGHT: Max Yasgur addressing the Woodstock generation camped out on his dairy farm. The man who made the world's biggest rock festival possible died just four years later, in 1973, from a heart attack.

Betty Friedan
Strike for Equality

(March 20, 1970)

When Betty Friedan retired as president of the National Organization of Women she was not content merely to bid farewell to the body of which she had been a cofounder. Instead, she propelled it into a new phase of activity with an announcement that took even her closest allies by surprise.

Betty Friedan's book *The Feminine Mystique* is credited with kick-starting the second wave of feminism in America. The first wave addressed the issues of suffrage and legal discriminations such as inheritance. Now women focused on equality at work and in the home. Although in the early 1960s some legislature was passed for equal opportunities and equal pay for women, it was rarely applied.

In response, Friedan and some of her fellow activists formed the National Organization for Women (NOW) in 1966. NOW put pressure on bodies such as the Equal Employment Opportunity Commission to enforce the 1963 Equal Pay Act and the 1964 Civil Rights Act. One of their early successes was the extension of affirmative action to include women as well as African Americans. It also won a ruling against gender-discriminatory employment advertisements.

Friedan was NOW's first president, and she pursued some policies that were not universally popular with her colleagues. Her support for legalized abortion offended pro-lifers; and many felt that affirmative action was more important for African Americans than for white women. Nevertheless, it was expected that her valedictory speech as president in 1970 would look back on the achievements of her term with some pride. Instead of basking in the past, however, Friedan chose the occasion to galvanize the women of America to future action.

Speaking for almost two hours at the NOW convention in Chicago, she did, indeed, review the progress of the feminist movement so far. But she also called for something extraordinary to take place on the fiftieth anniversary of the day when women got the vote: a strike by women. She appealed to "secretaries put the covers on their typewriters and close their notebooks and the telephone operators unplug their switchboards, waitresses, stop waiting, cleaning women, stop cleaning.

"[E]veryone who is doing a job for which a man would be paid more, stop!" It was unthinkable. How could a strike be defined by gender? Teamsters went on strike; sanitation workers went on strike; but women? She was not only talking about working women. "And when it begins to get dark," Friedan went on, "instead of cooking dinner or making love, we will assemble and we will carry candles alight in every city to converge the visible power of women at city hall."

It was to be nothing less than a complete withdrawal of female labor. "I have led you into history," she declared at the end. "I leave you now to make new history." She received a standing ovation, but it was, to say the least, an ambitious idea for a young organization with a little over 3,000 members and an annual budget of a little under $40,000. It certainly hadn't been discussed by the rest of the NOW office-bearers; and Friedan, whom the *New York Times*'s report of the speech called a "militant leader," had just five months to coordinate a national event.

The proposed strike was the object of mocking derision in the press. But Betty Friedan's call had struck a nerve. Quietly, more and more women decided to join the strike, no doubt goaded by the scorn of men at work. On the anniversary, August 26, 1970, men sat up and took notice when 50,000 women joined a march in New York City in support of the strike. There were sister events in forty-three of the fifty states of the US.

Betty Friedan's strike call shone a light on the role of women in society, making it impossible for men to continue to ignore their unthinking attitudes any longer. As the *New York Times*, in a revision of its earlier view of Friedan, wrote in her obituary in 2006, she "permanently transformed the social landscape of the United States."

I propose that the women who are doing menial chores in the offices as secretaries put the covers on their typewriters and close their notebooks and the telephone operators unplug their switchboards, the waitresses stop waiting, cleaning women stop cleaning and everyone who is doing a job for which a man would be paid more, stop!

And when it begins to get dark, instead of cooking dinner or making love, we will assemble and we will carry candles alight in every city to converge the visible power of women at city hall. Women will occupy for the night the political decision making arena and sacrifice a night of love to make the political meaning clear.

Legislators on vacation will be tracked down in the mountains and on the beaches and we will talk to that Senator through the night and follow him through the day until we have his commitment on the equal rights of women.

Our sisterhood is powerful. The awesome political power of 53 percent of the population is visible now and is being taken seriously as all of us who define ourselves as people now take the actions that need to be taken in every city and state and together make our voices heard.

I have led you into history. I leave you now to make new history.

Farewell speech as first president of the National Organization for Women, calling for women to go on strike for equal pay

LEFT: *By calling on women to abstain from making love in protest, Friedan was echoing the 411 BC play by Aristophanes,* Lysistrata.

John Kerry
Vietnam Veterans Against the War

(April 22, 1971)

John Kerry served with distinction in Vietnam. His service was on the Navy's Swift Boats, small vessels that patrolled Vietnam's rivers and coastal waterways. He received two medals for bravery. Having seen at first hand the pointless brutality and suffering he returned to America, determined to speak out.

His three Purple Hearts entitled John Kerry to an early return from his tour of duty in Asia, and he served out his time as a military aide in Brooklyn. On his release from active duty in January 1970, he joined Vietnam Veterans Against the War (VVAW) and participated in VVAW's Winter Soldier Investigation, an event designed to publicize the horrors of the war by encouraging veterans to give harrowing testimony of what they had seen.

In 1971, he was instructed to appear in front of the Senate Foreign Affairs Committee's Fulbright Hearings, which were taking evidence for a review of America's role in Vietnam. Kerry was the first veteran to speak to the committee. His testimony, backed up by what he had heard in the Winter Soldier Investigation, was graphic and shocking in its description of the brutalized behavior of American troops toward both the Vietcong and the innocent civilians of both North and South Vietnam.

Kerry expressed very frankly the anger of veterans returning to the United States, having committed war crimes in their country's name, to find that no one cared about their mental and physical injuries or their prospects in civilian life. Around 20 percent of veterans remained unemployed; over half of those entering VA (Veterans Affairs) hospitals talked of suicide, and over a quarter of them attempted it. "The country doesn't know it yet," he said, speaking of postcombat trauma, "but it's created a monster, in the form of millions of men who have been taught to deal and trade in violence."

Speaking directly to the purposes of the committee, Kerry questioned the validity of the war. "There is nothing in South Vietnam, nothing which could happen, that realistically threatens the United States of America."

And yet, he said, "we watched the falsification of body counts, in fact the glorification of body counts, because we couldn't lose, and we couldn't retreat, and because it didn't matter how many American bodies were lost to prove that point. Each day someone has to die so that President Nixon won't be—and these are his words—the first American President to lose a war."

The war was supposedly being fought to hold back the advance of communism so that the Vietnamese people could be free. "But they're not a free people now, under us," Kerry pointed out. "Most people," he reported, "didn't even know the difference between communism and democracy. They only wanted to work in rice paddies without helicopters strafing them and bombs with napalm burning their villages. We cannot fight communism all over the world, and I think we should have learnt that lesson by now." The war was being fought under that erroneous assumption; it was a mistake. "How do you ask a man to be the last man to die for a mistake?"

At the end of a long speech that was frequently interrupted by the applause and agreements of his fellow veterans in the public seating, Kerry also criticized military leaders who would not speak up for their returning troops' needs. "We do not need their testimony. Our own scars and stumps of limbs are witness enough. ... We wish that a merciful God could wipe away our own memories of that service as easily as this Administration has wiped their memories of us."

Although Americans returned Nixon to the White House in 1972, America finally agreed a ceasefire with North Vietnam in 1973. Some returning US prisoners of war claimed that Kerry's descriptions of US war

An American Indian friend of mine who lives on the Indian nation of Alcatraz put it to me very succinctly. He told me how as a boy on an Indian reservation he had watched television and he used to cheer the cowboys when they came in and shot the Indians. And then suddenly one day he stopped in Vietnam and he said, "My God, I'm doing to these people the very same thing that was done to my people"—and he stopped. And that's what we're trying to say, that we think this thing has to end.

We're also here to ask—We are here to ask and we're here to ask vehemently: where are the leaders of our country? Where is the leadership? We're here to ask: where are MacNamara, Rostow, Bundy, Kilpatrick and so many others? Where are they now that we the men whom they sent off to war have returned? These are commanders who have deserted their troops and there is no more serious crime in the law of war. The Army says they never leave their wounded. The Marines say they never leave even their dead. These men have left all the casualties and retreated behind a pious shield of public rectitude. They've left the real stuff of their reputations, bleaching in the sun in this country.

And finally, this Administration has done us the ultimate dishonor. They've attempted to disown us and the sacrifices we made for this country. In their blindness and fear, they have tried to deny that we are veterans or that we served in Nam. We do not need their testimony. Our own scars and stumps of limbs are witness enough for others and for ourselves. We wish that a merciful God could wipe away our own memories of that service as easily as this Administration has wiped their memories of us.

<small>TESTIMONY TO US CONGRESS ABOUT THE VIETNAM WAR, REPEATED IN THE KEN BURNS SERIES</small>

crimes had led to their torture at the hands of the Vietcong, but his testimony had a profound influence on the committee and on the wider American public's attitude to the war.

Kerry subsequently served five terms as a senator for Massachusetts. Thirty-three years after his Fulbright appearance, he was the Democratic candidate in the presidential race against George W. Bush. Kerry now found himself trading on his Vietnam service, which contrasted with Bush's relatively safe stint in the Texas Air National Guard. To the disappointment of many he voted in favor of the Iraq War, although he voted against the cost of it, a contradiction that may have cost him the election.

ABOVE: Kerry's powerful testimony to the Fulbright Hearings was highlighted in Ken Burns's landmark documentary series on Vietnam.

The detriment that the State would impose upon the pregnant woman by denying this choice [to abort] altogether is apparent. Specific and direct harm medically diagnosable even in early pregnancy may be involved. Maternity, or additional offspring, may force upon the woman a distressful life and future. Psychological harm may be imminent. Mental and physical health may be taxed by child care.

There is also the distress, for all concerned, associated with the unwanted child, and there is the problem of bringing a child into a family already unable, psychologically and otherwise, to care for it. In other cases, as in this one, the additional difficulties and continuing stigma of unwed motherhood may be involved. All these are factors the woman and her responsible physician necessarily will consider in consultation.

On the basis of elements such as these, appellant and some amici argue that the woman's right is absolute and that she is entitled to terminate her pregnancy at whatever time, in whatever way, and for whatever reason she alone chooses.

With this we do not agree. . . . The Court's decisions recognizing a right of privacy also acknowledge that some state regulation in areas protected by that right is appropriate. A State may properly assert important interests in safeguarding health, in maintaining medical standards, and in protecting potential life. At some point in pregnancy, these respective interests become sufficiently compelling to sustain regulation of the factors that govern the abortion decision. The privacy right involved, therefore, cannot be said to be absolute. . . .

We, therefore, conclude that the right of personal privacy includes the abortion decision, but that this right is not unqualified, and must be considered against important state interests in regulation.

ROE VS. WADE ABORTION RULING.

LEFT: Harry Blackmun was appointed by Republican Richard Nixon in 1970 but became one of the most liberal justices in the Supreme Court.

Harry Blackmun
Roe vs. Wade

(January 22, 1973)

A woman's right to an abortion is one of the most divisive issues in American social politics today. Opinions were polarized on both sides by the Supreme Court's ruling in the case of *Roe vs. Wade* in 1973, which was fought over the right of an unmarried woman to have an abortion in Texas.

The plaintiff, preserving her anonymity under the pseudonym Jane Roe, was denied an abortion in 1969, even though she told the authorities she was pregnant as a result of rape. Two young lawyers, Linda Coffee and Sarah Weddington, took Dallas county attorney Henry Wade to the US District Court for the Northern District Texas, which decided for Roe but did not enforce its decision.

Coffee and Weddington appealed to the Supreme Court where it was heard not once but twice during 1972. The first hearing had been unsatisfactory for several reasons, not least the opening remark of the defense counsel who launched his case by insensitively remarking to Chief Justice Warren Burger, presiding, "may it please the Court, it's an old joke, but when a man argues against two beautiful ladies like this, they are going to have the last word."

Aware of the importance of the decision, Harry Blackmun, Associate Justice of the Supreme Court and a close friend of Burger's, spent many months drafting the final opinion and researching the history of abortion law. It was finally published on January 22, 1973, when by a 7-2 majority the court found in favor of Jane Roe. It argued that a person's right to privacy, as defined in the Fourteenth Amendment, extended to a woman's right to make the very personal, private decision about whether to have an abortion.

"[T]he right of personal privacy includes the abortion decision," ruled Blackmun, in a decision that rendered illegal the laws in abortion on some forty-six states, "but that this right is not unqualified, and must be considered against important state interests in regulation." He balanced a woman's rights with the state's duty to consider both a woman's health and the potential for human life of the developing fetus.

To that end he limited abortion to the first trimester, a limit which is a constant subject of debate given the improvements in life-saving medical techniques. During the second trimester a woman's health becomes increasingly a factor in any decision; and the viability of the fetus is the overriding concern during the third. The application of the Fourteenth Amendment in this case is often cited in other issues where privacy is a consideration.

The abortion debate arouses fiercer emotions than most because, like the death penalty, it concerns the termination of life. There is no middle ground, no potential for compromise. The publicity attached to *Roe vs. Wade* sent Justice Blackmun death threats, and prompted the formation of several key pro-life and pro-choice groups. As so often in issues of great moral weight such as this, the fate of the individual is often overlooked.

Jane Roe identified herself soon after the publication of the ruling as Norma McCorvey. Norma had been abused as a child and beaten as a sixteen-year-old bride. The pregnancy that was the subject of *Roe vs. Wade* was her third; denied an abortion in 1969, the resulting child was adopted like the previous two. She later admitted that her rape had been a fabrication in the hope of being allowed to terminate the pregnancy.

Norma worked for a time in a Dallas abortion clinic, but in later life she came to regret the *Roe vs. Wade* decision. She converted to Roman Catholicism in 1994 and became an active pro-life supporter who campaigned for the overturning of the ruling made in her favor. She died in Texas of heart failure in February 2017.

Richard Nixon
Announcement of Resignation

(August 8, 1974)

We hold those in high office to high standards. When they fall, they fall farther than ordinary men and women. President Nixon's fall from grace from the highest office in the land was spectacular and fascinating, played out in detail in the pages of newspapers and on the screens of televisions.

Despite the rising tide of opposition to the Vietnam War, Richard Nixon was elected to a second term as president in 1972 in a landslide, defeating George McGovern, who campaigned on defense cuts and amnesty for draft dodgers. And so it fell to Nixon to withdraw from the East Asian arena and to forge new friendships with the communist heartlands of China and the Soviet Union, and with the previously hostile Arab nations. These international détentes, he had hoped, would be his presidential legacy.

As the Watergate scandal broke, however, it seemed more likely that he would be remembered by his less than flattering epithet—"Tricky Dicky." His complicity in the break-in of the Democratic offices in the Watergate building in Washington, D.C., and his dirty-tricks efforts against rivals and activists, undermined his support in government. Nixon claimed that the revelations were what today would be dismissed as "fake news" and insisted on his ignorance of the burglary. He told the American people defiantly that "there can be no whitewash at the White House."

Nixon fired the special counsel leading the Watergate

investigation after the existence of secret tapes of conversations in the Oval Office came to light. He was determined to tough it out. "People have got to know whether or not their President is a crook. Well, I'm not a crook." But when one of the tapes made it clear that he had known about Watergate, he was advised that he could count on less than half the Senate votes required to prevent his impeachment. To avoid that embarrassment, Nixon chose instead to resign.

In 1962, Nixon had lost his first bid for presidency against John F. Kennedy, in part because of his failure to master the medium of television. After that defeat he worked hard to make friends with the camera and used it to far better effect in 1968 and 1972. His resignation address to the nation was his thirty-seventh address from the Oval Office. "Each time I have done so to discuss with you some matter that I believed affected the national interest." He was relaxed in front of the lens, and calmly explained that "I have never been a quitter. But as President, I must put the interest of America first."

He urged Americans to support his vice president Gerald Ford, who would be sworn in the following day. "The first essential is to begin healing the wounds of this nation," he said, "to put the bitterness and divisions of the recent past behind us"—divisions, he might have added, sown by his duplicity. "If some of my judgments have been wrong, and some were wrong, they were made in the best interest of the nation."

This was the closest he got to an admission of any wrong-doing. The rest of his address was devoted to the achievements of his administration, as if he were not evading impeachment but concluding a successful presidency. "We have unlocked the doors that for a quarter of a century stood between the United States and the People's Republic of China"; "one hundred

In all the decisions I have made in my public life, I have always tried to do what was best for the Nation. Throughout the long and difficult period of Watergate, I have felt it was my duty to persevere, to make every possible effort to complete the term of office to which you elected me.

I would have preferred to carry on through to the finish whatever the personal agony it would have involved, and my family unanimously urged me to do so. But the interest of the nation must always come before any personal considerations. From the discussions I have had with Congressional and other leaders, I have concluded that because of the Watergate matter I might not have the support of the Congress that I would consider necessary to back the very difficult decisions and carry out the duties of this office in the way the interests of the Nation would require.

I have never been a quitter. To leave office before my term is completed is abhorrent to every instinct in my body. But as President, I must put the interest of America first. America needs a full-time President and a full-time Congress, particularly at this time with problems we face at home and abroad.

To continue to fight through the months ahead for my personal vindication would almost totally absorb the time and attention of both the President and the Congress in a period when our entire focus should be on the great issues of peace abroad and prosperity without inflation at home.

Therefore I shall resign the Presidency effective at noon tomorrow. Vice President Ford will be sworn in as President at that hour in this office.

RESIGNATION TV ADDRESS

million people in the Arab countries, many of whom considered us their enemy for nearly twenty years, now look on us as their friends"; "we have opened the new relation with the Soviet Union."

He spoke of world poverty and American affluence; and, having once hoped that he would not be the first American president to lose a war, he portrayed America's withdrawal from Vietnam as a victory for peace. "Living in peace, rather than dying in war—this, more than anything, is what I hope will be my legacy to you, to our country, as I leave the presidency."

By announcing his resignation at the start of his address, he hoped that most of the 110 million Americans who watched it live would have forgotten

it by the end. When he spoke at Oxford University in 1978, he took the same long view of his legacy, telling his audience, "I screwed it up. Mea culpa. But let's get on to my achievements. You'll be here in the year 2000 and we'll see how I'm regarded then."

In 2000 and beyond, we remember Watergate; and Nixon remains, at time of writing, the only president to be forced to resign from office.

OPPOSITE: In addition to lying about Watergate, it has subsequently emerged that Nixon worked behind the scenes to block the 1968 Paris Peace Accord that would have undermined his 1968 presidential campaign.

Harvey Milk
"You have to give people hope"

(June 25, 1978)

Calls for gay liberation only really began in 1969 after a police raid on the Stonewall Inn in New York put the issue in the public eye. The election of the first openly homosexual man to public office did not happen until 1977, when Harvey Milk was voted onto the San Francisco Board of Supervisors.

After Dade County, I walked among the angry and the frustrated night after night and I looked at their faces. And in San Francisco, three days before Gay Pride Day, a person was killed just because he was gay. And that night, I walked among the sad and frustrated at City Hall in San Francisco and later that night as they lit candles on Castro Street and stood in silence, reaching out for some symbolic thing that would give them hope. These were strong people, whose faces I knew from the shop, the streets, meetings and people who I never saw before but I knew. They were strong, but even they needed hope.

And the young gay people in Altoona, Pennsylvania, and Richmond, Minnesota, who are coming out and hear Anita Bryant on television and her story: the only thing they have to look forward to is hope. And you have to give them hope. Hope for a better world, hope for a better tomorrow, hope for a better place to come if the pressures at home are too great. Hope that all will be all right.

Without hope not only gays but the blacks, the seniors, the handicapped, the 'us'es — the 'us'es will give up. And if you help elect to the central committee and other offices, more gay people, that gives a green light to all who feel disenfranchised, a green light to move forward. It means hope to a nation that has given up, because if a gay person makes it, the doors are open to everyone.—If a gay person can be elected, it's a green light. And you and you and you, you have to give people hope. Thank you very much.

THE "HOPE" SPEECH, GIVEN AT SAN FRANCISCO'S GAY FREEDOM DAY PARADE IN THE YEAR HE WAS ASSASSINATED

OPPOSITE: Harvey Milk leading a parade in San Francisco.

As the center of early hippie counterculture, San Francisco became a magnet for all those with radical or alternative views and lifestyles. Harvey Milk moved there from New York in 1972 as part of the first wave of gay migrants seeking a tolerant society in which to live. He was disappointed to find persistent discrimination against homosexuals and found himself drawn into local politics in his desire to end it.

In 1977, at the third time of asking, he was elected as one of eleven members of the legislative body of local government, the board of supervisors—the San Francisco equivalent of a city council. By all accounts he served his district well, fighting not only for gay rights but for better provisions for all its residents. He was an impassioned speaker and campaigned against issues ranging from the problem of dog excrement to the plans of real estate developers.

But it was as a leader of the gay community that Milk attracted most attention. He was much in demand at gay liberation rallies, where he usually gave a version of what has become known as the "Hope" speech. It was this speech that he gave to a crowd on 1978's Gay Freedom Day in San Francisco, an annual event held on the anniversary of the Stonewall Inn raid, June 25.

He began by discussing the controversial success of Anita Bryant, noted opposer of gay rights, in overturning new antidiscrimination legislation in Miami-Dade County, Florida, in 1977. What could be seen as a setback for the gay community, Milk chose to celebrate,

because "the word 'homosexual' or 'gay' appeared in every single newspaper in this nation, in every radio station, in every TV station and in every household. Everybody was talking about it, good and bad. Once you have dialogue starting you can break down prejudice."

He compared the civil rights campaigns of gays and blacks. "Today the black community is not judged by its friends but by its black legislators and leaders." He celebrated his own achievement in getting elected in 1977 and urged other homosexuals to stand for office. There was a great difference between "friends"—supporters of the gay community—and gay people themselves. "Friends can't feel the anger and frustration. A friend has never gone through what is known as coming out." Coming out often left you feeling hopelessly alone.

The Miami-Dade legislation was the first in America to restrict discrimination on grounds of sexuality, and Bryant's actions had robbed homosexuals of the hope it gave them. Milk spoke at length about the need for hope. After Dade County and the recent murder of a gay man in San Francisco, Milk said, "I walked among the angry and the frustrated, and the sad and frustrated, as they lit candles and stood in silence. These were strong people whose faces I knew, but even they needed hope."

"[Y]ou have to give them hope," he concluded. "Hope for a better world, hope for a better tomorrow, hope for a better place to come if the pressures at home are too great. Without hope, not only gays but the blacks, the seniors, the handicapped—the 'us'es will give up. And if you help elect more gay people, that gives a green light to all who feel disenfranchised. And you and you and you, you have to give people hope."

In the same supervisor elections that Harvey Milk won, the first African American woman, the first Chinese American, and the first single mother were also elected to the board. The civil rights movement gave millions of people hope. But as with racial discrimination, the fight for gay rights cost lives. Five months after Gay Freedom Day 1978, a fellow supervisor named Daniel White, who had campaigned on family values and whom Milk had opposed in a planning decision, shot Milk dead in city hall. A candlelit vigil that night packed the streets of San Francisco, and Harvey Milk became an icon of the gay community. He had given them hope.

It is not the State that creates a healthy society. When the State grows too powerful people feel that they count for less and less. The State drains society, not only of its wealth but of initiative, of energy, the will to improve and innovate as well as to preserve what is best. Our aim is to let people feel that they count for more and more.

... A healthy society is not created by its institutions, either. Great schools and universities do not make a great nation any more than great armies do. Only a great nation can create and involve great institutions—of learning, of healing, of scientific advance. And a great nation is the voluntary creation of its people—a people composed of men and women whose pride in themselves is founded on the knowledge of what they can give to a community of which they in turn can be proud.

If our people feel that they are part of a great nation and they are prepared to will the means to keep it great, a great nation we shall be, and shall remain. So, what can stop us from achieving this? What then stands in our way? The prospect of another winter of discontent? I suppose it might.

But I prefer to believe that certain lessons have been learnt from experience, that we are coming, slowly, painfully, to an autumn of understanding. And I hope that it will be followed by a winter of common sense. If it is not, we shall not be—diverted from our course.

To those waiting with bated breath for that favorite media catchphrase, the 'U' turn, I have only one thing to say. 'You turn if you want to. The lady's not for turning.'

"THE LADY'S NOT FOR TURNING" SPEECH

LEFT: "The lady's not for turning" was a pun on the title of a popular West End play from 1948 by Christopher Fry entitled The Lady's Not For Burning.

Margaret Thatcher
"The lady's not for turning"

(October 10, 1980)

Margaret Thatcher polarized British politics with her attacks on trade union power and privatization of publicly owned transport and utility companies. Early in her premiership, at a time of recession, many even in her own party hoped she might soften her monetarist approach and reverse some of her policies.

At its annual conference in 1980, the Conservative Party celebrated their first seventeen months in power after half a decade in opposition to the Labour Party. They had returned to government under the leadership of Britain's first female prime minister (although Thatcher herself was more proud of being the first prime minister with a science degree).

Despite rising unemployment in a deepening recession, Thatcher stuck to counterinflationary policies, which some, including her predecessor Edward Heath, felt were doing more harm than good. There was much speculation in the national press about the possibility of a U-turn, and the prime minister's conference speech was eagerly awaited.

Speaking the week after the Labour Party conference, she characterized socialism as the enemy within, blaming (as all incoming regimes do) present ills on the outgoing administration. Her approach, she explained, had been one of removing legislative obstacles to economic success. "Prosperity comes not from grand conferences of economists but by countless acts of personal self-confidence and self-reliance." Hers was to be a government for the individual achiever, not the massed ranks.

She ran through the restrictions on trade union practice that her government had already put in place, and its first steps to break up nationalized monopolies. The social landscape was further being transformed by giving tenants in council housing the right to buy their homes. While Labour were speaking of the death of Capitalism, Thatcher retorted: "if this is the death of Capitalism, I must say that it's quite a way to go."

Deregulation, hands-off government, and unfettered free enterprise were to be the future. But the key to Thatcher's economic policy was the reduction of inflation at all costs. "Inflation destroys nations and societies as surely as invading armies do."

Unemployment levels had reached two million during her first year. Thatcher professed her concern, but used the greater security of workers in the public sector as an argument not for extending the public sector but for cutting public funding in order to level the playing field. "Those in the public sector," she suggested, "have a duty to those in the private sector not to take out so much in pay that they cause others unemployment."

She warmed to this theme. High public sector wage settlements meant less public money to purchase goods from private sector companies. "It is not the state that creates a healthy society," she said, an idea she would make more specific in the future when she declared that there was "no such thing as society." "A healthy society is not created by its institutions either."

To her critics: "those who urge us to relax the squeeze [on public spending]," she insisted that the defeat of inflation would bring about the defeat of unemployment. "To those waiting with baited breath for that favorite media catchphrase, the 'U' turn, I have only one thing to say. 'You turn if you want to. The lady's not for turning.'"

The gag won a standing ovation and was widely reported in the papers the following day, reinforcing as it did Thatcher's reputation as an unbending "Iron Lady."

During her first term Thatcher displayed strong leadership in the Falklands War of 1982. She was returned by a landslide for a second term as prime minister, during which she resolutely crushed the mining communities that had thwarted her in 1981. A third term followed, but her position on Europe and her introduction of the unpopular "poll tax" lost her the support of her party and forced her resignation.

Ronald Reagan
"Tear down this wall!"

(June 12, 1987)

Divided by a wall in 1961; given hope by President Kennedy's declaration that "ich bin ein Berliner" in 1963—East and West Berlin were symbols of the standoff between communism and capitalism throughout the 1970s and 1980s.

By the time of his 1987 visit, hastily arranged on the back of an economic summit in Venice, Ronald Reagan and Soviet president Mikhail Gorbachev had established a good working relationship. At their Reykjavik summit meeting eight months earlier, Gorbachev was preaching a new Soviet approach to diplomacy: glasnost [transparency] and perestroika [reconstruction]. Although their talks in Reykjavik on arms limitation stalled because of Reagan's pursuit of the militarization of space, the two men developed a strong mutual respect and understanding.

In part because of Reagan's so-called "star wars" program, there were large demonstrations in West Berlin against his visit. West German police made large parts of the city no-go areas for fear that further protests would drown out Reagan's speech. Ironically, in East Berlin, East German police were doing the same thing for fear that his speech would be heard there.

Reagan spoke at the Brandenburg Gate, in full view of East German border guards and shielded by a double layer of bulletproof but transparent glass. Evoking memories of Kennedy's morale-boosting appearance in the city twenty-six years before, he praised the city's unique attractions by using a couple of German phrases: "*Ich hab' noch einen Koffer in* Berlin" [I still keep a suitcase in Berlin], the title of a song sung by Marlene Dietrich, and "*es gibt nur ein* Berlin" [there's only one Berlin], despite its division in two by the Berlin Wall.

He praised the economic recovery of West Germany and West Berlin since the war, achieved—he quietly reminded them—with the support of America's Marshall Plan.

Referring to glasnost and perestroika, Reagan reported on Russia's release of some political prisoners and an end to the jamming of some western broadcasts.

"Are they the beginnings of profound changes in the Soviet state, or are they token gestures?" he asked. "There is one sign the Soviets can make that would be unmistakable, that would advance dramatically the cause of freedom and peace."

And then he indicated the Brandenburg Gate, which stood on the border of east and west and had been closed since the building of the Berlin Wall. "General Secretary Gorbachev, if you seek peace, if you seek prosperity for the Soviet Union and Eastern Europe, if you seek liberalization: Come here to this gate! Mr. Gorbachev, open this gate! Mr. Gorbachev—tear down this wall!"

The inclusion of such a direct demand by the speechwriter Peter Robinson had been hotly debated in the corridors of the White House. President Reagan insisted on keeping it in, despite the advice of aides who felt that it was "unpresidential" and potentially inflammatory. The Soviet news agency TASS responded as feared, describing Reagan's address as "an openly provocative, war-mongering speech." Gorbachev's personal response is not recorded.

In the West, Reagan's remark was largely ignored as rhetoric; but two years later East Germany relaxed border controls and allowed visits back and forth between the two halves of the city. For some Berliners this meant seeing relatives for the first time in more than twenty years. Reagan's remark was rediscovered and hailed as a diplomatic landmark, confirming his reputation as the Great Communicator. In the same year, borders fell and more or less bloodless revolutions toppled communism all across Eastern Europe. The wall was finally torn down in 1990, and East and West Germany were reunited as one country with one Berlin as its capital.

In the 1950s, Khrushchev predicted: 'We will bury you.' But in the West today, we see a free world that has achieved a level of prosperity and well-being unprecedented in all human history. In the Communist world, we see failure, technological backwardness, declining standards of health, even want of the most basic kind—too little food. Even today, the Soviet Union still cannot feed itself. After these four decades, then, there stands before the entire world one great and inescapable conclusion: Freedom leads to prosperity. Freedom replaces the ancient hatreds among the nations with comity and peace. Freedom is the victor.

And now the Soviets themselves may, in a limited way, be coming to understand the importance of freedom. We hear much from Moscow about a new policy of reform and openness. Some political prisoners have been released. Certain foreign news broadcasts are no longer being jammed. Some economic enterprises have been permitted to operate with greater freedom from state control.

Are these the beginnings of profound changes in the Soviet state? Or are they token gestures, intended to raise false hopes in the West, or to strengthen the Soviet system without changing it? We welcome change and openness; for we believe that freedom and security go together, that the advance of human liberty can only strengthen the cause of world peace. There is one sign the Soviets can make that would be unmistakable, that would advance dramatically the cause of freedom and peace.

General Secretary Gorbachev, if you seek peace, if you seek prosperity for the Soviet Union and Eastern Europe, if you seek liberalization: Come here to this gate! Mr. Gorbachev, open this gate! Mr. Gorbachev, tear down this wall!

"TEAR DOWN THIS WALL!" SPEECH AT BRANDENBURG GATE

RIGHT: Ronald Reagan speaking in front of the Brandenburg Gate in 1987. Berlin's most famous landmark lay on the other side of the Berlin Wall.

Nelson Mandela
"We have waited too long for our freedom"

(February 11, 1990)

The release from prison of Nelson Mandela was a moment that few in South Africa could have imagined. His emergence from Victor Verster prison at the age of seventy-one was a defining moment not only of the twentieth century but in the history of civil rights. It was the symbolic end of apartheid.

Incarcerated since 1962, a time before television came to South Africa, Nelson Mandela had spent eighteen years of his imprisonment in the harsh Robben Island prison. His first cell had no bed, and neither basin nor toilet; and he had to do hard labor in the island's stone quarry. Conditions there gradually improved following complaints and hunger strikes, and Mandela spent his free time reading and studying for a University of London law degree by correspondence course.

Under the slogan "Free Mandela," an international campaign for his release began in 1980, backed by the United Nations. It was opposed by Margaret Thatcher and Ronald Reagan, key allies of South Africa who still considered Mandela a terrorist. He was moved to a mainland jail in 1982 to prevent him from influencing younger prisoners on Robben Island, and rejected a conditional offer of release by South African president P. W. Botha in 1985. "What freedom am I being offered while the organization of the people [the African National Congress, ANC] remains banned? Only free men can negotiate. A prisoner cannot enter into contracts."

Beyond the prison walls violent unrest was spreading through South Africa, met with equal violence by the police. Mandela's seventieth birthday was celebrated in his absence by a concert in London's Wembley Stadium, watched by a television audience of 200 million. In 1989, F. W. de Klerk succeeded Botha as president, and as the Berlin Wall fell he decided that in a changing political world, apartheid was no longer sustainable. ANC prisoners were released, and the organization legalized; and on February 11, 1990, Mandela, a free man

at last, was driven the forty miles to Cape Town, where he spoke to supporters and the world's media from a balcony of city hall.

He was unrepentant. He began by saluting the ANC, the South African Communist Party, and those who had died in the cause of abolishing apartheid. He also thanked the Black Sash and the National Union of South African Students, white organizations that had "acted as the conscience of white South Africans." He praised the working classes, the young, and all women—"the rock-hard foundation of our struggle. Apartheid has inflicted more pain on you than on anyone else."

Mandela called for peace and security, but made it clear that he would not renounce violence until the South African state did so. "The factors which necessitated the armed struggle still exist today," he said, as they had done when he was imprisoned in 1964. "I am a loyal and disciplined member of the African National Congress. I am therefore in full agreement with all of its objectives, strategies and tactics." He insisted that he had not conducted any negotiations on the ANC's behalf while in prison, only called for them to begin. And in calling for democracy and an end to apartheid, he praised Mr. de Klerk, "a man of integrity [who] has gone further than any other Nationalist president in taking real steps to normalize the situation."

But there was still work to be done. "We have waited too long for our freedom," Mandela told the crowd and the world. "We can no longer wait. Now is the time to intensify the struggle on all fronts." And he concluded by quoting his own words spoken at his trial twenty-six years earlier. "I have cherished the ideal of a democratic and free society in which all persons live together in

Our struggle has reached a decisive moment. We call on our people to seize this moment so that the process towards democracy is rapid and uninterrupted. We have waited too long for our freedom. We can no longer wait. Now is the time to intensify the struggle on all fronts. To relax our efforts now would be a mistake which generations to come will not be able to forgive. The sight of freedom looming on the horizon should encourage us to redouble our efforts.

It is only through disciplined mass action that our victory can be assured. We call on our white compatriots to join us in the shaping of a new South Africa. The freedom movement is a political home for you too. We call on the international community to continue the campaign to isolate the apartheid regime. To lift sanctions now would be to run the risk of aborting the process towards the complete eradication of apartheid.

Our march to freedom is irreversible. We must not allow fear to stand in our way. Universal suffrage on a common voters' role in a united democratic and non-racial South Africa is the only way to peace and racial harmony.

In conclusion I wish to quote my own words during my trial in 1964. They are true today as they were then:

'I have fought against white domination and I have fought against black domination. I have cherished the ideal of a democratic and free society in which all persons live together in harmony and with equal opportunities. It is an ideal which I hope to live for and to achieve. But if needs be, it is an ideal for which I am prepared to die.'

RELEASE SPEECH

harmony and with equal opportunity. It is an ideal which I hope to live for and to achieve. But, if needs be, it is an ideal for which I am prepared to die."

A turbulent and bloody few years followed of in-fighting within the black African community. Mandela's measured, moderate tone frustrated many who had continued the fight during his imprisonment and envisioned different ends to apartheid. But in 1994, South Africa held its first fully free and democratic general election. The ANC won a convincing victory, and Nelson Mandela became the country's first black president, an international symbol of the power of mass action, patience, and hope.

RIGHT: *Nelson Mandela makes his first speech after release from prison from the balcony of Cape Town City Hall.*

Mikhail S. Gorbachev
Farewell Address

(December 25, 1991)

The speed of the Soviet Union's collapse took commentators by surprise. President Gorbachev, born in the Stalinist era, fought to reform the only political system he had known. But as his power base and the union itself disintegrated, the eighth and last leader of the USSR was forced to acknowledge the inevitable end.

"Speaking to you for the last time as President of the USSR, I consider it necessary to express my assessment of the path traversed since 1986. Especially since there are a good many contradictory, superficial and unobjective opinions on this score.

Fate ordained that when I became head of state it was already clear that things were not going well in the country. We have a great deal of everything—land, petroleum, gas and other natural resources—and God has endowed us with intelligence and talent, too, but we live much worse than people in the developed countries do, and we are lagging further and further behind them.

The reason was evident-society was suffocating in the grip of the command-bureaucratic system. Doomed to serve ideology and to bear the terrible burden of the arms race, it had been pushed to the limit of what was possible.

All attempts at partial reforms—and there were a good many of them—failed, one after the other. The country had lost direction. It was impossible to go on living that way. Everything had to be changed fundamentally.

That is why I have never once regretted that I did not take advantage of the position of General Secretary just to 'reign' for a few years. I would have considered that irresponsible and immoral. . . .

I want to thank from the bottom of my heart those who during these years stood with me for a right and good cause. Certainly some mistakes could have been avoided, and many things could have been done better. But I am sure that sooner or later our common efforts will bear fruit and our peoples will live in a prosperous and democratic society."

RESIGNATION SPEECH DISSOLVING THE USSR

RIGHT: Mikhail Gorbachev speaking in 1991.

Mikhail Gorbachev was the only leader of the Soviet Union to be born after its birth in the Russian Revolution of 1917. He was twenty years younger than Konstantin Chernenko, the man who preceded him in the role. Although he might have been expected to think only in terms of totalitarian government, his relative youth and distance from the revolution gave him the flexibility to think outside the ideological box. "Society was suffocating," as he recalled in his televised final address to the Union, "in the grip of the command-bureaucratic system, doomed to serve ideology and to bear the terrible burden of the arms race."

The Soviet economy was as stagnant as the form of government that regulated it, and Gorbachev tried to liberalize both in an effort to stimulate them. He replaced political officials who were too set in their ways, such as foreign minister Gromyko, and introduced valuable reforms to the centralized economy, allowing some state producers to set their own production targets and expanding the private sector. "The totalitarian system which for a long time deprived the country of the opportunity to become prosperous and flourishing, has been eliminated," he told viewers.

Gorbachev instigated press and religious freedoms, a multiparty system, and some curbs on the power of the Communist Party of the Soviet Union (CPSU). But there was strong opposition from traditionalists in the party. "The changes ran up against our intolerance, low level of political sophisticationand fear of change," he said. It was as if the Soviet Union, immature and overprotected, was not ready for "grown-up," late-twentieth-century government. "The old system collapsed before a new one had time to start working."

To make matters worse, the economy did not flourish under Gorbachev's *perestroika* [reconstruction]; in fact, it shrank. And all those new freedoms only encouraged freedoms of thought and expression. One by one the countries of the eastern bloc began to set their own laws and to secede from

the Soviet Union. The opening of the borders between East and West Germany released a tide of independent, nationalist expression behind the Iron Curtain, which no amount of social or economic reform could hope to hold back.

As the Soviet Union shrank, its government held little sway beyond Moscow, and there were increasing clashes between Gorbachev, president of the Union, and his counterpart Boris Yeltsin, president of Russia. The final blow to Gorbachev came in the form of an attempted coup d'état in August 1991 by hard-liners in the CPSU. For two days he was held under house arrest until Yeltsin came to his rescue. The coup was suppressed, but Yeltsin had gained enormously in power and influence as a result.

The CPSU's control collapsed, and the remaining Soviet states formed a new alliance as the Commonwealth of Independent States. The Soviet Union was dead in all but name, and Gorbachev's admission that "certainly some mistakes could have been avoided, and many things could have been done better" seemed irrelevant from the president of a country that no longer really existed. He announced his resignation on Christmas Day 1991, and the following day the USSR was formally abolished. "I am leaving my post with a feeling of anxiety," Gorbachev told viewers, "but we are heirs to a great civilization and its rebirth into a new, up-to-date and fitting life now depends on each and every one of us."

In the years since the death of the USSR, many of its former states and satellites, finding their way in a capitalist world, have begun to long for the old certainties of a centralized economy. Russia, resurgent under Vladimir Putin, is extending its influence on the western world as never before in a very modern reinvention of the totalitarian state of which Gorbachev was so critical. In Russia, he has said, "politics is increasingly turning into imitation democracy," with all power in the "hands of the executive branch." It seems little changed, in many ways, from the time of Gorbachev's birth.

Maya Angelou
"On the Pulse of Morning"

(January 20, 1993)

Maya Angelou spent her childhood in the Arkansas town of Stamps, only twenty-five miles from Hope, birthplace of then President-Elect Bill Clinton. During the planning of his Inauguration Day, he decided that he wanted poetry to be represented, and he looked no further than Angelou.

A poet has been part of inaugural celebrations only five times in America's history, and for only three presidents, all of them Democrats—John F. Kennedy's was the first, more than 180 years after the founding of the nation, when Robert Frost read his poem "The Gift Outright" in 1961. It took another thirty-two years and seven presidents before the next, Bill Clinton.

Angelou was by the 1990s a well-known author. She published her first volume of an autobiography, *I Know Why the Caged Bird Sings*, in 1971, and since then she had been publishing alternately further volumes of autobiography (five by 1991 of her eventual seven) and of poetry. Known as both a writer and a performer, she drew a clear distinction between the spoken and the written word; her poem "On the Pulse of Morning," written for the Clinton inauguration, was designed to be read aloud. It was full of words for the voice—words about crying, singing, hearing, speaking, Angelou's theme for the day, as might be expected at the installation of a new president, was hope and a fresh start.

And new beginnings were required. She began with a reference to fossils: "the mastodon, the dinosaur who left dry tokens of their sojourn here"; and to polluted land where toxic waters "have left collars of waste upon my shore, currents of debris upon my breast." She spoke of the many nationalities of immigrants who came to America for new beginnings, but also of the slaves who were forced to come, "sold, stolen, arriving on a nightmare, praying for a dream"; and the native Americans driven from their lands, "forced on bloody feet." All were welcome in America now:

"History, despite its wrenching pain,
Cannot be unlived, but if faced
With courage, need not be lived again."

The recurring metaphors of the poem were, as the first line announced, "A Rock, A River, A Tree." They connected her to ancient gospel songs of which there are echoes in the poem—"I went to the rock to hide my face; the rock cried out 'No hiding place!'" for example, and "I'm gonna lay down my burden, down by the riverside, ain't gonna study war no more." The rock is the permanence of the land and of the god of Angelou's deeply held Christian faith. The river is the cleansing movement of people and time. The tree puts down roots, nourished by land and water, and shelters the traveler. Together, the three represent America, and

"Here on the pulse of this fine day
You may have the courage
To look up and out and upon me, the
Rock, the River, the Tree, your country."

Clinton described the poem as "an eternal gift to America," and its clarity of image and message were well received. Poetry critics, who only read the text without considering it as spoken words, did not rate it highly; but Maya Angelou's public profile soared afterward. Her publishers sold more of her books in that month than in the whole of the previous year. When the poem itself was published, it hit the best-seller lists immediately, and the audio recording of it won a Grammy.

Bill Clinton invited another poet, Miller Williams, to be part of his second inauguration, and Obama included poets Elizabeth Alexander and Richard Blanco in his two ceremonies. Maya Angelou was the first woman poet, and the first black poet, to read at a presidential inauguration.

ABOVE AND RIGHT: Maya Angelou: "People will forget what you said . . . but people will never forget how you made them feel."

Chris Patten
"A very Chinese city with British characteristics"

(June 30, 1997)

Hong Kong became a British colony in 1841. Its return to Chinese control in 1997 marked the final end of the British Empire, which had been divesting itself of its territories since the end of World War II. It was, for good or ill, the end of an era.

What we celebrate this evening is the restless energy, the hard work, the audacity of the men and women who have written Hong Kong's success story. Mostly Chinese men and Chinese women. They were only ordinary in the sense that most of them came here with nothing. They are extraordinary in what they have achieved against the odds.

As British administration ends, we are, I believe, entitled to say that our own nation's contribution here was to provide the scaffolding that enabled the people of Hong Kong to ascend. The rule of law. Clean and light-handed government. The values of a free society. The beginnings of representative government and democratic accountability. This is a Chinese city, a very Chinese city with British characteristics. No dependent territory has been left more prosperous, none with such a rich texture and fabric of civil society, professions, churches, newspapers, charities, civil servants of the highest probity and the most steadfast commitment to the public good.

I have no doubt that, with people here holding on to these values which they cherish, Hong Kong's star will continue to climb. Hong Kong's values are decent values. They are universal values. They are the values of the future in Asia as elsewhere, a future in which the happiest and the richest communities, and the most confident and the most stable too, will be those that best combine political liberty and economic freedom as we do here today.

HANDING OVER HONG KONG TO CHINA, "ONE COUNTRY, TWO SYSTEMS"

OPPOSITE: Chris Patten, a former cabinet minister under Margaret Thatcher and last governor of Hong Kong, speaking at the official handover ceremony.

It was reported that Chris Patten spent his last day as Britain's last governor of Hong Kong in tears. Certainly, he was visibly distressed during the farewell speech that he gave to British troops that afternoon. "Today," he began, "is a cause for celebration, not sorrow. But here and there perhaps there will be a touch of personal sadness as is true for any departure."

British rule, he acknowledged, was not the whole of Hong Kong's history—only a little over 150 years of it—which began with "events that, from today's vantage point, none of us here would seek to condone." China had ceded Hong Kong Island to Britain in perpetuity in 1841 as part compensation for the blow to British merchants of China's clampdown on the opium trade.

Hong Kong harbor afforded British vessels a fine harbor within reach of Canton, and the colony expanded, eventually annexing the Kowloon area of the nearby Chinese mainland. Temporary Japanese occupation of the city during World War II gave Chinese businesses there the opportunity to flourish without British intervention.

After the Japanese surrender, mainland China was distracted by the civil war that led to the declaration of the People's Republic of China. Hong Kong provided a haven for some Chinese who did not welcome communist rule, and Patten noted that "most of those who live in Hong Kong now do so because of events in our own century which would today have few defenders."

But there were also calls from both sides of the border for Hong Kong and China to be reunited. Britain responded by extending the right to vote in the colony. But as China made it clear that it would take Hong Kong back anyway, negotiations began under Margaret Thatcher's leadership to plan an orderly handover.

The primary concern in the west was that Hong Kong's booming capitalist economy be allowed to continue under

that enemy of capitalism: communism. A deal was struck whereby the city would be guaranteed its economic and political freedoms for fifty years after the handover, a settlement described as "One Country, Two Systems." Much of Patten's speech was aimed at reassuring Hong Kong residents and reminding Chinese officials of this point. He talked of "a very Chinese city with British characteristics," of its people "holding on to these values which they cherish," and of Hong Kong's values being "universal values . . . the values of the future of Asia as elsewhere."

In later years Patten would express regret that Britain did not do more to guarantee those values. Elections, for example, were not introduced in Hong Kong until after the 1984 agreement with China. Within twenty years of the handover, many of the freedoms that agreement sought to guarantee had been eroded. Dissident voices were being suppressed. In 2017, when a group of political booksellers were arrested, Patten commented that "I think we have got a big responsibility to behave more honorably to Joshua Wong [a student demonstrator] and his generation than we behaved to his parents' generation."

After Patten's speech to the troops, it was left to Prince Charles and Britain's new prime minister Tony Blair to represent their country at the formal handover ceremony. At one minute to midnight, the Union Jack was lowered while the band played "God Save the Queen." It was over. On the stroke of midnight, while the rest of the world slept, seven hours of celebrations and fireworks began in Tiananmen Square in Beijing, and in Hong Kong the Chinese flag was raised over the country's new region to the tune of the Chinese national anthem "March of the Volunteers." A convoy of 500 vehicles of the People's Liberation Army had already crossed the border three hours earlier.

Charles Spencer
"The most hunted person of the modern age"

(September 6, 1997)

The death of Diana, Princess of Wales, in a car crash in Paris prompted an outpouring of public grief in Britain and around the world. At her televised state funeral, six days after her death, her younger brother Earl Spencer stood up to deliver her eulogy.

Born into British nobility as the daughter of a viscount, Lady Diana Spencer was thrust onto the world stage in February 1981, when she became engaged to Charles, Prince of Wales, heir to the British throne. The wedding attracted an estimated global audience of a billion people, where she became Princess of Wales. She was a popular figure worldwide, despite (or perhaps because of) intense media scrutiny of her reported infidelities, the breakdown of her marriage, and subsequent divorce. She was especially prominent in the support of people with HIV/AIDS and the International Campaign to Ban Landmines.

On the evening of August 31, 1997, with the paparazzi in close pursuit, the car in which Diana was traveling struck the wall of the Pont de l'Alma tunnel in Paris, killing the princess. The crash also resulted in the death of her companion Dodi Fayed, the son of a British/Egyptian businessman, and the driver Henri Paul. Her bodyguard survived by the simple expedient of wearing a seat belt but was still badly injured. The apparent coldness of the queen toward the tragedy was ascribed to Charles and Diana's divorce and widely reported as being out of step with public feeling.

At her funeral, Earl Spencer was visibly emotional but demonstrated the classic stiff upper lip of the British peerage. His eulogy for his

sister set out to separate Diana from her previous role and marriage as a princess of the House of Windsor and redefine her by her independent, international legacy. "All over the world," he said, "she was a symbol of selfless humanity, a standard bearer for the rights of the truly downtrodden, a very British girl who transcended nationality."

Purposefully impassioned to emphasize the gulf between the public and royal reactions to her death, Spencer directed thinly veiled barbs at the queen and her family, sitting only feet away, in the church where Diana was married. He painted the princess as an ordinary person, emphasizing her international work and her charity, humanity, and frailty. She was, he said, "an insecure person, the very essence of compassion, of duty, of style, of beauty. She needed no royal title to continue."

As Earl Spencer brought the eulogy to a close, he turned from the public image of Diana to her private reality as a member of two families and mother of another. He spoke as an uncle to her sons William, heir to the British throne, and Harry; and as a brother of his sister, part of his Spencer "blood family." Further distancing her from her public life as a royal princess, he insisted she was "at her most beautiful and radiant and when she had joy in her private life."

It is a point to remember that of all the ironies about Diana, perhaps the greatest was this: a girl given the name of the ancient goddess of hunting was, in the end, the most hunted person of the modern age.

She would want us today to pledge ourselves to protecting her beloved boys, William and Harry, from a similar fate. And I do this here, Diana, on your behalf. We will not allow them to suffer the anguish that used regularly to drive you to tearful despair.

And beyond that, on behalf of your mother and sisters, I pledge that we, your blood family, will do all we can to continue the imaginative and loving way in which you were steering these two exceptional young men, so that their souls are not simply immersed by duty and tradition but can sing openly as you planned.

We fully respect the heritage into which they have both been born, and will always respect and encourage them in their royal role. But we, like you, recognize the need for them to experience as many different aspects of life as possible, to arm them spiritually and emotionally for the years ahead. I know you would have expected nothing less from us.

William and Harry, we all care desperately for you today. We are all chewed up with sadness at the loss of a woman who wasn't even our mother. How great your suffering is we cannot even imagine.

I would like to end by thanking God for the small mercies He's shown us at this dreadful time; for taking Diana at her most beautiful and radiant and when she had joy in her private life.

Above all, we give thanks for the life of a woman I'm so proud to be able to call my sister: the unique, the complex, the extraordinary and irreplaceable Diana, whose beauty, both internal and external, will never be extinguished from our minds.

EULOGY ON DEATH OF PRINCESS DIANA

In the days that followed, the world's press was torn between sensationalizing the very pointed criticism of the queen, her family, and her son and examining the media's own role in her death, through their relentless pursuit of Diana. One phrase in Earl Spencer's eulogy, which described her as "the most hunted person of the modern age," came to define Diana's tragic end: it cemented in the public eye the ruthless pursuit of their

quarry by the paparazzi, their chase through the streets of Paris, and the devastating wreckage in the tunnel under the Pont de l'Alma.

OPPOSITE: Earl Spencer reading the eulogy to his sister at Westminster Abbey; a speech which brought spontaneous cheers and applause from the crowds gathered outside.

Bill Clinton
"I have sinned"

(September 11, 1998)

During the first year of President Clinton's second term, allegations surfaced of an affair between him and a White House intern named Monica Lewinsky. His evasive responses to this and other accusations of misconduct left the American public unsatisfied and hungry for greater truth and contrition from their leader.

I don't think there is a fancy way to say that I have sinned.

It is important to me that everybody who has been hurt know that the sorrow I feel is genuine: first and most important, my family; also my friends, my staff, my Cabinet, Monica Lewinsky and her family, and the American people. I have asked all for their forgiveness.

But I believe that to be forgiven, more than sorrow is required—at least two more things. First, genuine repentance—a determination to change and to repair breaches of my own making. I have repented. Second, what my bible calls a 'broken spirit,' an understanding that I must have God's help to be the person that I want to be; a willingness to give the very forgiveness I seek; a renunciation of the pride and the anger which cloud judgment, lead people to excuse and compare and to blame and complain.

Now, what does all this mean for me and for us? First, I will instruct my lawyers to mount a vigorous defense, using all available appropriate arguments. But legal language must not obscure the fact that I have done wrong. Second, I will continue on the path of repentance, seeking pastoral support and that of other caring people so that they can hold me accountable for my own commitment.

Third, I will intensify my efforts to lead our country and the world toward peace and freedom, prosperity and harmony, in the hope that with a broken spirit and a still strong heart I can be used for greater good, for we have many blessings and many challenges and so much work to do.

"I HAVE SINNED" APOLOGY DELIVERED AT THE ANNUAL WHITE HOUSE PRAYER BREAKFAST

OPPOSITE: Bill Clinton's confession didn't spare him impeachment proceedings,
but did help restore some of his public profile.

Bill Clinton's denials in January 1998 were unconvincing and based on technical, legal definitions of the act of sex. An admission wrung out of him in August that he did have an inappropriate relationship with Lewinsky was accompanied more by self-justification than by apology. "While my answers were legally accurate," he told Americans by television on August 17, "I did not volunteer information."

He was speaking then after an extraordinary event, the first time a sitting president had testified to a grand jury that was investigating his own behavior. In his address to the nation afterward he confirmed that "indeed I did have a relationship with Ms. Lewinsky that was not appropriate," having in January said emphatically, "I did not have sexual relations with that woman." However, he focused not on his own acts but on his right to privacy, and on political rivalries who he claimed were conducting a witch hunt against him.

The public wanted to see some humility from a man whose pejorative nickname was Slick Willie. Two days later it was confirmed that he had been required to supply a DNA sample for testing against a stain on a blue dress belonging to Lewinsky. Clinton must have been quite sure what the result would be, and he decided on a more humble, confessional approach to his guilt for the sake of his reputation and his chances of remaining unimpeached in the White House.

The perfect opportunity came at the White House Prayer Breakfast three weeks later on September 11. This annual event brought an audience of over a hundred priests and ministers into the East Room; who better to confess to? On the same morning a report had concluded that Clinton was guilty of perjury and other offenses for having tried to conceal his relationship with Lewinsky. This extra pressure on top of the smoking gun of the blue dress stain convinced Clinton to come clean.

"In my first statement after I testified," he began, "I was not contrite enough. I don't think there

is a fancy way to say that I have sinned." He continued, as he had noticeably not done in August, by apologizing to all concerned—"first and most important, my family; also my friends, my staff, my Cabinet, Monica Lewinsky and her family, and the American people."

He hoped that "with a broken spirit and a still strong heart I can be used for greater good." Although he still insisted that "the bounds of privacy have been excessively and unwisely invaded, in this case it may have been a blessing, because I still sinned."

He wound up with a passage from the Yom Kippur liturgy that was apt for the autumn season and for his own fall. "Now is the time for turning. The leaves are beginning to turn from green to orange. The animals are beginning to turn to storing their food for the winter." Humans, he said, find it harder to turn than wild nature does. "It means starting all over again; it means saying I am sorry. But unless we turn, we will be trapped forever in yesterday's ways. Turn us around, O Lord, and bring us back toward you."

At that prayer breakfast, President Clinton certainly used all the right words and could scarcely have expressed more contritely or apologetically his guilt and humility. For some it was altogether too good to be true, coming after so many of his attempts to avoid the truth of what he had done. Nevertheless, widely reported, his speech did some good in turning public opinion—and more importantly in preserving his marriage to Hillary Clinton.

President Clinton was impeached in December 1998 for perjury and obstruction of justice, only the second president to be so indicted. After a twenty-one-day trial in the Senate, enough Republicans voted with the Democrats to ensure that he was cleared of both charges. The right to privacy for public figures remains a hotly contested principle, given the hypocrisy of men such as Speaker of the House Newt Gingrich, who were having their own affairs with White House staff while hounding Clinton about his.

Tony Blair
Address to Irish Parliament
(November 26, 1998)

Despite a shared cultural experience going back millennia, the political relationship between Ireland and Britain has always been one of tension. Ireland's independence was won through the barrel of a gun, with such bitterness that Tony Blair's speech to the Irish parliament was the first by a serving British prime minister.

Britain has treated Ireland very badly over the centuries, ruthlessly crushing any resistance to the imposition of its laws and customs.

Rule from Dublin was finally achieved by the Irish War of Independence in 1921. But in the county of Ulster, which had the greatest density of Protestants, a majority wished to remain British. Thus, the separate country or province of Northern Ireland was created, tied to Britain by allegiance but separated by sea, bound to the Republic of Ireland by geology and history but divided by a border.

Violence flared between so-called Loyalists who favored union with Britain, and Republicans who sought a reunification of all Ireland, at a high human and economic cost to the region. A bitter sectarian war of attrition had reached a stalemate by the late 1990s, when changes of leadership in many of the political and military factions made peace talks a real possibility.

Unimaginable concessions by hard-liners on all sides brought about the Belfast Agreement on Good Friday, April 10, 1998. It was signed by both governments and by all the political parties in Northern Ireland except the Democratic Unionists. It recognized the desire of Northern Ireland to remain British, but also the desire of all Ireland to be reunited. It established new forums for peaceful discussion, both between north and south Ireland and between Northern Ireland and Great Britain.

After years of direct rule from London, the Good Friday Agreement also established a new devolved government structure for Northern Ireland based not on majority rule but on a consensus of majorities within each party. A week after the signing, Irish prime minister Bertie Ahern told the Irish people, "The British Government are effectively out of the equation and neither the British parliament nor people have any legal right under this agreement to impede the achievement of Irish unity if it had the consent of the people North and South."

Tony Blair's invitation to address the Irish parliament was a sign of just how far all sides had moved their positions in order to reach agreement. "Politics is replacing violence," he said, "as the way people do business." He had a difficult job: on the one hand emphasizing positive connections between the two countries while on the other not ignoring the historical antagonism between them. "We need not be prisoners of our history. Now the UK and Ireland are two modern countries, we can try to forgive and forget those age-old enmities." And for Northern Irish ears he had to pitch the agreement as a win for two sides notoriously resistant to any forgive-and-forget approach. "I'm not asking anyone to surrender," said Blair. "I am asking everyone to declare the victory of peace."

And so it was. There were teething problems, including the reluctance of some paramilitary units to disarm. A great deal of instinctive suspicion and mistrust slowed the move toward any political normality, and a second agreement at St. Andrews in Scotland was necessary. But in due course the sight on television of Unionist and Republican leaders cooperating on the day-to-day affairs of a Northern Irish government—little short of miraculous—was a reality. The IRA formally laid down its arms in 2005, and since then, the prosperity and quality of life of Northern Irish people has improved beyond measure.

Britain's impending departure from the European Union has placed new strains on the relationship between Northern and Southern Ireland (where the Irish Republic is a committed member of the EU),

It is time now for all the parties to live up to all their commitments. Time for North/South bodies to be established to start a new era of co-operation between you and Northern Ireland—I hope agreement on these is now close. Time to set up the institutions of the new government. Time for the gun and the threat of the gun to be taken out of politics once and for all; for decommissioning to start.

I am not asking anyone to surrender. I am asking everyone to declare the victory of peace.

In Belfast or Dublin, people say the same thing: make the agreement work.

It is never far from my mind. My sense of urgency and mission comes from the children in Northern Ireland. I reflect on those who have been victims of violence, whose lives are scarred and twisted through the random wickedness of a terrorist act, on those who grow up in fear, those whose parents and loved ones have died.

And I reflect on those, who though untouched directly by violence, are nonetheless victims—victims of mistrust and misunderstanding who through lack of a political settlement miss the chance of new friendships, new horizons, because of the isolation from others that the sectarian way of life brings.

I reflect on the sheer waste of children taught to hate when I believe passionately children should be taught to think.

No one should ignore the injustices of the past, or the lessons of history. But too often between us, one person's history has been another person's myth. We need not be prisoners of our history.

SPEAKING ABOUT THE GOOD FRIDAY AGREEMENT. THE FIRST SERVING
BRITISH PRIME MINISTER TO ADDRESS IRISH PARLIAMENT

and between Ulster Unionists and mainland Britain. New uncertainty about the future has resulted in a resurgence of violence within Northern Ireland. But life in Ulster is infinitely better and safer than before the Belfast Agreement. Good Friday 1998 was a very good Friday indeed.

RIGHT: *From left to right; Irish prime minister Bertie Aherne; US Senator George Mitchell, who helped broker the deal; and Tony Blair.*

George W. Bush
Address to the Nation
(September 11, 2001)

On a clear, bright morning, September 11, 2001, four passenger jets were hijacked, midair, by nineteen Al-Qaeda terrorists. By the end of the day, nearly 3,000 people had been killed, and over 6,000 injured. Never did the American people need more urgently the strong, comforting assurances of their president.

Two of the planes were crashed into the Twin Towers of the World Trade Center, in lower Manhattan, New York. At first, the buildings stood, allowing many to flee from the fires. But in just under two hours, both had collapsed, killing all those who could not escape and destroying many buildings around them.

The third plane was crashed into the Pentagon, near Arlington, Virginia, the headquarters of the Department of Defense, destroying part of the building. The fourth plane never reached its intended target of the Capitol in Washington, home of the US Congress, and crashed into a field in rural Pennsylvania, brought down in a struggle between the terrorists and passengers, who mounted an attack on their hijackers. From phone records, it has been established that once the hijackers realized the passengers were going to regain control, they flew the airplane into the ground.

That morning, President George W. Bush had been visiting an elementary school in Florida. Initial reports were confused, describing the first attack as a terrible accident. As the truth emerged, Bush recorded a short speech that played on national TV channels. He spoke of the security measures being taken. "Make no mistake, the United States will hunt down and punish those responsible for these cowardly acts," he promised. "Freedom itself was attacked this morning by a faceless coward. And freedom will be defended."

Returning to the White House, the president and his speech-writing team sat down to craft a more measured response. Bush, father of the nation, had to gauge the tone of the speech as carefully as the words he used. By now it was clear that this series of attacks was the worst peacetime loss of life in American history. From a president with a reputation for verbal blunders, Americans required clear, focused, reassuring, and resolute leadership.

TV schedules across America were cleared for 8:30 p.m. George W. Bush addressed the nation from the Oval Office. He spoke briefly and directly, for a little over four minutes. His delivery was calm; his tone carried authority, but he was audibly and visibly experiencing the same mixture of rage and loss as his audience.

He described the nation's "terrible sadness and quiet, unyielding anger," and despite the enormity of the day's events, he insisted that the attacks, designed to terrorize, had failed, because "our country is strong." The twin towers of the World Trade Center might have fallen, but America would be open for business tomorrow.

Anticipating the coming war on terror, he reported the messages of support and sympathy from other nations. "We stand together to win the war against terrorism," he said. And in a message to nations sympathetic to Al-Qaeda, he made it clear that: "We will make no distinction between the terrorists who committed these acts and those who harbor them."

Bush contrasted the heroic acts of the first responders with the "evil, the very worst of human nature" of the terrorists. "A great people has been moved to defend a great nation. . . . None of us will ever forget this day."

Bush's address was perfectly judged. A man often mocked for his inability to express himself clearly had spoken with clarity for America. His approval rating climbed to over 90 percent in the aftermath of the attacks. America was as good as his word in hunting down the terrorists responsible. Many of them were incarcerated in Guantanamo Bay detention camp, where many remain imprisoned. In 2011, Osama bin Laden, the leader of Al-Qaeda, was finally tracked to a house in Pakistan and killed.

Today, our fellow citizens; our way of life, our very freedom came under attack in a series of deliberate and deadly terrorist acts. These acts of mass murder were intended to frighten our nation into chaos and retreat. But they have failed. Our country is strong.

A great people has been moved to defend a great nation. Terrorist attacks can shake the foundations of our biggest buildings, but they cannot touch the foundation of America. These acts shatter steel, but they cannot dent the steel of American resolve. America was targeted for attack because we're the brightest beacon for freedom and opportunity in the world. And no one will keep that light from shining. Today, our nation saw evil—the very worst of human nature—and we responded with the best of America. With the daring of our rescue workers, with the caring for strangers and neighbors who came to give blood and help in any way they could.

Immediately following the first attack, I implemented our government's emergency response plans. Our military is powerful, and it's prepared. . . . The functions of our government continue without interruption. Federal agencies in Washington which had to be evacuated today are reopening for essential personnel tonight and will be open for business tomorrow. Our financial institutions remain strong, and the American economy will be open for business as well.

The search is underway for those who were behind these evil acts. I have directed the full resources of our intelligence and law enforcement communities to find those responsible and to bring them to justice. We will make no distinction between the terrorists who committed these acts and those who harbor them.

ADDRESS TO THE NATION POST 9/11

RIGHT: George W. Bush addresses the nation.

Osama bin Laden
Address to the United States

(October 29, 2004)

High on the Most Wanted Fugitive list after Al-Qaeda's attacks against the US on September 11, Osama bin Laden often seemed to mock America's attempts to capture him. In a rambling video message to the American people broadcast on the Al Jazeera TV network in 2004, he finally admitted responsibility.

I say to you, Allah knows that it had never occurred to us to strike the towers. But after it became unbearable and we witnessed the oppression and tyranny of the American/Israeli coalition against our people in Palestine and Lebanon, it came to my mind.

The events that affected my soul in a direct way started in 1982 when America permitted the Israelis to invade Lebanon and the American Sixth Fleet helped them in that. This bombardment began and many were killed and injured and others were terrorized and displaced.

I couldn't forget those moving scenes, blood and severed limbs, women and children sprawled everywhere. Houses destroyed along with their occupants and high-rises demolished over their residents, rockets raining down on our home without mercy.

The situation was like a crocodile meeting a helpless child, powerless except for his screams. Does the crocodile understand a conversation that doesn't include a weapon? And the whole world saw and heard but it didn't respond.

In those difficult moments many hard-to-describe ideas bubbled in my soul, but in the end they produced an intense feeling of rejection of tyranny, and gave birth to a strong resolve to punish the oppressors.

And as I looked at those demolished towers in Lebanon, it entered my mind that we should punish the oppressor in kind, and that we should destroy towers in America in order that they taste some of what we tasted, and so that they be deterred from killing our women and children.

OSAMA BIN LADEN ADDRESS (VIA VIDEO)

OPPOSITE: A still image taken from the
Bin Laden video message.

in Laden released as many as thirty video and audio tapes between the Twin Towers attacks and his death in 2011, mostly through the Arabic news channel Al Jazeera. In the first, only four weeks after 9/11, he rejoiced that "America has been hit by Allah at its most vulnerable point, destroying, thank God, its most prestigious buildings," but stopped short of accepting culpability. He spoke, naturally, in Arabic, and in the war of words, English translations were sometimes willfully inaccurate in their efforts to prove his guilt.

Bin Laden's guilt was put beyond doubt by the 2004 video. While most later "videos" were, in fact, only audio recordings played over still photographs of the Al-Qaeda leader, he was distinctly animated in this tape, probably a deliberate response to rumors that he had been injured in an air strike. He grabbed the attention of Americans from his opening declaration: "People of America, this talk of mine is for you and concerns the ideal way to prevent another Manhattan."

He claimed that "it had never occurred to us to strike the towers" until he had witnessed civilian casualties, "high-rises demolished over their residents" during the American-backed Israeli invasion of Lebanon in 1982. "[A]s I looked at those demolished towers in Lebanon, it entered my mind that we should punish the oppressor in kind." Al-Qaeda had been justifying innocent civilian deaths of its own terrorist actions since it bombed a hotel in Aden in 1995; it argued that such casualties would either benefit by going to heaven as good Muslims, or go to hell as infidels and therefore deserve to die.

Bin Laden claimed to have given plenty of warning to the US in interviews with Western journalists during the 1990s but to have been ignored by leaders who were "characterized by pride, arrogance, greed and misappropriation of wealth." America fought wars, he said, "to keep busy their various corporations in the field of arms or oil or reconstruction." The 9/11 attacks had cost Al-Qaeda a mere $500,000, but in its aftermath, America had spent over $500 billion. "So we are continuing this policy," said Bin Laden, referring to Al-Qaeda terrorist attacks, "in bleeding America to the point of bankruptcy. The real loser is you, the American people and their economy."

He taunted President George W. Bush by suggesting that, knowing an attack would come, he had deliberately abandoned the occupants of the World Trade Center to their fate while he made an appearance at a school in Miami. "Talking to the little girl about the goat and its butting was more important than occupying himself with the planes and their butting of the skyscrapers. Bush's hands are stained with the blood of all those killed on both sides, all for the sake of oil."

The video was released four days before a US presidential election, and it has been suggested that it was in Bin Laden's interest to get Bush reelected since he would be more determined at any cost to pursue Al-Qaeda. Bush's opponent was the Democrat John Kerry, who had in the past been an outspoken critic of American military involvement overseas. Bush received a 6 percent boost in opinion polls taken immediately after the release of the video and won the election with a comfortable majority of both the electoral and the popular votes.

This was the last verified video footage of Bin Laden to be released. One other tape, in 2007, included a short clip of him in motion, which it was suspected might be old footage. Photographic stills continued to provide proof of his survival, but America pursued him with such vigor that he was forced to live underground for a time.

Eventually, he found sanctuary in Pakistan, where he was able to build himself a fortified compound near the Pakistan Military Academy. It was there that US Navy SEALs found and killed him on May 2, 2011. It fell to President Obama to break the news to the American people, which he did that evening, concluding, "To those families who have lost loved ones to Al-Qaeda's terror, justice has been done."

Barack Obama
Keynote Address at the Democratic National Convention

(July 27, 2004)

In March 2004, excitement started to spread through the Democratic Party about a senator from Illinois who had won a landslide victory in a primary election. Party officials and the media began to take an interest in this young black politician, aged only forty-two, and his star began to rise. Only four months later Barack Obama was chosen to deliver the keynote address at the 2004 Democratic National Convention.

The pundits, the pundits like to slice-and-dice our country into Red States and Blue States; Red States for Republicans, Blue States for Democrats. But I've got news for them, too:

We worship an awesome God in the Blue States, and we don't like federal agents poking around in our libraries in the Red States. We coach Little League in the Blue States and yes, we've got some gay friends in the Red States. There are patriots who opposed the war in Iraq and there are patriots who supported the war in Iraq.

We are one people, all of us pledging allegiance to the stars and stripes, all of us defending the United States of America. In the end, that's what this election is about. Do we participate in a politics of cynicism or do we participate in a politics of hope?

I'm not talking about blind optimism here—the almost willful ignorance that thinks unemployment will go away if we just don't think about it, or the health care crisis will solve itself if we just ignore it. That's not what I'm talking about. I'm talking about something more substantial.

It's the hope of slaves sitting around a fire singing freedom songs. The hope of immigrants setting out for distant shores. The hope of a young naval lieutenant bravely patrolling the Mekong Delta. The hope of a millworker's son who dares to defy the odds. The hope of a skinny kid with a funny name who believes that America has a place for him, too.

Hope in the face of difficulty. Hope in the face of uncertainty. The audacity of hope!

"I Don't See Red America or Blue America" speech, which launched his national visibility

John Kerry was the Democratic nominee for the forthcoming presidential contest against the incumbent George W. Bush. The keynote speech was his to give by rights, but with the agreement of the party's executive he yielded the spotlight to Obama. It was not an entirely selfless act. Democrats recognized Obama's political talent, and if his speech was well received, he had the potential to become a future black presidential candidate, something unprecedented. Such a nominee would secure widespread media attention and cross-community support for the party. If the convention got behind Obama, the American political landscape might never be the same again.

Obama had a lot going for him. He was handsome, articulate, and clear in his ideas; confident and relaxed, whether on a podium, at a press conference or in an impromptu interview in a hotel lobby. He was media friendly and charismatic, reminiscent of a young JFK. It was a powerful cocktail.

During the day, Obama rehearsed his speech in front of party dignitaries. At the climax of a passage intended to unite Americans of all political hues, he said, "We're not red states and blue states; we're all Americans, standing up together for the red, white, and blue." One of John Kerry's aides interrupted to say he would have to cut the line because it resembled one from Kerry's later convention speech accepting his party's nomination.

On the journey back to the hotel, Obama was furious, aware that the keynote speech was a golden opportunity to advance his career, and feeling that Kerry was stealing his best line. Arguably, the passage with which he replaced it was even stronger and more inclusive. "The pundits like to slice-and-dice our country," Obama said in his revised speech, "into Red States and Blue States; Red States for Republicans, Blue States for Democrats. But I've got news for them, too. We worship an awesome God in the Blue States, and we don't like

federal agents poking around in our libraries in the Red States. We coach Little League in the Blue States and, yes, we've got some gay friends in the Red States."

Despite the absence of the phrase, Barack Obama's speech has become known for declaring "I don't see red America or blue America." Obama himself reclaimed it in a CNN interview in 2007, a year before his own nomination for the presidency, when he prefaced an answer with "when I said in 2004 that there were no red states or blue states, there are United States of America."

Elsewhere in his 2004 speech, Barack Obama spoke of his own heritage and America's, using himself as a model of American aspiration and achievement. He was an example of inclusion, and expanding on his theme, he said that "there is not a liberal America and a conservative America—there is the United States of America. We are one people, all of us pledging allegiance to the stars and stripes."

The speech was very well received by convention delegates. Although it was not broadcast live on national TV, news of it spread by word of mouth. Soon, clips were being shown on TV and transcripts published in print. Obama's refreshing appeals for unity and hope were good news for a nation polarized by Iraq, another American war overseas.

John Kerry's acceptance speech included the sentence "Maybe some just see us divided into those red states and blue states, but I see us as one America: red, white, and blue." But Bush's approval ratings were still high in the patriotic aftermath of 9/11, and when Kerry lost the presidential race later that year, it was clear to Democrats who would be their next hope. Obama's 2004 convention rhetoric propelled him to the White House only four years later.

LEFT: *Barack Obama delivers the keynote speech on the second night of the Democratic National Convention at the Fleet Center in Boston.*

Steve Jobs
"Today Apple is going to reinvent the phone"

(January 9, 2007)

Macworld was an annual trade show held in San Francisco every January from 1987 to 2014 to celebrate the technology of Apple Inc. From 1997 the highlight was a keynote address from Apple cofounder Steve Jobs who used the occasion to announce developments and new products.

Apple's Steve Jobs and Steve Wozniak have left behind them a trail of groundbreaking personal microcomputing devices as testament to their technological flair and marketplace savvy. As Jobs noted during his 2007 Macworld keynote talk: "Every once in a while, a revolutionary product comes along that changes everything. . . . Apple's been very fortunate. It's been able to introduce a few of these into the world."

From the first Apple computer to the iMac via the Graphical User Interface, which allowed users to do more than type, from radical laser printers to world domination with the iPod—which held over 60 percent of the MP3 player market in 2007—Apple was a pioneer. During his twelve-year estrangement from the company between 1985 and 1997, Jobs found time to transform the world of computer-generated image-making too, by funding Pixar and the world's first fully computer-animated feature film, *Toy Story*.

Back at the helm of Apple, Jobs continued to develop technology by looking at its applications from the user's perspective. This ability to understand the demands and wishes of the marketplace also made him a first-class communicator. His Macworld lectures, sometimes called Stevenotes, were unmissable, not just for the latest Apple innovations but because of his obvious delight in sharing them with his audience.

In 2007, he took great pleasure in demonstrating the ease of use of the new Apple TV interface and was positively gleeful in telling the audience of iTunes's expansion and the iPod's prevalence over Microsoft's then new Zunes player. But all this was just a warm-up for what he was about to unveil. "This is a day I've been looking forward to for two-and-a-half years," he

confided, half an hour into his notes. "Well, today, we're introducing three revolutionary products."

Jobs listed them—a widescreen iPod with touch controls, a revolutionary mobile phone, and a breakthrough Internet communications device. He listed them again, and again, and again, before interrupting himself: "Are you getting it? These are not three separate devices, this is one device, and we are calling it iPhone. Today, today Apple is going to reinvent the phone, and here it is."

Jobs had a teacher's technique for getting information across: tell them what you're going to teach them, teach them, then tell them again what you've taught. For the next hour Steve Jobs excitedly showed off the new device's capabilities with the help of a giant screen linked to the iPhone in his hand. The term "smartphone" already existed, but as he reminded his audience with reference to his rivals at Motorola, Blackberry, and elsewhere, they were neither very smart nor very easy to use.

By contrast, the iPhone's fingertouch technology ("let's not use a stylus—we're gonna use the best pointing device in the world"), its large screen size ("highest resolution we've ever shipped"), and its ability to synchronize content to the user's computer was intuitively simple. In prearranged exchanges with colleagues at Apple, he demonstrated its phone, text and email functions; its capacity and quality for music and video, and its potential for powerful apps, including Google Maps.

"We've been innovating like crazy for the last few years on this," he said with obvious pride, "and we filed for over 200 patents for all the inventions in iPhone,

This is a day I've been looking forward to for two-and-a-half years.

Every once in a while, a revolutionary product comes along that changes everything. And Apple has been—well, first of all, one's very fortunate if you get to work on just one of these in your career.

Apple's been very fortunate. It's been able to introduce a few of these into the world. In 1984, we introduced the Macintosh. It didn't just change Apple, it changed the whole computer industry. In 2001, we introduced the first iPod, and it didn't just—it didn't just change the way we all listen to music, it changed the entire music industry.

Well, today, we're introducing three revolutionary products of this class. The first one: is a widescreen iPod with touch controls. The second: is a revolutionary mobile phone. And the third is a breakthrough Internet communications device.

So, three things: a widescreen iPod with touch controls; a revolutionary mobile phone; and a breakthrough Internet communications device. An iPod, a phone, and an Internet communicator. An iPod, a phone . . . are you getting it? These are not three separate devices, this is one device, and we are calling it iPhone. Today, today Apple is going to reinvent the phone, and here it is.

. . . You know, there's an old Wayne Gretzky quote that I love: 'I skate to where the puck is going to be, not where it has been.' And we've always tried to do that at Apple.

MACWORLD SPEECH LAUNCHING THE NEW APPLE PHONE

and we intend to protect them. After today, I don't think anyone is gonna look at these phones quite the same way again."

It's easy to forget, now that genuinely smartphones are such an integral part of our lives, just how innovative the iPhone was. It is now in its eleventh generation, with many imitators, but by general consensus still the market leader. There are nearly two and a half million apps for the iPhone in Apple's App Store. As Steve Jobs boasted presciently in 2007, "iPhone is like having your life in your pocket. It's the ultimate digital device."

RIGHT: *Steve Jobs, in trademark black turtleneck and jeans, presents his vision of the future.*

Bill Gates
Commencement Address at Harvard

(June 7, 2007)

Bill Gates achieved spectacular success through the ubiquity of Microsoft's software, a business that made him the world's richest man. Together with his wife, Melinda, he set about sharing that wealth, and at a commencement addresss at Harvard University, he explained the ethos of his Giving Pledge.

Bill Gates, "Harvard's most successful dropout" as the university's student newspaper described him, quit his studies there after two years to found Microsoft with an old school friend, Paul Allen. At last in 2007, he was awarded an honorary diploma, and afterward gave a graduation address to students who had managed to stay the distance. "I'm changing my job next year," he joked with them, "and it'll be nice to finally have a college degree on my résumé."

Microsoft grew rapidly from its inception in 1975, working first with Altair and then with IBM, for whom it developed the MS-DOS operating system. The company launched its Windows operating system in 1985, and Gates continued to write software for that until the end of the decade when he settled on a fully managerial role.

At its height, Windows ran on over 90 percent of all personal computers (PCs). The success of Windows was assisted by Microsoft's aggressively protective strategies, which gave many users no option but to adopt it; and in 1998 Microsoft was successfully prosecuted under antitrust laws. Although Google's Android system now dominates the market for tablets and smartphones, Windows remains the most popular system for PCs. It has made Gates a very, very wealthy man.

Gate's theme at Harvard's graduation day was philanthropy. "I left Harvard with no real awareness of the awful inequities in the world," he said. "It took me decades to find out. Imagine that you had a few hours a week and a few dollars a month to donate to a cause. Where would you spend it? For [my wife] Melinda and me the challenge is the same: how can we do the most good for the greatest number with the resources we have?"

The new job to which Gates referred was his transition from entrepreneur to fulltime philanthropist. "Humanity's greatest advances are not its discoveries," said the man who had transformed the world through the spread of PCs. "Whether through democracy, strong public education, quality healthcare or broad economic opportunity, reducing inequity is the highest human achievement." He explained to students the ease with which many millions of deaths in the world could be prevented but were not, because the victims had "no power in the market and no voice in the system. But you and I have both."

Convinced that most people did care about preventable death, Gates analyzed the process of turning caring into action—"see a problem, see a solution, see the impact." PCs assisted the process, increasing dramatically "the number of brilliant minds we can have working together on the same problem."

Gates has always had a reputation for being tough in the boardroom, and now he issued a direct challenge to

Let me make a request of the deans and the professors—the intellectual leaders here at Harvard: As you hire new faculty, award tenure, review curriculum, and determine degree requirements, please ask yourselves:

Should our best minds be dedicated to solving our biggest problems?

Should Harvard encourage its faculty to take on the world's worst inequities? Should Harvard students learn about the depth of global poverty . . . the prevalence of world hunger . . . the scarcity of clean water . . . the girls kept out of school . . . the children who die from diseases we can cure?

Should the world's most privileged people learn about the lives of the world's least privileged? These are not rhetorical questions—you will answer with your policies.

My mother, who was filled with pride the day I was admitted here—never stopped pressing me to do more for others. A few days before my wedding, she hosted a bridal event, at which she read aloud a letter about marriage that she had written to Melinda. My mother was very ill with cancer at the time, but she saw one more opportunity to deliver her message, and at the close of the letter she said: 'From those to whom much is given, much is expected.'

When you consider what those of us here in this Yard have been given—in talent, privilege, and opportunity—there is almost no limit to what the world has a right to expect from us.

COMMENCEMENT ADDRESS AT HARVARD

the intellectual leaders of Harvard University. "Should our best minds be dedicated to solving our biggest problems? . . . Should the world's most privileged people learn about the lives of the world's least privileged? These are not rhetorical questions—you will answer with your policies." And he reminded all present of their ivory-towered good fortune. "When you consider what those of us here in this Yard have been given—in talent, privilege, and opportunity—there is almost no limit to what the world has a right to expect from us."

He closed by urging each graduate: "Be activists. Take on the big inequities. Judge yourselves not on your professional accomplishments alone, but also on how well you have addressed the world's deepest inequities . . . on how well you treated people a world away who have

nothing in common with you but their humanity."

In 2010, Gates and his fellow billionaire Warren Buffett devised The Giving Pledge, a moral commitment by the wealthiest in the world to donate half of their fortunes to good causes, either during their lifetimes or after their deaths. To date there are over 150 signatories to the pledge, committing in total over $365 billion dollars. As Bill Gates told students in 2007, quoting his mother who was fond of quoting the Gospel according to Luke, "From those to whom much is given, much is expected."

OPPOSITE: Bill Gates prepares to give the commencement speech at Harvard University, June 7, 2007, in Cambridge, Massachusetts.

Barack Obama
"Yes, We Can!"

(November 4, 2008)

It is impossible to overstate the significance of the moment when Barack Obama, the freshman senator from Illinois, was elected as America's forty-fourth president. The first nonwhite occupant of the Oval Office was put there not just by the landslide of 2008 but by 250 years of campaigns against denials of human rights.

Barack Obama's political ascendency was swift. Elected to the Senate only four years before he was elected to the White House, he had the savvy and charisma of a much-more-experienced politician. His presidential campaign was for inclusion in society and against the war in Iraq, opposite Republican candidate John McCain, a veteran of the Vietnam War. Twenty-five years younger than McCain, Obama emphasized his youthful energy by often appearing without a tie, looking like a man prepared to roll his sleeves up and do the work that needed to be done. The election took place against the backdrop of crippling global recession.

When McCain conceded defeat on the evening of November 4, 2008, Obama chose to make his acceptance speech not from Democratic party HQ but from Grant Park in Chicago, where nearly a quarter of a million supporters had gathered. "If there is anyone out there," he began, "who still doubts that America is a place where all things are possible, who still wonders if the dream of our founders is alive in our time; who still questions the power of our democracy, tonight is your answer." Most memorably he told the crowd: "Tonight, because of what we did on this day, in this election, at this defining moment, change has come to America."

Obama looked to the future: America at war and going through the worst financial crisis in a century. Several times he returned to the thought that winning the election was not an end in itself: "I know you didn't

[vote for me] just to win an election"; "this victory alone is not the change we seek."

In the depths of recession, Obama metaphorically rolled up his sleeves as he urged all Americans "to join in the work of remaking this nation block by block, brick by brick, calloused hand by calloused hand. We cannot have a thriving Wall Street," he said, "while Main Street suffers. We rise or fall as one nation, one people."

Addressing an even larger audience, he turned to the world: "to all those watching tonight from beyond our shores, from parliaments and palaces to those who are huddled around radios in the forgotten corners of the world—our stories are singular, but our destiny is shared."

Evocative and poetic as much of his address to the crowd was, the closing section of Barack Obama's acceptance speech was a masterpiece of oratory. He switched from the billions who were watching and listening to him that night, to just one person. One voter. "She's a lot like the millions of others who stood in line to make their voice heard in this election, except for one thing—Ann Nixon Cooper is 106 years old. She was born just a generation past slavery; a time . . . when someone like her couldn't vote for two reasons—because she was a woman and because of the color of her skin."

Through Ms. Cooper's life, Obama showed his American audience the struggles of a century "when women's voices were silenced . . . when there was despair in the dust bowl and depression across the land . . . when bombs fell on our harbor." After each of "the times we

Ann Nixon Cooper is 106 years old.

She was born just a generation past slavery; a time when there were no cars on the road or planes in the sky; when someone like her couldn't vote for two reasons—because she was a woman and because of the color of her skin.

And tonight, I think about all that she's seen throughout her century in America—the heartache and the hope; the struggle and the progress; the times we were told that we can't, and the people who pressed on with that American creed: Yes, we can.

At a time when women's voices were silenced and their hopes dismissed, she lived to see them stand up and speak out and reach for the ballot. Yes, we can.

When there was despair in the dust bowl and depression across the land, she saw a nation conquer fear itself with a New Deal, new jobs, a new sense of common purpose. Yes, we can.

When the bombs fell on our harbor and tyranny threatened the world, she was there to witness a generation rise to greatness and a democracy was saved. Yes, we can.

She was there for the buses in Montgomery, the hoses in Birmingham, a bridge in Selma, and a preacher from Atlanta who told a people that 'We Shall Overcome.' Yes, we can.

A man touched down on the moon, a wall came down in Berlin, a world was connected by our own science and imagination. And this year, in this election, she touched her finger to a screen, and cast her vote, because after 106 years in America, through the best of times and the darkest of hours, she knows how America can change. Yes, we can.

"Yes, We Can" victory speech

were told that we can't, the people pressed on with that American creed"—and he turned to the people—"YES, WE CAN!"

Seven times he said it, gradually shifting from America's trials to its triumphs—"a preacher from Atlanta who told a people that 'We Shall Overcome,'" a man on the moon, the end of the Berlin wall—"because after 106 years in America, through the best of times and the darkest of hours, she knows how America can change. YES, WE CAN!"

When President Obama was reelected in 2012, he became the first Democratic president since FDR to win with an absolute majority of the popular vote twice. Although his successor President Trump moved quickly to dismantle many of the inclusive innovations that he had introduced, Obama is considered among the ten best presidents that America ever had.

OPPOSITE: The historic headline from USA Today.

We call upon the developed nations to support the expansion of education opportunities for girls in the developing world. We call upon all communities to be tolerant, to reject prejudice based on caste, creed, sect, color, religion or agenda to ensure freedom and equality for women so they can flourish. We cannot all succeed when half of us are held back. We call upon our sisters around the world to be brave, to embrace the strength within themselves and realize their full potential.

Dear brothers and sisters, we want schools and education for every child's bright future. We will continue our journey to our destination of peace and education. No one can stop us. We will speak up for our rights and we will bring change to our voice. We believe in the power and the strength of our words. Our words can change the whole world because we are all together, united for the cause of education. And if we want to achieve our goal, then let us empower ourselves with the weapon of knowledge and let us shield ourselves with unity and togetherness.

Dear brothers and sisters, we must not forget that millions of people are suffering from poverty and injustice and ignorance. We must not forget that millions of children are out of their schools. We must not forget that our sisters and brothers are waiting for a bright, peaceful future.

So let us wage a glorious struggle against illiteracy, poverty and terrorism, let us pick up our books and our pens, they are the most powerful weapons. One child, one teacher, one book and one pen can change the world. Education is the only solution. Education first. Thank you. **"**

"WORLDWIDE ACCESS TO EDUCATION" SPEECH, GIVEN ON HER SIXTEENTH BIRTHDAY

LEFT: Malala attended Edgbaston High School before taking up a degree in Philosophy, Politics and Economics (PPE) at Lady Margaret Hall, Oxford University—the same degree and college as Benazir Bhutto.

Malala Yousafzai
"The right of education for every child"
(July 12, 2013)

Malala Yousafzai was already a confident, outspoken individual when she was the target of a Taliban murder attempt at the age of fifteen. Surviving that attack, she attracted the world's attention, of which she took full advantage to argue for women's right to education.

Malala Yousafzai was born in Khyber Pakhtunkhwa, formerly known as the North-West Frontier, a region of northern Pakistan. It has been an area of military conflict since the terrifying events of September 11, 2001. When she was ten, Taliban forces overran Malala's home district of Swat. They imposed Sharia law on the area for the next two years.

The BBC Urdu service persuaded her to write a blog about life for a schoolgirl under the Taliban (which was opposed to education for girls). Malala, whose father ran schools in Swat, was a fierce advocate of education for women and a persistent critic of life under the Taliban. The resulting international interest in her young but articulate voice persuaded the Taliban to mount an assassination attempt, and she was shot through the head on a school bus on October 9, 2012. She was fifteen.

Remarkably, she survived, and after treatment in Pakistan and England, which included reconstructive surgery on her skull and a cochlear implant to restore her damaged hearing, she made a full recovery. The attack on a schoolgirl caused outrage around the world. In Pakistan the protests by millions led directly to the country's first ever bill guaranteeing the right to education. In Britain and America politicians expressed their disgust, and United Nations Secretary-General Ban Ki-moon condemned the crime as a cowardly act.

Malala, released from hospital in January 2013, was invited to address UN delegates on July 12 that year. The date was her sixteenth birthday and the first time she had spoken publicly since she was shot. For the occasion she wore a shawl that had belonged to her childhood hero Benazir Bhutto, the outspoken female former prime minister of Pakistan who was assassinated in 2007 while campaigning in Rawalpindi.

Malala spoke in measured tones and with a remarkably mature sense of oratory. In one moving, rhythmic passage she said she wished no revenge on her attacker. "Even if there was a gun in my hand and he was standing in front of me, I would not shoot him. This is the compassion I have learned from Mohamed, the prophet of mercy, Jesus Christ and Lord Buddha. This is the legacy of change I have inherited from Martin Luther King, Nelson Mandela and Mohammed Ali Jinnah. This is the philosophy of nonviolence that I have learned from Gandhi, Bacha Khan and Mother Teresa. And this is the forgiveness that I have learned from my father and from my mother. This is what my soul is telling me: be peaceful and love everyone."

In an impassioned plea for education rather than warfare, especially for women, she concluded: "[L]et us wage a global struggle against illiteracy, poverty and terrorism, let us pick up our books and our pens, they are the most powerful weapons. One child, one teacher, one book and one pen can change the world."

A year later that plea, and the campaign that supported it, led to an extraordinary honor for Malala—the 2014 Nobel Prize for Peace. She, a Muslim Pakistani, shared it with Kailash Satyarthi, a Hindu Indian who also fought for children's rights. He was sixty years old, she—at seventeen—the youngest ever recipient of a Nobel Prize. Malala Yousafzai is now reading politics at Oxford University.

"Emily Doe"
Stanford Rape Trial
(June 2, 2016)

When a Stanford student was raped on campus, the prosecution belittled the victim in court an attempt to get their privileged client a lenient sentence. The presiding judge duly obliged, despite a powerful speech delivered by the victim that struck an immediate chord with thousands of victims of sexual violence.

Two male Stanford University students were riding their bikes on campus around 1 a.m. on January 18, 2015, when they witnessed a man on top of what appeared to be an unconscious and partially naked woman behind a dumpster. The concerned students approached the scene and chased the man when he attempted to flee, holding him down until the police arrived.

The victim, who became known as "Emily Doe," had attended the same party earlier in the evening as the accused, Brock Turner. Both were heavily intoxicated, with Doe's blood alcohol content found to be three times the legal driving limit. However, while Turner later claimed that she had consented to his sexual advances, Doe had no memory of ever even having met him. When she regained consciousness at a local hospital, there was dried blood on her hands and elbows, and pine needles in her hair. A nurse who performed an examination determined that she had experienced significant (physical injury and bruising) and penetrating trauma.

During the criminal case, formally known as *People of the State of California vs. Brock Allen Turner*, Turner's lawyers made every attempt to discredit Doe, portraying Brock as an all-American athlete with a promising future ahead of him, and Doe as a willing participant.

Turner was ultimately found guilty on three counts: assault with intent to rape an intoxicated woman, sexually penetrating an intoxicated person with a foreign object, and sexually penetrating an unconscious person with a foreign object. Although he faced up to fourteen years in a state prison, Santa Clara county's Superior Court Judge Aaron Persky sentenced Turner to only six months in county jail and probation, saying that a more severe sentence could have a drastic, negative impact on the aspiring Olympic swimmer. Turner was also ordered to register as a sex offender for life. The backlash from the public was severe, the sentencing viewed as a light slap on the wrist by a judge showing bias in favor of a privileged, young white man.

During the sentencing on June 2, 2016, Emily Doe read aloud to Turner an emotional 7,244-word letter she had written, recounting her ordeal and its devastating effects that continued to impact her daily life. The letter was published in its entirety on BuzzFeed the following day. Heartbreaking lines such as "in newspapers my name was 'unconscious intoxicated woman,' ten syllables, and nothing more than that. For a while, I believed that that was all I was" resonated deeply with people, particularly other victims of sexual abuse, and the letter soon spread like wildfire on social media, resulting in eight million views in only three days.

On June 4, another letter, by Brock Turner's father, was released. It pleaded with the judge to be lenient with his son, claiming the sentence was a "steep price to pay for 20 minutes of action," inciting even more anger and criticism against the Turners.

Doe's speech continued to circulate, and showings of support poured in from around the globe, among them a letter from Vice President Joe Biden titled "An Open Letter to a Courageous Young Woman," which included impassioned words such as "I am filled with furious anger—both that this happened to you and that our culture is still so broken that you were ever put in the position of defending your own worth."

At Stanford's 2016 commencement ceremony, members of the graduating class expressed their anger and frustration at the verdict by carrying handmade posters protesting rape culture and wearing signs with the fraction "1/3" on top of their mortarboards, representing the ratio of women statistically likely to

Your Honor, if it is all right, for the majority of this statement I would like to address the defendant directly

You don't know me, but you've been inside me, and that's why we're here today. . . .

I want to show people that one night of drinking can ruin two lives. You and me. You are the cause, I am the effect. You have dragged me through this hell with you, dipped me back into that night again and again. You knocked down both our towers, I collapsed at the same time you did. If you think I was spared, came out unscathed, that today I ride off into sunset, while you suffer the greatest blow, you are mistaken. Nobody wins. We have all been devastated, we have all been trying to find some meaning in all of this suffering. Your damage was concrete; stripped of titles, degrees, enrollment. My damage was internal, unseen, I carry it with me. You took away my worth, my privacy, my energy, my time, my safety, my intimacy, my confidence, my own voice, until today.

See one thing we have in common is that we were both unable to get up in the morning. I am no stranger to suffering. You made me a victim. In newspapers my name was "unconscious intoxicated woman", ten syllables, and nothing more than that. For a while, I believed that that was all I was. I had to force myself to relearn my real name, my identity. To relearn that this is not all that I am. That I am not just a drunk victim at a frat party found behind a dumpster, while you are the All-American swimmer at a top university, innocent until proven guilty, with so much at stake. I am a human being who has been irreversibly hurt, my life was put on hold for over a year, waiting to figure out if I was worth something. . . .

(ADDITIONAL EXCERPTS ON PAGE 214)

EMILY DOE STATEMENT TO COURT

suffer sexual or physical violence in their lifetime.

The effects of *The People vs. Turner* and Doe's speech continued to make an impact long after the trial ended. California state legislature eventually passed two bills that would toughen sexual assault law; the first expanded California's definition of rape by including nonconsensual digital penetration and the second mandated a minimum prison sentence of three years for assault of an unconscious victim.

The anger toward Judge Aaron Persky eventually boiled over, and an online petition to recall the judge gathered more than 1.3 million signatures. Ultimately, he was removed from his position on June 5, 2018, the first judge to be recalled in California in more than 80 years.

Meanwhile, Doe's powerful and moving address to the court, which has been read more than eleven million times, has changed the conversation about sexual assault and rape culture forever.

Stephen Hawking
"AI will be either the best, or the worst thing, ever to happen to humanity"
(October 19, 2016)

In his final years the physicist Stephen Hawking gave considerable public thought to the future of artificial intelligence (AI). The wheelchair-bound author of A Brief History of Time was invited to speak at the opening of the new Leverhulme Centre for the Future of Intelligence, in Cambridge, England, in 2016.

Diagnosed with motor neuron disease in 1963 and given two years to live, Stephen Hawking died fifty-five years later at the age of seventy-six. One by one his muscles stopped functioning, and for speech he relied on a computer-activated voice synthesizer, which he controlled at first by hand and later by a single muscle in his cheek.

His robotic "voice" was familiar to millions through his public comments on science issues of the day and his guest appearances on TV shows such as *The Big Bang Theory*. As technology advanced he was offered other voices that sounded more human, but he chose to retain the metallic tone that was by then recognizably his.

In 2014, Hawking and space travel entrepreneur Elon Musk both expressed concerns about the dangers of uncontrolled research into AI. Both men sat on the board of the Boston-based Future of Life Institute, which kept a watch on developments in AI that might compromise human existence. They were among the signatories to a public letter in January 2015, which included the observation that "because of the great potential of AI, it is important to research how to reap its benefits while avoiding potential pitfalls."

The pitfalls included creating machines and systems that could not be controlled by a human being after they had been set up and might make "wrong" decisions, for example, based purely on statistical analysis of data and not on the moral dimensions of a given situation. In a road accident for example, should a self-driving car swerve to avoid killing someone if that meant causing lesser injuries to many more bystanders?

The letter called for more investigation of this difficult area, and at the opening of the new AI research center in Cambridge, Hawking quipped, "I am very glad someone was listening to me." It's not easy to tell jokes with a voice synthesizer, but he welcomed the establishment of the research center with another wry comment: "We spend a great deal of time studying history, which, let's face it, is mostly the history of stupidity. So it's a welcome change that people are studying instead the future of intelligence."

Hawking was enthusiastic about the potential for computers to imitate human intelligence and even surpass it. "The potential benefits of creating intelligence are huge," he said. "We cannot predict what we might achieve, when our own minds are amplified by AI." He stressed the noble uses to which AI might be put in improving the environment damaged by the earlier technological revolution of the industrial age. "And surely," he pleaded, "we will aim to eradicate disease and poverty?"

But limits should be placed on AI's ability to think entirely for itself. "Alongside the benefits, AI will also bring dangers, like powerful autonomous weapons, or new ways for the few to oppress the many. It will bring great disruption to our economy. And in the future, AI could develop a will of its own—a will that is in conflict with ours."

"In short," Hawking finished, "the rise of powerful AI will be either the best, or the worst thing, ever to happen to humanity. We do not yet know which." In the spring of 2018, stories began to appear in the press of deaths caused by driverless cars.

I believe there is no deep difference between what can be achieved by a biological brain and what can be achieved by a computer. It therefore follows that computers can, in theory, emulate human intelligence—and exceed it.

Artificial intelligence research is now progressing rapidly. Recent landmarks such as self-driving cars, or a computer winning at the game of Go, are signs of what is to come. Enormous levels of investment are pouring into this technology. The achievements we have seen so far will surely pale against what the coming decades will bring.

The potential benefits of creating intelligence are huge. We cannot predict what we might achieve, when our own minds are amplified by AI. Perhaps with the tools of this new technological revolution, we will be able to undo some of the damage done to the natural world by the last one—industrialization. And surely we will aim to finally eradicate disease and poverty. Every aspect of our lives will be transformed. In short, success in creating AI, could be the biggest event in the history of our civilization.

But it could also be the last, unless we learn how to avoid the risks. Alongside the benefits, AI will also bring dangers, like powerful autonomous weapons, or new ways for the few to oppress the many. It will bring great disruption to our economy. And in the future, AI could develop a will of its own—a will that is in conflict with ours.

In short, the rise of powerful AI will be either the best, or the worst thing, ever to happen to humanity. We do not yet know which.

EXPLORING THE IMPACT OF ARTIFICIAL INTELLIGENCE SPEECH

The Leverhulme Centre for the Future of Intelligence declares its aims as, "to bring together the best of human intelligence so that we can make the most of machine intelligence," drawing on "a global community to ensure that Artificial Intelligence benefits all humankind." It's a pity that Stephen Hawking's very human intelligence is no longer around to contribute to the subject.

RIGHT: Born on January 8, 1942, the 300th anniversary of Galileo Galilei's death, Stephen Hawking died on March 14, 2018, the 139th anniversary of Albert Einstein's birth.

Ashley Judd
"I am a nasty woman"

(January 21, 2017)

The 2016 US election was an ill-tempered affair. Republican candidate Donald Trump had no political experience and did not play by the rules; Democrat Hillary Clinton came across as elitist and out of touch. But Trump's insults to her and other women triggered the biggest political protest ever seen in the capital.

During the campaign, a 2005 audio recording surfaced of Donald Trump, then the star of reality TV series *The Apprentice*, describing in the lewdest terms his attempted physical advances on women. He shrugged off his remarks as locker room banter, but two weeks later during the final election debate, he interrupted Hillary Clinton to call her "a nasty woman." The term became a badge of honor for many of Clinton's female supporters. Feminists around the world responded to Trump's perceived misogyny by holding 673 Women's Marches in eighty-two countries on the day after his inauguration.

The largest Women's March was in Washington, where estimates of the number of protesters range from half a million to a million. The size of the crowd was all the more impressive in comparison to the relatively poor turnout for the inauguration ceremony the day before. Speakers included the feminist figurehead Gloria Steinem, documentary filmmaker Michael Moore and celebrities like Scarlett Johansson.

Ashley Judd, best known for screen roles—including the film *Double Jeopardy* and the TV series *Missing*—gave one of the most impassioned speeches of the day. It consisted of a poem that she had seen performed by its nineteen-year-old author Nina Donovan some weeks earlier, called "Nasty Woman." As Donovan told her local newspaper in Franklin, Kentucky, "The second he called Hillary a nasty woman, I said: 'Oh man, I've got to write a nasty woman piece.' I reclaimed it."

"I am a nasty woman," it began. "I'm not as nasty as a man who looks like he bathes in Cheetos dust." Trump's hair color has been compared to the corn-based snack.

"I'm not as nasty as racism, fraud, conflict of interest, homophobia, sexual assault, white supremacy, misogyny; yeah, I'm a nasty woman—a loud, vulgar, proud woman."

Trump's casual sexism had, it seemed, reignited the frustrated anger of women who, more than fifty years after the publication of Betty Friedan's feminist classic *The Feminine Mystique*, couldn't believe they still had to fight this battle. "I'm nasty like the battles my grandmothers fought to get me into that voting booth. I'm nasty like the fight for wage equality." Donovan reclaimed the explicit terms that Trump had used in his locker room banter, then asked rhetorically, "Tell me why pads and tampons are taxed when Viagra and Rogaine are not? Is the bloodstain on my jeans more embarrassing than the thinning of your hair?"

Confronting Trump's inappropriate sexual behavior directly, Donovan's poem said she spent half her life lowering her eyes, "hoping you don't mistake eye contact for wanting physical contact. Half my life I have been zipping up my smile hoping you don't think I want to unzip your jeans." Trump during his campaign unleashed a particularly feminist fury. Women's bodies, Donovan had written, were not for grabbing but for raising new generations of nasty women. "So if you are a nasty woman, or you love someone who is, let me hear you say HELL YEAH!"

As Ashley Judd finished, the million-strong crowd responded in kind: "HELL YEAH!" Video of her performance of Nina Donovan's poem went viral on social media. It was one of the outstanding addresses of the Women's March, which, sadly, served to heighten the divisive nature of Trump's presidency. Judd received praise and abuse in equal measure on Twitter, and was moved later in the year to describe her own experiences of abuse at the hands of disgraced movie mogul Harvey Weinstein. There were, it became clear in 2017, a lot of nasty men out there.

I am a nasty woman.

I'm not as nasty as a man who looks like he bathes in Cheetos dust. A man whose words are a distract to America; Electoral College-sanctioned hate speech contaminating this national anthem.

I am not as nasty as Confederate flags being tattooed across my city. Maybe the South actually is gonna rise again; maybe for some it never really fell. Blacks are still in shackles and graves just for being Black. Slavery has been re-interpreted as the prison system in front of people who see melanin as animal skin.

I am not as nasty as a swastika painted on a pride flag. And I didn't know devils could be resurrected, but I feel Hitler in these streets—a mustache traded for a toupee; Nazis re-named the cabinet; electro-conversion therapy the new gas chambers, shaming the gay out of America turning rainbows into suicide notes.

EXTRACT FROM WOMEN'S MARCH SPEECH, "NASTY WOMAN," BY NINA DONOVAN

LEFT: Ashley Judd speaking at the Women's March in Washington, D.C.

Mark Zuckerberg
Commencement Address at Harvard

(May 25, 2017)

Following in Bill Gates's footsteps, Facebook founder Mark Zuckerberg dropped out of Harvard University to set up the business that made his fortune. Zuckerberg returned to Harvard in 2017, as Gates had done ten years earlier, to collect an honorary degree and to address that year's graduating students.

As of January 2018, there were 2.2 billion active Facebook accounts. That's enough for more than one in every four people on the planet. Facebook's reach to the farthest corners of our world must surely exceed even Mark Zuckerberg's wildest dreams. "I remember telling [my friend] I was excited to connect the Harvard community, but one day someone would connect the whole world," he told Harvard graduates on his return. "It never occurred to me that someone might be us."

The market access that Facebook provides to advertisers, based on data about those users, is its main source of revenue and helped its market value pass the $500 billion mark in 2017—by coincidence in the same week that Amazon reached the same milestone. Only Google, Apple, and Bill Gates's Microsoft were worth more at the time.

The social networking Internet site began life as a facility for Harvard students in 2004, gradually expanding to include universities across northern America. By 2006, it was open to anyone over the age of thirteen. And, it seems, everyone over the age of thirteen wanted to sign up. To be "Facebook-Friends" with someone meant to be part of a community, and it was to community and communal purpose that Zuckerberg devoted his speech.

"I'm not here," he began, "to give you the standard commencement. 'Finding your purpose' isn't enough.

The challenge for our generation is creating a world where everyone has a sense of purpose." People lacked purpose, he argued, because of changes in society and in work practices. "Purpose is that sense that we are part of something bigger than ourselves. Today, many people are disconnected."

He proposed three ways to redress that disconnection. First, come up with "big meaningful projects"—public works. He gave the example of the 300,000 people who worked toward putting a man on the moon, a task that not only gave them purpose but "gave our whole country a sense of pride that we could do great things." Great things start small. "Ideas don't come out fully formed. You just have to get started," Zuckerberg said, giving Facebook as the obvious illustration. "The idea of a single eureka moment is a dangerous lie," he added, one that discouraged people from beginning for fear of being ridiculed or of making mistakes.

In an entrepreneurial society, Zuckerberg's second idea was to redefine equality as the right of everyone, not just the wealthy, to "take lots of shots" at success. "Every generation expands its definition of equality," he observed. "Previous generations fought for the vote and civil rights. Now it's time to define a new social contract for our generation." Borrowing from Bill Gates's graduation address ten years earlier, he appealed for a society

Every generation has its defining works. More than 300,000 people worked to put a man on the moon—including that janitor. Millions of volunteers immunized children around the world against polio. Millions of more people built the Hoover dam and other great projects.

These projects didn't just provide purpose for the people doing those jobs, they gave our whole country a sense of pride that we could do great things. Now it's our turn to do great things. I know, you're probably thinking: I don't know how to build a dam, or get a million people involved in anything.

But let me tell you a secret: no one does when they begin. Ideas don't come out fully formed. They only become clear as you work on them. You just have to get started.

Movies and pop culture get this all wrong. The idea of a single eureka moment is a dangerous lie. It makes us feel inadequate since we haven't had ours. It prevents people with seeds of good ideas from getting started.

It's good to be idealistic. But be prepared to be misunderstood. Anyone working on a big vision will get called crazy, even if you end up right. Anyone working on a complex problem will get blamed for not fully understanding the challenge, even though it's impossible to know everything upfront. Anyone taking initiative will get criticized for moving too fast, because there's always someone who wants to slow you down.

In our society, we often don't do big things because we're so afraid of making mistakes that we ignore all the things wrong today if we do nothing. The reality is, anything we do will have issues in the future. But that can't keep us from starting.

COMMENCEMENT ADDRESS AT HARVARD

"that measures progress not just by economic metrics but by how many of us have a role we find meaningful."

It was a surprisingly idealistic address from the Facebook founder, who has often been accused of breaching the trust of his Facebook community by harvesting information about them purely for the benefit of his advertisers and the income they bring him. But he acknowledged the luck, wealth, and privilege that gave him and his fellow Harvard students the capacity to succeed. "Giving everyone the freedom to pursue purpose isn't free," he admitted. "People like me should pay for it. Many of you will do well and you should too.

"The third way we can create a sense of purpose for everyone is by building community," he continued. Again he offered Facebook as an example. "This is my story too. A student in a dorm room, connecting one community at a time and keeping at it until one day we connect the whole world. Class of 2017, you are graduating into a world that needs purpose. It's up to you to create it."

OPPOSITE: Mark Zuckerberg speaking at Harvard University.

James Comey
Senate Testimony

(June 8, 2017)

In September 2013, President Barack Obama appointed James Comey, a former US deputy attorney general, to be director of the FBI. It was a ten-year fixed term appointment. Comey replaced Robert Mueller, who would later come to public attention as Special Counsel in the investigation of Russian interference in the 2016 presidential election. Comey ruffled feathers on both sides of the House and Senate.

Iunderstood what he wanted me to do was drop any investigation connected to Flynn's account of his conversations with the Russians.

SENATOR FEINSTEIN: But why didn't you stop and say, 'Mr. President, this is wrong. I cannot discuss this with you'?

COMEY: Maybe if I were stronger, I would have. I was so stunned by the conversation that I just took in. I was playing in my mind, what should my response be? That's why I carefully chose the words. Look, I've seen the tweet about tapes. Lordy, I hope there are tapes! I remember saying, 'I agree he is a good guy,' as a way of saying, I'm not agreeing with what you asked me to do. Again, maybe other people would be stronger in that circumstance. Maybe if I did it again, I'd do it better.

SENATOR FEINSTEIN: You describe two phone calls that you received from President Trump. He, quote, 'described the Russia investigation as a cloud that was impairing his ability.' end quote, as president, and asked you, quote, 'to lift the cloud,' end quote. How did you interpret that? What did you believe he wanted you to do?

COMEY: I interpreted that as he was frustrated that the Russia investigation was taking up so much time and energy. I think he meant of the executive branch, but what he asked me was actually narrowing than that. I think what he meant by the cloud—and, again, I could be wrong—but the entire investigation is taking up oxygen and making it hard for me to focus on what I want to focus on. The ask was to get it out that I, the president, am not personally under investigation.

SENATE TESTIMONY IMPLICATING DONALD TRUMP

OPPOSITE: There was global press coverage of James Comey's testimony before the Senate Intelligence Committee. It was the first weighty blow against the president in what has been a steadily unfolding drama.

Although James Comey had been a registered Republican, he later declared himself unaffiliated to either party. He felt the full force of the Democrats' anger when he reopened an investigation into presidential candidate Hillary Clinton's use of a public email server for classified information, just weeks before the conclusion of the 2016 presidential election. He then faced similar wrath from the Republican side when it was revealed that he had drafted a letter exonerating Clinton before the investigation had been completed.

Comey's investigation tainted Clinton but concluded without recommending criminal charges. Both parties were indignant and frustrated at not being able to identify any demonstrably partisan behavior on Comey's part. From the public and the press, it won him a reputation for independence and impartiality.

In early 2017, reports emerged that President Trump's National Security advisor Michael Flynn had conducted meetings with the Russian ambassador. Following suggestions that he had subsequently misled Vice President Mike Pence about the nature and occasion of these meetings, Trump accepted Flynn's resignation. It was under James Comey that the FBI began an investigation into Flynn's activities.

Trump fired Comey on May 9, only four years into his contract—something that Comey only discovered when he saw a newsflash on a TV screen in the FBI's Los Angeles office. The grounds were unclear: Trump first cited Comey's handling of the Hillary Clinton probe, and later suggested it was because of his inquiries into Russian collusion. At other times Trump told the media that Comey simply "wasn't doing a good job."

The White House press secretary claimed to have heard from "countless members of the FBI that are grateful and thankful for the President's decision," although two days later, acting FBI director Andrew McCabe reported that "Director Comey enjoyed broad support within the FBI and still does."

On June 8, 2017, Comey was invited to testify about his dismissal before the Senate Intelligence Committee. During his testimony, he answered quesions from Senator Dianne Feinstein and talked about a memo that he had circulated among his immediate colleagues, detailing a private conversation between himself and Trump. The president, Comey claimed, had directly asked him to drop the investigation into Flynn, saying, "I hope you can see your way clear to letting this go, to letting Flynn go. He is a good guy. I hope you can let this go."

Comey explained to the committee that he had made notes at the time about several of his conversations with Trump because "I was honestly concerned that he might lie about the nature of our meeting, so I felt the need to document it," adding that he had not felt the need to do so with the two previous presidents under whom he had served. He was, he had recorded, stunned by the request and had replied carefully that Flynn was a good guy, without suggesting that he was going to drop the case. President Trump told a reporter on May 18 that he had not in any way, shape, or form asked Comey to close down the investigation.

As is Trump's habit, he had conducted a war of words with James Comey on Twitter after Comey's firing. At his hearing Comey quoted one tweet posted by the president on May 12, which read "James Comey better hope that there are no 'tapes' of our conversations before he starts leaking to the press!" His comment to the committee, "Lordy, I hope there are tapes!" made headlines across all media.

James Comey's testimony was a pivotal moment in the public's perception of the integrity of the Trump administration. He seemed to be describing, live on TV, a prima facie case for a charge of obstruction of justice against the president of the United States. At time of writing, investigations into the Trump campaign's connections with Russia continue.

Fundamentally, the future is vastly more exciting and interesting if we are a spacefaring civilization and a multiplanet species than if we are not. You want to be inspired by things, you want to wake up in the morning and think the future is going to be great. That is what being a spacefaring civilization is all about. It's about believing in the future and thinking the future is better than the past. And I can't think of anything more exciting than going out there and being amongst the stars.

[this from later in the speech, editing out technical detail to make it interesting] Becoming a multi-planetary species beats the hell out of being a single planet species. We would start off by sending a mission to Mars where it would be obviously just landing on rocky ground or dusty ground. I feel fairly confident that we can complete the ship and be ready for a launch in about five years. Five years seems like a long time to me.

Then in 2024 we want to try to fly four ships—two cargo and two crew. The goal of the first mission is to find the best source of water, and for the second mission, the goal is to build the propellant plant. The base starts with one ship, then multiple ships, then we start building out the city and making the city bigger, and even bigger. Over time terraforming Mars and making it a really nice place to be.

It is quite a beautiful picture. You know that on Mars, dawn and dusk are blue. The sky is blue at dawn and dusk and red during the day. It's the opposite of Earth.

SPACEX SPEECH EXPANDING ON HIS VISION OF HUMANITY AS A "MULTIPLANETARY SPECIES"

RIGHT: Elon Musk presenting his Mars ambitions in Adelaide, Australia.

Elon Musk
Becoming a Multiplanet Species
(September 28, 2017)

Elon Musk, CEO of SpaceX, Tesla Motors, and more, writes the same way he speaks and thinks—impatiently. When at the sixty-eighth International Astronautical Congress (IAC) in 2017, he announced plans to send an unmanned mission to Mars in only five years' time, he added that "five years seems like a long time for me."

Elon Musk made his early fortune with Internet services such as PayPal. He founded SpaceX in 2002, with the intention of rekindling the public's excitement about space travel. Falcon 1, SpaceX's first rocket, named after the Millennium Falcon from *Star Wars*, was almost as unreliable as its namesake and failed its first three launches. The fourth attempt, with the last of Musk's budget riding on it, succeeded on September 28, 2008. As an aide pointed out to him when he addressed IAC 2017 in Adelaide, he was doing so on the ninth anniversary of that maiden flight.

Musk's desire to go to Mars has been no secret for many years. His speech at Adelaide went into detail about his ambition and his plans, particularly about the new vehicle that he has designed for the task. He presented SpaceX's latest rocket, code-named the BFR, standing for Big [Expletive] Rocket. The BFR will be 106m (348ft) long and 9m (30ft) in diameter with a payload of 150 tons, room for forty cabins for the three-to-six month voyage to Mars carrying up to 200 passengers.

A key plank of Musk's approach to space travel, he explained, is cost and reusability. "It is really crazy," he complained, "that we build these sophisticated rockets and then crash them every time we fly. This is mad." He showed delegates film of some of the sixteen consecutive flights of the reusable Falcon 9 rocket, which have returned to Earth, not on runways like NASA's space shuttles, but vertically, emulating take-off in reverse. "It will literally land with so much precision that it will land back on its launch mounts."

A lot of Elon Musk's talk in Adelaide was couched in technical terms that only IAC delegates would understand. But whether he was speaking in jargon or in lay terms, his enthusiasm for his sphere of activity was unmistakable. His ambition to establish a colony on Mars isn't just the theoretical pipedream of a scientist, or the because-it's-there idealism of a Kennedy. He argues that a human settlement on another planet may be essential to the survival of the species. If earth becomes uninhabitable, either through mankind's own folly or a mutant disease or the sort of impact that killed the dinosaurs, relocation to another planet may be our last, best hope.

So Musk is determined to make human beings an interplanetary species. If the worst never happens, so much the better. "You want to wake up in the morning and think the future is going to be great," he said. "And that's what being a space-faring nation is all about. It's about believing in the future and thinking the future will be better than the past. And I can't think of anything more exciting than going out there and being amongst the stars."

SpaceX intends to send two cargo BFRs to Mars in 2022, followed by four BFRs two years later, two of them carrying the first explorers of Mars. Construction is already underway, and Musk has already proved he can deliver. He has held a contract with NASA to ferry supplies to the International Space Station since the Space Shuttle program ended.

In February 2018, SpaceX took a significant step toward realizing Musk's ambition when a Falcon Heavy—a Falcon 9 with two additional Falcon 9 first-stage rockets strapped to its sides—was successfully launched into outer space. It is expected to reach Mars at the planet's farthest orbit from the sun. It carries a modest dummy payload in the form of Elon Musk's own Tesla Roadster car, which was launched with its sound system playing—what else?—David Bowie's "Life on Mars."

Oprah Winfrey
"Their time is up"

(January 7, 2018)

The Oprah Winfrey Show ran for twenty-five years and elevated her to the status of national institution. In 2018, she received the Cecil B. DeMille Award at the Golden Globes Awards ceremony. She used her acceptance speech to comment on the 2017 exposure of routine sexual abuse within the entertainment industry.

Oprah Winfrey was the fourteenth woman in sixty-six years to receive the Cecil B. DeMille Award for an outstanding contribution to the entertainment industry. Her acceptance speech began with her recollections as a young girl of watching Sidney Poitier become the first African American to win an Oscar, and later the first to win the award she was now receiving. The sight of a black man accepting an award was a remarkable moment, and Oprah was aware, she said, "that at this moment there are some little girls watching as I become the first black woman to be given this same award."

She took advantage of the fact that the Globes are awarded by the Hollywood Foreign Press Association to praise the press's "insatiable dedication to uncovering the absolute truth that keeps us from turning a blind eye to corruption and injustice and tyrants and victims and secrets and lies." In the preceding year President Trump had devoted considerable time to demonizing the press for spreading "fake news" about his administration.

The truth was powerful, Oprah said, especially at the end of a year in which, instead of telling stories, the entertainment industry had become the story. Movie magnate Harvey Weinstein had been the subject of accusations of regular abuses of power on the casting couch. More and more women came forward with their own stories of assault, not only at his hands and not only in entertainment. A tipping point was reached, after which women who had previously been afraid or ashamed to come forward were now empowered to do so, under the banner "Me Too."

Oprah used her speech to praise women from all walks of life "who have endured years of abuse and assault because they, like my mother, had children to feed and bills to pay and dreams to pursue. And there's

someone else." She reminded her audience of the story of Recy Taylor, abducted in 1944, gang-raped, and left blindfolded by the side of the road in Alabama by six white men who threatened to kill her if she told anyone.

Bravely, she pursued a prosecution, and although the men eventually confessed, no court would convict them. She died on December 28, 2017, three days short of her ninety-eighth birthday. Oprah described Taylor as living, "as we all have lived, too many years in a culture broken by brutally powerful men. But their time is up. Their time is up. And I just hope that Recy Taylor died knowing that her truth—like the truth of so many other women who [have been] tormented, goes marching on."

Oprah said that her guests on *The Oprah Winfrey Show* had taught her "something about how men and women really behave. . . . but the one quality all of them seem to share is an ability to maintain hope for a brighter morning—even during our darkest nights." Turning to her younger viewers again, she continued, "I want all the girls watching here and now to know that a new day is on the horizon! And when that day finally dawns, it will be because a lot of magnificent women . . . and some pretty phenomenal men, [have] become the leaders who take us to the time when nobody ever has to say, 'Me Too' again."

The Oprah Winfrey Show holds the record for the highest-rated daytime show in American TV history. Her position of considerable power within the entertainment industry has given her the right and the responsibility to speak, as she did at the Golden Globes, for many—women, black Americans, victims of abuse. Commentators have, however, suggested that in the aspirational tone of her speech, particularly in its evocative closing section, she was aiming for a higher level of representation, and perhaps testing the waters.

Recy Taylor died 10 days ago, just shy of her 98th birthday. She lived, as we all have lived, too many years in a culture broken by brutally powerful men. And for too long, women have not been heard or believed if they dared to speak their truth to the power of those men. But their time is up. Their time is up. Their time is up.

And I just hope that Recy Taylor died knowing that her truth—like the truth of so many other women who were tormented in those years, and even now tormented—goes marching on. It was somewhere in Rosa Parks's heart almost 11 years later, when she made the decision to stay seated on that bus in Montgomery. And it's here with every woman who chooses to say, 'Me too.' And every man—every man—who chooses to listen. In my career, what I've always tried my best to do, whether on television or through film, is to say something about how men and women really behave: to say how we experience shame, how we love and how we rage, how we fail, how we retreat, persevere, and how we overcome. And I've interviewed and portrayed people who've withstood some of the ugliest things life can throw at you, but the one quality all of them seem to share is an ability to maintain hope for a brighter morning—even during our darkest nights.

So I want all the girls watching here and now to know that a new day is on the horizon! And when that new day finally dawns, it will be because of a lot of magnificent women, many of whom are right here in this room tonight, and some pretty phenomenal men, fighting hard to make sure that they become the leaders who take us to the time when nobody ever has to say, 'Me too,' again. Thank you.

AT THE GOLDEN GLOBES, "A NEW DAY IS ON THE HORIZON" SUMMARIZING THE METOO MOVEMENT

RIGHT: *Although many thought that Oprah's Golden Globes speech had a presidential feel, friends were quick to say that was not where her ambitions lay.*

Continued from p.201

. . . On that morning, all that I was told was that I had been found behind a dumpster, potentially penetrated by a stranger, and that I should get retested for HIV because results don't always show up immediately. But for now, I should go home and get back to my normal life. Imagine stepping back into the world with only that information. They gave me huge hugs and I walked out of the hospital into the parking lot wearing the new sweatshirt and sweatpants they provided me, as they had only allowed me to keep my necklace and shoes.

My sister picked me up, face wet from tears and contorted in anguish. Instinctively and immediately, I wanted to take away her pain. I smiled at her, I told her to look at me, I'm right here, I'm okay, everything's okay, I'm right here. My hair is washed and clean, they gave me the strangest shampoo, calm down, and look at me. Look at these funny new sweatpants and sweatshirt, I look like a P.E. teacher, let's go home, let's eat something. She did not know that beneath my sweatsuit, I had scratches and bandages on my skin, my vagina was sore and had become a strange, dark color from all the prodding, my underwear was missing, and I felt too empty to continue to speak. That I was also afraid, that I was also devastated. That day we drove home and for hours in silence my younger sister held me. . . .

I tried to push it out of my mind, but it was so heavy I didn't talk, I didn't eat, I didn't sleep, I didn't interact with anyone. After work, I would drive to a secluded place to scream. I didn't talk, I didn't eat, I didn't sleep, I didn't interact with anyone, and I became isolated from the ones I loved most. For over a week after the incident, I didn't get any calls or updates about that night or what happened to me. The only symbol that proved it hadn't just been a bad dream, was the sweatshirt from the hospital in my drawer. . . . .

One day, I was at work, scrolling through the news on my phone, and came across an article. In it, I read and learned for the first time about how I was found unconscious, with my hair disheveled, long necklace wrapped around my neck, bra pulled out of my dress, dress pulled off over my shoulders and pulled up above my waist, that I was butt naked all the way down to my boots, legs spread apart, and had been penetrated by a foreign object by someone I did not recognize. This was how I learned what happened to me, sitting at my desk reading the news at work. I learned what happened to me the same time everyone else in the world learned what happened to me. That's when the pine needles in my hair made sense, they didn't fall from a tree. He had taken off my underwear, his fingers had been inside of me. I don't even know this person. I still don't know this person. When I read about me like this, I said, this can't be me, this can't be me. I could not digest or accept any of this information. I could not imagine my family having to read about this online. I kept reading. In the next paragraph, I read something that I will never forgive; I read that according to him, I liked it. I liked it. Again, I do not have words for these feelings. . . .

I thought there's no way this is going to trial; there were witnesses, there was dirt in my body, he ran but was caught. He's going to settle, formally apologize, and we will both move on. Instead, I was told he hired a powerful attorney, expert witnesses, private investigators who were going to try and find details about my personal life to use against me, find loopholes in my story to invalidate me and my sister, in order to show that this sexual assault was in fact a misunderstanding. That he was going to go to any length to convince the world he had simply been confused.

I was not only told that I was assaulted, I was told that because I couldn't remember, I technically could not prove it was unwanted. And that distorted me, damaged me, almost broke me. It is the saddest type of confusion to be told I was assaulted and nearly raped, blatantly out in the open, but we don't know if it counts as assault yet. I had to fight for an entire year to make it clear that there was something wrong with this situation.

When I was told to be prepared in case we didn't win, I said, I can't prepare for that. He was guilty the minute I woke up. No one can talk me out of the hurt he caused me. Worst of all, I was warned, because he now knows you don't remember, he is going to get to write the script. He can say whatever he wants and no one can contest it. I had no power, I had no voice, I was defenseless. My memory loss would be used against me. My testimony was weak, was incomplete, and I was made to believe that perhaps, I am not enough to win this. His attorney constantly reminded the jury, the only one we can believe is Brock, because she doesn't remember. That helplessness was traumatizing. Instead of taking time to heal, I was taking time to recall the night in excruciating detail, in order to prepare for the attorney's questions that would be invasive, aggressive, and designed to steer me off course, to contradict myself, my sister, phrased in ways to manipulate my answers. Instead of his attorney saying, Did you notice any abrasions? He said, You didn't notice any abrasions, right? This was a game of strategy, as if I could be tricked out of my own worth. The sexual assault had been so clear, but instead, here I was at the trial, answering questions like:

How old are you? How much do you weigh? What did you eat that day? Well what did you have for dinner? Who made dinner? Did you drink with dinner? No, not even water? When did you drink? How much did you drink? . . . I was pummeled with narrowed, pointed questions that dissected my personal life, love life, past life, family life, inane questions, accumulating trivial details to try and find an excuse for this guy who had me half naked before even bothering to ask for my name. After a physical assault, I was assaulted with questions designed to attack me, to say see, her facts don't line up, she's out of her mind, she's practically an alcoholic, she probably wanted to hook up, he's like an athlete right, they were both drunk, whatever, the hospital stuff she remembers is after the fact, why take it into account, Brock has a lot at stake so he's having a really hard time right now.

And then it came time for him to testify and I learned what it meant to be revictimized. My family had to see pictures of my head strapped to a gurney full of pine needles, of my body in the dirt with my eyes closed, hair messed up, limbs bent, and dress hiked up. And even after that, my family had to listen to your attorney say the pictures were after the fact, we can dismiss them. . . .

I want to show people that one night of drinking can ruin two lives. You and me. You are the cause, I am the effect. You have dragged me through this hell with you, dipped me back into that night again and again. You knocked down both our towers, I collapsed at the same time you did. If you think I was spared, came out unscathed, that today I ride off into sunset, while you suffer the greatest blow, you are mistaken. Nobody wins. We have all been devastated, we have all been trying to find some meaning in all of this suffering. Your damage was concrete; stripped of titles, degrees, enrollment. My damage was internal, unseen, I carry it with me. You took away my worth, my privacy, my energy, my time, my safety, my intimacy, my confidence, my own voice, until today. . . .

I can't sleep alone at night without having a light on, like a five-year-old, because I have nightmares of being touched where I cannot wake up. I did this thing where I waited until the sun came up and I felt safe enough to sleep. For three months, I went to bed at six o'clock in the morning. . . .

I used to pride myself on my independence, now I am afraid to go on walks in the evening, to attend social events with drinking among friends where I should be comfortable being. I have become a little barnacle always needing to be at someone's side, to have my boyfriend standing next to me, sleeping beside me, protecting me. It is embarrassing how feeble I feel, how timidly I move through life, always guarded, ready to defend myself, ready to be angry. . . .

You have no idea how hard I have worked to rebuild parts of me that are still weak. It took me eight months to even talk about what happened. I could no longer connect with friends, with everyone around me. I would scream at my boyfriend, my own family whenever they brought this up. You never let me forget what happened to me. At the of end of the hearing, the trial, I was too tired to speak. I would leave drained, silent. I would go home, turn off my phone and for days I would not speak. You bought me a ticket to a planet where I lived by myself. Every time a new article come out, I lived with the paranoia that my entire hometown would find out and know me as the girl who got assaulted. I didn't want anyone's pity and am still learning to accept 'victim' as part of my identity. You made my own hometown an uncomfortable place to be. . . .

When I see my younger sister hurting, when she is unable to keep up in school, when she is deprived of joy, when she is not sleeping, when she is crying so hard on the phone she is barely breathing, telling me over and over again she is sorry for leaving me alone that night, sorry sorry sorry, when she feels more guilt than you, then I do not forgive you. That night I had called her to try and find her, but you found me first. Your attorney's closing statement began, "[Her sister] said she was fine and who knows her better than her sister." You tried to use my own sister against me? Your points of attack were so weak, so low, it was almost embarrassing. You do not touch her.

You should have never done this to me. Secondly, you should have never made me fight so long to tell you, you should have never done this to me. But here we are. The damage is done, no one can undo it. And now we both have a choice. We can let this destroy us, I can remain angry and hurt and you can be in denial, or we can face it head on, I accept the pain, you accept the punishment, and we move on.

Your life is not over, you have decades of years ahead to rewrite your story. The world is huge, it is so much bigger than Palo Alto and Stanford, and you will make a space for yourself in it where you can be useful and happy. But right now, you do not get to shrug your shoulders and be confused anymore. You do not get to pretend that there were no red flags. You have been convicted of violating me, intentionally, forcibly, sexually, with malicious intent, and all you can admit to is consuming alcohol. Do not talk about the sad way your life was upturned because alcohol made you do bad things. Figure out how to take responsibility for your own conduct. . . .

Most importantly, thank you to the two men who saved me, who I have yet to meet. I sleep with two bicycles that I drew taped above my bed to remind myself there are heroes in this story. That we are looking out for one another. To have known all of these people, to have felt their protection and love, is something I will never forget. . . .

And finally, to girls everywhere, I am with you. On nights when you feel alone, I am with you. When people doubt you or dismiss you, I am with you. I fought everyday for you. So never stop fighting, I believe you. As the author Anne Lamott once wrote, "Lighthouses don't go running all over an island looking for boats to save; they just stand there shining." Although I can't save every boat, I hope that by speaking today, you absorbed a small amount of light, a small knowing that you can't be silenced, a small satisfaction that justice was served, a small assurance that we are getting somewhere, and a big, big knowing that you are important, unquestionably, you are untouchable, you are beautiful, you are to be valued, respected, undeniably, every minute of every day, you are powerful and nobody can take that away from you. To girls everywhere, I am with you. Thank you.

"EMILY DOE" STATEMENT TO COURT

Acknowledgments

Speech sources: The Internet Classics Archive; The Art of Manliness; Patrick Fraser Tytler, *Lives of Scottish Worthies* (1831); James Harvey Robinson, *Readings in European History* (1906); The Constitution Society; World Future Fund; Papers of George Washington held at University of Virginia; University College London; University of Maryland; Socialist Worker; Oxford University Museum of Natural History; Civilwarcauses.org; American Battlefield Trust; The Avalon Project of Yale Law School; The History Place; University of Missouri; Speeches on Social Justice; Eleanor Hull, *A History of Ireland* (1931), Marxists Internet Archive; American Rhetoric; Samuel Rosenman, (ed.), *The Public Papers of Franklin D. Roosevelt, Volume Two: The Years of Crisis* (1933); Brigham Young University; *Washington Times*; Fordham University; *The Guardian*; The Churchill Society; George Mason University; BBC School Radio; National Diet Library of Japan; Israel Ministry of Foreign Affairs; Socialist Health Association; US Supreme Court; School for Champions; South African History Online; NASA; University of Nottingham; Sony Music; Digital History; *The Beatles Bible*; Cornell Law School, Speech Vault; *Birmingham Mail*; CNN; *Poughkeepsie Journal*; *New York Times*; PBS; Boston Museum of Fine Arts; Margaret Thatcher Foundation; *Washington Post*; Michigan State University; William J. Clinton Presidential Library; Université de Sherbrooke; *Town and Country Magazine*; *The Irish Times*; BBC News; Al Jazeera; Engadget; *The Harvard Gazette*; *Daily Telegraph*; BuzzFeed, University of Cambridge; SpaceX; *Daily Mail*.

Photo sources: Getty images, Alamy.com, Library of Congress, National Gallery, Mary Evans Picture Library, New York State Library, Penguin Books, Pavilion Image Library, Christian Action.

Cover images: Front cover—Barack Obama, Vladimir Lenin, Malala Yousafzai, Martin Luther King Jr., Winston Churchill, Nelson Mandela, Oprah Winfrey, Mark Zuckerberg, Betty Friedan, John F. Kennedy, Eva Perón, Mark Twain, Elizabeth I, Edward VIII, Steve Jobs, Neil Armstrong.
Back cover—Elon Musk, Elvis Presley, Sojourner Truth, Timothy Leary, Harvey Milk, General Charles de Gaulle, Chief Joseph, Lou Gehrig, Ronald Reagan, Franklin D. Roosevelt, Neville Chamberlain, Malcolm X, Emmeline Pankhurst.

Index

African National Congress (ANC) 140, 141, 172

Ahern, Bertie 184

"Ain't I a woman?" (Truth) 38–39

Alabama 37, 45, 133, 143

Aldrin, Buzz 155

Alexander III, King 23

Alexander the Great 16–17

Alexander, Elizabeth 177

Ali, Muhammad 136–37

Allen, Paul 194

America First 81

American Civil Liberties Union (ACLU) 146

American Civil War 44–45, 46–47, 48–49

Angelou, Maya 176–77

Anti-Slavery Bugle 39

Antony, Mark 19

Apology of Socrates (Plato) 14

Apple Corps. 192–93, 206

Aristobulus 16

Armenian massacre 76

Armstrong, Neil 129, 154–55

Arrian of Nicomedia 16

"Ask not what your country can do for you; ask what you can do for your country" (Kennedy) 126–27

Attlee, Clement 106

Baldwin, Stanley 71

Balfour Declaration 105

Baliol, King John 23

"Ballot or the Bullet, The" (Malcolm X) 138–39

Baltic States 90

Bannockburn, Battle of 23

Barrow, Ed 74

Barrow, Tony 142

Batista, Fulgencio 122

Battle of Britain 86–87

Bay of Pigs invasion 123, 129

Bazile, Leon 146

Beatles, The 142–43

Ben-Gurion, David 104–05

Berlin 130–31, 170–71

Bevan, Aneurin 106–107

Bhutto, Benazir 199

Biden, Joe 200

bin Laden, Osama 186, 188–89

Black Sash 172

Blackmun, Harry 162–63

Blair, Tony 179, 184–85

Blanco, Richard 177

"Blood, toil, tears and sweat" (Churchill) 82–83

Booth, John Wilkes 48

Botha, P. W. 172

Bowie, David 211

Bradford, William 129

Brandenburg Gate 170

British Association for the Advancement of Science 43

British Science Festival 43

Brown, Oliver 114

Brown vs. Board of Education 114–15

Bryant, Anita 167

Buckingham Palace 79

Buffett, Warren 195

Burger, Warren 163

Burns, Robert 23

Bush, George W. 161, 186–187, 189, 191

Carter, D. H. 36

Caspian Sea 16

Castro, Fidel 122–23, 126, 141

Catiline 18

Catiline Orations (Cicero) 18–19

Chamberlain, Neville 73–73, 76, 77, 79

Chaplin, Charlie 65

Chapman, Mark 143

Charles I, King 26–27

Charles II, King 27

Charles, Prince of Wales 71, 179, 180

Charles, Tommy 142

Chernenko, Konstantin 175

Cherokee Nation 37

Cheyenne Nation 51
Chiang Kai-shek 108
Chickasaw Nation 37
Choctaw Nation 37
Churchill, Winston 55, 65, 71, 72, 89, 95
    "Blood, toil, tears and sweat" 82–83
    Iron Curtain speech 98–99
    "This was their finest hour" 86–87
    "We shall fight on the beaches" 84–85
Cicero 18–19
Clarke, Thomas 58, 59
Cleave, Maureen 142
Clinton, Bill 126, 176, 177, 182–83
Clinton, Hillary 183, 204, 209
Cocker, Joe 156
Coffee, Linda 163
Collins, Michael 155
Comey, James 208–209
Committee of Public Safety 32
Commonwealth of Independent States 175
Cooper, Ann Nixon 196, 197
Cornerstone Speech (Stephens) 44-45
Cromwell, Oliver 27
Cuba 122–123, 126, 127, 129
Cultural Revolution 108
Curtis, Edward 50

D–Day landings 94–95
Danton, Georges 32, 33
Darien Scheme 23
Darwin, Charles 43
"date which will live in infamy, A" (Roosevelt) 92–93
Datebook 142
Davis, Jefferson 45
de Gaulle, Charles 88–89, 95
de Klerk, F. W. 172
Declaration of Independence 29, 34, 40, 45
Diana, Princess 180–181
Disraeli, Benjamin 72
Doe, Emily 200–01
Donovan, Nina 204
Douglas, Lord Alfred 53
Douglas-Home, Alec 135
Douglass, Frederick 40–41
Dublin 59

Easter Rising 59
Eavis, Michael 157
Edward I, King 23
Edward VIII, King 70–71, 79, 112
Eisenhower, Dwight D. 94–95
Elizabeth, Queen Mother 79, 113
Elizabeth I, Queen 24–25, 113
Elizabeth II, Queen 71, 112–13, 180, 181
Eritrea 118
Everett, Edward 46

Facebook 206–07
Falkirk, Battle of 23
Falklands War 169
Feminine Mystique, The (Friedan) 158
Fayed, Dodi 180
Feinstein, Dianne 208
Finland 90
Flynn, Michael 209
Ford, Gerald 164
Fourteen Points (Wilson) 62–63
"Freedom or Death" (Pankhurst) 56–57
Freisinger, Franz Gabriel 33
French Revolution 32–33
Friedan, Betty 158–59
Frost, Robert 176
Future of Life Institute 202

Gagarin, Yuri 129
Gage, Frances Dana Barker 39
Gaitskell, Hugh 134
Galilee 21
Gandhi, Mahatma 21, 64–65, 102, 103
Ganges 16
Gates, Bill 194–95, 206
Gehrig, Eleanor 75
Gehrig, Lou 74–75
General Strike of 1926 65
George V, King 71, 125
George VI, King 71, 78–79, 112, 113
Georgia 37, 45
Gettysburg Address (Lincoln) 35, 46–47
Gettysburg, Battle of 46–47
Ghana 118
Gill, C. F. 52

Gingrich, Newt 183

Ginsberg, Allen 122

Glastonbury Festival 157

Gorbachev, Mikhail 170, 171, 174–75

Gordimer, Nadine 141

Göring, Hermann 76, 77, 81

Graceland 120–21

Great Depression 67, 69

Greece, Ancient 14–15, 16–17, 19

Greeley, Horace 49

Gretzky, Wayne 193

Griffith-Jones, Mervyn 124–25

Gromyko, Andrei 175

Guantanamo Bay 186

Hallett, Maurice 102

Hamilton, Alexander 35

Harry, Prince 71, 180, 181

Harvard University 194–95, 206–07

Hawking, Stephen 202–03

Heath, Edward 153

Hebrew Technical School for Girls 55

Hemmings, Sally 147

Henry, Patrick 28–29, 56

Hephaestion 17

Himmler, Heinrich 100

Hindenburg, Paul von 67

Hirohito, Emperor 96–97

Hiroshima 96

Hitler, Adolf 2, 73, 77, 81, 86, 87, 90, 100, 101, 105

    first speech as Chancellor 66–67

    foreign policy speech 76–77

Hong Kong 119, 178–79

Howard, Oliver Otis 51

Huggins, Miller 74, 75

Humphrey, Hubert 149

Huxley, Thomas Henry 42–43

Hydaspes River 16

"I am the greatest!" (Ali) 136–37

"I am a nasty woman" (Judd) 204–05

"I have a dream" (King) 132–33

"Ich bin ein Berliner" (Kennedy) 130–31

Idaho 51

"ideal for which I am prepared to die, An" (Mandela) 140–141

Importance of Being Earnest, The (Wilde) 53

Indian National Congress 102

Indian Ocean 16

Irish Republican Brotherhood (IRB) 58

Iron Curtain speech (Churchill) 98–99

"I've been to the mountaintop" (King) 150–51

Jackson, Andrew 36–37

Japan 77, 93, 93, 96–97

Jefferson, Thomas 29, 35, 147

Jesus Christ 20–21

Jewish Agency 105

Jhelum River 16

Jobs, Steve 192–93

John the Baptist 21

Johnson, Lyndon B. 133, 149

Jordan 105

Joseph, Chief 50–51

Judd, Ashley 204–05

Kansas 51

Kennedy, John F. 114, 133, 135, 138, 139, 149, 155, 164, 170, 176

    "Ask not what your country can do for you; ask what you can do for your country" 126–27

    "Ich bin ein Berliner" 130–31

    "We choose to go to the moon" 128–29

Kerry, John 160–161, 189, 191

Khan, Genghis 76

Khrushchev, Nikita 116–17, 122–23, 130, 139, 171

King, Ernest 95

King, Martin Luther Jr. 138

    "I have a dream" 132–33

    "I've been to the mountaintop" 150–151

King's Speech, The 79

Kingsley Hall 65

La Guardia, Fiorello 75

Lady Chatterley's Lover (Lawrence) 124–25

"lady's not for turning, The" (Thatcher) 168–69

Lang, Mike 156

Langdon, Olivia 55

Lawrence, D. H. 125

Lawson, James 151

League of Nations 62–63, 105

League for Spiritual Discovery 145
Leary, Timothy 144–45
Lenin, Vladimir 60–61, 117
Lennon, John 142–43
Lester, Doris 65
Lester, Muriel 65
Leverhulme Centre for the Future of Intelligence
    202–03
Lewinsky, Monica 182–83
Lincoln, Abraham 35, 45
    Gettysburg Address 46–47
Second Inaugural Speech 48–49
Lindbergh, Charles 80–81
Liston, Sonny 137
Liverpool 30
Lloyd George, David 62, 65
Logue, Lionel 79
Louis XVI, King 32
Loving, Mildred 146–47
Loving, Richard 146–47
Loving vs. Virginia 146-47

MacArthur, Douglas 96, 97
Macedonia 16
Macmillan, Harold 118–19
Malcolm X 122, 138–39
Mallory, George 129
Mandela, Nelson
    'An ideal for which I am prepared to die' 140–41
    speech after release from prison 172–73
Mao Zedong 108–109
Mary I, Queen 25
Mau Mau uprising 118
McCain, John 196
McCarthy, Eugene 148–149
McCarthy, Joe 74, 75
McCorvey, Norma 163
McGovern, George 164
Midway, Battle of 96
Miles, General 51
Milk, Harvey 166–67
Mississippi River 37
Missouri Democrat 55
Molotov, Vyacheslav 90–91
Molotov-Ribbentrop Pact 90

Monday Evening Club of Hartford 55
Montana 51
Moscow 61
Mountbatten, Lord 102
Muhammad, Elijah 138
Munich conference 72
Muscogee-Creek Nation 37
Musk, Elon 202, 210–11
Mussolini, Benito 81
"My Spiritual Message" (Gandhi) 64–65

Nagasaki 96
Nation of Islam 138, 139
National Association for the Advancement of Colored
    People (NAACP) 114
National Convention 32
National Health Service 106–07
National Organization for Women (NOW) 159–59
National Socialist German Workers' Party (NSDAP)
    66, 67
National Union of South African Students 172
Nehru, Jawaharlal 102–03
New Deal 69
New York Giants 74
New York Times 158
New York Yankees 75
Nez Perce tribe 50–51
Nicholas II, Tsar 60
Nixon, Richard 126, 145, 149, 160, 162, 164–65
Norris, Mr. 30
North Atlantic Treaty Organization (NATO) 35
Nuremberg trials 100–01, 125

Obama, Barack 123, 126, 133, 177, 189
    address to Democratic Convention 190–91
    "Yes, We Can!" 196–97
"On the Pulse of Morning" (Angelou) 176–77
"only thing we have to fear is fear itself, The"
    (Roosevelt) 68–69
O'Donovan Rossa, Jeremiah 58, 59
Oklahoma 51
"One small step for [a] man, one giant leap for mankind"
    (Armstrong) 154–55
Oracle of Delphi 15
Oregon 51